Abolition and Social Justice
in the Era of Reform

the text of this book is printed
on 100% recycled paper

Abolition and Social Justice in the Era of Reform

Edited by
LOUIS FILLER

HARPER & ROW, PUBLISHERS
New York, Evanston, San Francisco, London

CONTENTS

PART III: REFORM AT HIGH NOON

PART IV: THE CRISIS

PART V: REVOLUTIONS AND AFTERMATH

The watchword of the nineteenth century is
BROTHERHOOD.

Horace Greeley

INTRODUCTION

The 1830–1860 era of reform was the most momentous of all eras since the Revolution, and not solely because it stirred the nation to deeds and asseverations which brought on civil war. It also raised fundamental questions respecting the nature of our civilization. Americans had always been, as a nation, partial to reforms simply because they were constantly disturbed by western movements and new influxes of population. They were thus subject to fluidity and change. A wide open frontier and an eager people unleashed from constrictive European circumstances made for a seething, anticipating society: one receptive to reform and also to counter-demands for law and order.

There were probably as many reformers during the preceding decade as during the 1830s, yet the later time was one of turmoil and challenge not found earlier. The problem which faced contemporaries of the reform era was to determine which factors had created the difference. The 1820s could claim vigorous and distinguished partisans of reform.[1] They could still claim the vision and prospects of Thomas Jefferson and Dr. Benjamin Rush, the latter a reform movement in himself, favoring the products of science and of liberal religion, of temperance, antislavery, education and other causes including women's rights. Those times could claim Robert Owen and his son Robert Dale Owen, the latter's associate Frances Wright, a feminist as well as a utopian, and Ann Royall, who was no feminist but pioneered woman's work in journalism. Rev. Samuel A. Worcester in the 1820s became conspicuous for his efforts to aid the Cherokee Indians,

---

1. For an overview of the more purely moral aspects of reform in the period, Clifford S. Griffin, *Their Brothers' Keepers* (New Brunswick, N.J.: Rutgers University Press, 1960).

beset by state and federal authorities anxious for their removal. Joshua Leavitt made his first reputation as a moral reform leader concerned for the well-being of sailors and seriously determined to thwart prostitutes in New York. The 1820s saw the beginnings of the lyceum movement and the free school movement, the movement for institutional reform and for male suffrage reform; a time which found farmers in upper New York resisting their feudal obligations to landowners, and others joining to put Andrew Jackson in the White House.

Such a time were the 1820s. Yet those who observed events in the decade following sensed that times had changed, and these changes posed staggering questions to the nation.

The arresting issue was the fate of the Negro. The issue had once seemed secondary to the fate of democracy in general. Many Americans had assumed that slavery would not survive the generous slogans of the Revolution. It would dwindle and deteriorate, they believed, if only because it could not endure the competition created by free labor. Instead, the slavery economy had been reactivated by the advent of the cotton gin in 1793, and the quarrel over the admission to the Union of Missouri as a slave state in 1819–1820 had revealed an aggressive proslavery party in the South which had no intention of helping to destroy its own labor system. On the contrary, it was determined to advance it in full array in the West.

Though the antislavery crusade preempted public concern in the 1830s, it was far from being the only issue to seize attention. The 1830s and beyond were a time of ferment in every human field, from prisons to the proper rearing of children. Public unrest raised momentous questions for religion and, indeed, created a host of human experiments which agitated the church establishments at every turn. Without such stirrings and attendant eloquence, it is difficult to see how, in a nation of sweat and labor, of contracts and traditions which chained its citizens to duties and obligations, slave labor could have become the moral issue which abolitionists proposed.

William Jay, who possessed a great name which he gave to the abolitionist cause, nevertheless feared the spiritual unrest which accompanied it. He feared its effects on morals and religion. Whether experiments in cooperative living, the proliferation of "free love" colonies and the emergence of new religious sects and ideas—including Mormonism, spiritualism and perfectionism —loosened the fabric of society was a question which the future would inherit. But the moral earnestness of the major leaders of reform and the incomparable eloquence of their spokesmen were factors which helped determine the course of reform and maintain them as a challenge to posterity.

It is this eloquence, this sense of issues and conclusions, this probing of human beliefs and endeavor which inform the following pages. They help distinguish rhetoric from art—words which led to deeds from words which were merely promises. They make our greatest reform movement ever relevant, ever new respecting the nature of human beings and especially of Americans.

LOUIS FILLER

Let not the "thin ears" of intellectual pursuits "devour the full ears" of religious feeling; but, after the example of Paschal [sic] subordinate science to religion.

Elizur Wright, Sr. to Elizur Wright, Jr.
November 20, 1829

The heritage of good works . . . of which neither principalities nor powers, nor any other creature, can dispossess the present and future generations of mankind.

Elihu Burritt

Though all American eras harbored reformers, their causes and particular personalities highlighted this one segment of time more than any previous. The "Jefferson Revolution" of 1800 which placed the brilliant Virginia statesman in the presidency promised to mark a milestone for the common man. Instead, Jefferson's administration was one of party animosities and great events featuring the Louisiana Purchase, a major attack on the Supreme Court, accused of being an agency of reaction, and desperate wars during which the British claimed to defend civilization against the assaults of Napoleon Bonaparte. Jefferson was victimized by these European disorders. His Embargo of 1807–1809 was sincerely intended to maintain the peace by keeping American shipping out of the Atlantic war zone. Unhappily it mainly affected New England's trade and shippers. These Federalists, in retaliation, vengefully plotted treason and a new New England Confederation which would rid them of the hated Southerners. When the "Virginia dynasty" under James Madison as President led the nation into the War of 1812, New England produced the world's first peace movement which included the much-admired Reverend William Ellery Channing as well as pious businessmen of lesser note.

Nevertheless, such reformers were obscured by war heroes, by western expansionists, and in the 1820s by the harbingers of "Flush Times": speculators, bankers and adventurers. The times gave prominence to such magnetic figures as General Andrew Jackson in politics, imposing figures of the quality of John Jacob Astor in business, Robert Fulton who made steamboats practical

and Moses Austin who led a few hundred American families to
settle in what was then Mexican territory which later became the
Republic of Texas. When Felix Walker of North Carolina in the
early 1820s declared in Congress that he was making a speech
only to please his constituents of Buncombe County, the nation
was pleased and amused by his candor and immortalized what it
recognized to be an inevitable facet of democratic life.

Yet those same citizens knew that "buncombe," or "bunk" as it
later became, far from satisfied all their needs. Their spiritual
gropings produced the revivalist enthusiasm of Reverend Charles
C. Finney in Pennsylvania, New York and Massachusetts. The
Finger Lakes region of western New York became particularly
famous for the religious passion there unveiled and attracted
social and spiritual experimenters of every stripe. Such traveling
preachers as Peter Cartwright moved their followers in the
Midwest. Great camp meetings continued the tradition set in
1801 at Cane Ridge, Kentucky, where for some six frenzied days
up to 25,000 participants had prayed, sung, groaned, cried aloud
for mercy and expressed feelings which ranged from ecstasy to
horror. Sexual misconduct at revivals has been overstressed; yet it
was more than coincidental that "[at Cane Ridge,] this largest of
all encampments the greatest number of sexual irregularities
occurred."[1] Quarrels over doctrine in 1828 split the Presbyterians, and other denominations suffered differences between
their liberal and conservative branches.

The continuing impulse to expand democratic opportunities in
the 1820s gave the suffrage to a majority of white male citizens,
and with increased suffrage came in 1828 the "Jackson Revolution." How much it served the "common man" for whom the
event was alleged to speak is moot. The "spoils system" of the
new administration did not honor competence. The Peggy Eaton

1. Charles A. Johnson, *The Frontier Camp Meeting: Religion's Harvest
Time* (Dallas, Tex.: Southern Methodist University Press, 1955), p. 65. See
also Whitney R. Cross, *The Burned-Over District: the Social and Intellectual
History of Enthusiastic Religion in Western New York, 1800–1850* (Ithaca,
N.Y.: Cornell University Press, 1950).

controversy, which split Washington high society on the issue of whether the Secretary of War's new, young wife was respectable, highlighted a woman of undistinguished qualities. Jackson was a Tennessee slaveholder, and his administration honored slavery, to which, to be sure, the common man was little opposed.

Nevertheless, the "Jackson era" was not untinged by reform. Generally, Jacksonians were antipathetic to any continuation of the debtors' prison system and helped speed its deterioration. Robert Rantoul, Jr. (1805–1852) of Massachusetts was a Democrat and also an outstanding reformer, not only opposing monopoly—a major Jacksonian issue—but also supporting the fight against capital punishment and against anti-Catholic prejudice. Rantoul also favored temperance and an expanded public school system. Although some of the Jacksonian creed had a political base—for example, some of their constituents were Irish Catholic immigrants—it also served practices and ideals of democracy.

At the same time, it could be distinguished from other tendencies within the same era which were distinctly of a more reformist character. They were intended not only to modify patent injustice but to change the world. They were concerned not only for the economic man and the political man but for his dignity and hopes. They did not hesitate to ponder the state of his soul. Jacksonians, on the contrary, were usually alert to the separation of church and state and tolerant of human peccadilloes. They were not interested in interfering with the drinking habits of their constituents, though these were generally excessive and brought tragedy to promising young men and whole families of every social class. The moral reformers, on the other hand, thought it proper not only to be concerned for intemperance but to consider and review religious principles as a matter of general interest. They saw the physical world in the light of the world which was to come. They sought to impress upon others their concern for religion and social questions.

Joshua Leavitt (1794–1873) was one of numerous reformers in

the 1820s. While others argued about tariff, road-building and other temporal questions, he assayed the state of his own soul and that of others. This New Englander and Yale graduate, who had returned to school to become a Congregational minister, became a general agent of the Seamen's Friend Society and labored to curb the common sailor's often self-destructive social behavior. Leavitt also became active, and even notorious, for his efforts to end prostitution in New York. Although such enterprises roused the contempt and hatred of more worldly persons, they to an extent served humanitarian ends, saved lives and succored individual ambitions. Leavitt, in this stage of his career, was not strongly inclined against slavery. He deplored it but was no more willing than the majority of Americans to demand drastic action to eradicate it.

Lewis and Arthur Tappan, New York merchants, like many such, were originally from New England. They were religious seekers to whom orthodox tenets and religiously-motivated good works became vastly more satisfying than the benign and optimistic outlook of Boston Unitarians. They were eager to help build churches, advance missionary work at home and abroad and raise the moral standards of businessmen and their employees. The Tappans instituted the one-price system of buying and selling, sought a substitute for wine in church services and otherwise meddled with the preferences of others. But their religious preoccupations also caused them to brood upon the nature of the slave system and what it threatened to do to the human soul.

In the 1820s they supported the colonization scheme which promised to end slavery painlessly. In theory it was to have inspired slaveholders to release their slaves for service in Africa. There the emancipated Negroes would advance Christianity and their own individual capacities, and, in the process, depart from a United States in which the white citizens did not make them welcome.

Colonization in the 1830s received a bad name for not seriously retarding development of the slave system in America and as having as its prime mission the ridding of the country of *free* Negroes. Yet colonization drew sincere support and raised some splendid advocates. Typical was Elliott Cresson, a Philadelphia philanthropist, who succeeded in founding a Negro colony at Bassa Cove, Liberia, and who gave money to advance Negro religious and educational ventures. More notable was James G. Birney (1792–1857) during the first phase of this great Alabaman's crusade against slavery. Birney probed as deeply as any American to uncover the antislavery potential of colonization, in the process committing his fortune and reputation to the work, as agent and organizer. His disillusionment closed a chapter in hopes for what the plan could accomplish. Colonization took its most attractive form in the labors of Benjamin Lundy, the greatest abolitionist figure before Garrison.

Lundy (1789–1839), a Quaker, early assumed it would be possible to build an ever-increasing company of antislavery workers, particularly in the Border States and farther south, which would exercise greater and greater moral weight upon slaveholders. Hence, he pushed antislavery enterprises in Ohio and in Baltimore, Maryland, where he issued *The Genius of Universal Emancipation.* He also traveled in Kentucky, Tennessee, Virginia and North Carolina to encourage the building of antislavery societies. He sought unsuccessfully to colonize Negroes as far apart as Texas, Canada and Haiti, hoping to demonstrate their competence for free and independent human projects and to hasten the emancipation of their brothers in slavery. Lundy's was a brave endeavor, and if it did not fulfill his dreams of emancipation, it laid much of the groundwork for what was to follow.

Thus it would appear that reform in the 1820s was a minor pursuit beside such enterprises as making money, building the Erie Canal and concluding treaty and other operations which cleared Ohio of Indians. And yet it is also evident, at least from hindsight, that Americans were troubled by other questions besides those relating to material ends. The future of women and children solicited attention as cities grew and industries, which viewed the workers in them and the workers' families with increased impersonality, expanded. The low state of the free Negro community, rumors and incidents respecting slaves which suggested repression and cruelty among slaveholders, the degraded position of the criminal and insane—such topics and others reached legislators and some of their constituents and resulted in pamphlets and appeals.

Yet hope, if not certitude, continued to pervade the American community. It had endured the shock of an unpopular and even humiliating war and come out of it stronger than before. The aged John Adams's words, expressed in 1813 to his troubled friend Dr. Rush, still seemed true: "I acknowledge all the blunders you have hinted at, and a thousand more. But I say we do not make more mistakes now than we did in 1774, '5, '6, [to '83]. It was patched and piebald policy then, as it is now, ever was, and ever will be, world without end. The essential stamina remain and will remain. Health will be restored. The main pillars are founded on a rock. Winds and flood will not shake them."[2]

Citizens maintained faith in the republic. Vital, too, was their religious dream of a good time coming. It was a dream which in the 1840s would produce the Millerites. William Miller (1782–1849) was an earnest, intelligent former soldier who in the 1820s was persuaded that he had from Bible reading determined the date when Christ would return to earth and claim his kingdom. October 23, 1844, was the date which stirred thousands to exalted expectations. Malice and excitement produced the fantasy or falsehood that Millerites had awaited the coming of Christ adorned in white "ascension robes."[3]

2. John A. Schutz and Douglass Adair, *The Spur of Fame, Dialogues of John Adams and Benjamin Rush, 1805–1813* (San Marino, Calif.: Huntington Library, 1966), p. 242.

3. See Francis D. Nichol, *The Midnight Cry, a Defense of William Miller and the Millerites* (Washington, D.C.: Review and Herald Publishing Association, 1944), for a carefully researched study of the subject.

There can be no denying, however, the genuine hope Miller inspired and the disappointment which followed the uneventful passing of the great day.

The hope did not die. It continued directly in the career of the Seventh-Day Adventists and other religious sects. In a larger sense it expressed a hope that life was no meaningless succession of events and competitive actions, but rather a promise and fulfillment. As early as 1818, a vision of the "millennium" by a distinguished educator, Joseph Emerson (1777–1833), a kinsman of Ralph Waldo Emerson, anticipated Christ's coming and a spirit of brotherhood which directed many of the efforts of partisans of the reform era.

1.

WILLIAM ELLERY CHANNING:
"Hold Fast This Freedom"

Reverend William Ellery Channing (1780–1842) held a unique position in the America of his time. Though a New Englander in temperament and an intellectual in approach, he won almost universal approbation for kindly and distinguished qualities. A leader of Unitarians, he decried Calvinism, deplored war, and though sickly and retiring, took active measures to aid the poor. He was a major influence on Dorothea L. Dix and also on Elizabeth Palmer Peabody, who did much to create the kindergarten, and his views were respected in the South as well as in his native section. His conclusion in Slavery *(1835) that human bondage was a sin impressed numerous Northerners who had been unimpressed by abolitionists and constituted a moral defeat for defenders of the "patriarchal institution." The following is from his sermons on "Duties of the Citizen in Times of Trial or Danger," following the American declaration of war against Great Britain in 1812.*

In all circumstances, at all times, war is to be deprecated. The evil passions which it excites, its ravages, its bloody conflicts, the distress and terror which it carries into domestic life, the tears which it draws from the widow and fatherless, all render war a tremendous scourge.

There are indeed conditions in which war is justifiable, is necessary. It may be the last and only method of repelling law-

SOURCE: William Ellery Channing, *Works* (Boston: James Munroe and Co., 1848), vol. XV, pp. 411 ff.

less ambition, and of defending invaded liberty and essential rights. It may be the method which God's providence points out by furnishing the means of success. In these cases we must not shrink from war; though even in these we should deeply lament the necessity of shedding human blood. In such wars our country claims and deserves our prayers, our cheerful services, the sacrifice of wealth and even of life. In such wars, we have one consolation, when our friends fall on the field of battle; we know that they have fallen in a just cause. Such conflicts, which our hearts and consciences approve, are suited to call forth generous sentiments, to breathe patriotism and fortitude through a community. Could I view the war in which we are engaged in this light, with what different feelings, my friends, should I address you! We might then look up to God and commit to him our country with a holy confidence. But, in our present state, what can I say to you? I would, but I cannot address you in the language of encouragement. We are precipitated into a war, which, I think, cannot be justified, and a war which promises not a benefit, that I can discover, to this country or to the world.

A solemn question now offers itself. What conduct belongs to a good citizen in our present trying condition? To this subject I call your serious attention.

Our condition induces me to begin with urging on you the important duty of cherishing respect for civil government, and a spirit of obedience to the laws. I am sensible, that many whom I address consider themselves as called to oppose the measures of our present rulers. Let this opposition breathe nothing of insubordination, impatience of authority, or love of change. It becomes you to remember, that government is a divine institution, essential to the improvement of our nature, the spring of industry and enterprise, the shield of property and life, the refuge of the weak and oppressed. . . .

It is impossible that all the regulations of the wisest government should equally benefit every individual; and sometimes the general good will demand arrangements, which will interfere with the interests of particular members or classes of the nation. In such circumstances, the individual is bound to regard the inconveniences under which he suffers, as inseparable from a social, connected state, as the result of the condition which God has appointed, and not as the fault of his rulers; and he should cheerfully submit, recollecting how much more he receives from the community than he is called to resign to it. Disaffection towards a government which is administered with a view to the general welfare, is a great crime; and such opposition, even to a bad government, as springs from and spreads a restless temper, an unwillingness to yield to wholesome and necessary restraint, deserves no better name. In proportion as a people want a conscientious regard to the laws, and are prepared to evade them by fraud, or to arrest their operation by violence—in that proportion they need and deserve an arbitrary government, strong enough to crush at a blow every symptom of opposition.

These general remarks on the duty of submission, are by no means designed to teach that rulers are never to be opposed. Because I wish to guard you against that turbulent and discontented spirit, which precipitates free communities into an anarchy, and thus prepares them for chains, you will not consider me as asserting that all opposition to government, whatever be the occasion, or whatever the form, is to be branded as a crime. The citizen has rights as well as duties. Government is instituted for one and a single end, the benefit of the governed, the protection, peace, and welfare of society; and when it is perverted to other objects, to purposes of avarice, ambition, or party spirit, we are authorized and even bound to make such opposition, as is suited to restore it to its proper end, to render it as pure as the imperfection of our nature and state will admit. . . .

Resistance of established power is so great an evil, civil commotion excites such destructive passions, the result is so tremendously uncertain, that every milder method of relief should first be tried, and fairly tried. The last dreadful resort is never justifiable, until the injured members of the community are brought to despair of other relief, and are so far united in views and purposes as to be authorized in the hope of success. Civil commotion should be viewed as the worst of national evils, with the single exception of slavery. I know that this country has passed through one civil war, without experiencing the calamitous consequences of which I have spoken. But let us not forget, that this was a civil war of a very peculiar character. The government which we shook off was not seated in the midst of us. Our struggle was that of nation with nation, rather than of fellow-citizens with one another. Our manners and habits tended to give a considerateness and a stability to the public mind, which can hardly be expected in a future struggle. And, in addition to these favorable circumstances, we were favored by Heaven with a leader of incorruptible integrity, of unstained purity; a patriot who asked no glory, but that of delivering his country, who desired to reign only in the hearts of a free and happy people, whose disinterestedness awed and repressed the selfish and ambitious, who inspired universal confidence, and thus was a centre and bond of union to the minds of men in the most divided and distracted periods of our country. The name of WASHINGTON I may pronounce with reverence even in the temple of the Almighty; and it is a name which revives the sinking spirits in this day of our declining glory. From a revolution, conducted by such a man, under such circumstances, let no conclusions be hastily drawn on the subject of civil commotion.

It becomes us to rejoice, my friends, that we live under a constitution, one great design of which is, to prevent the necessity of appealing to force, to give the people an opportunity of removing, without violence, those rulers from whom they suffer or apprehend an invasion of rights. This is one of the principal advantages of a republic over an absolute government. In a despotism, there is no remedy for oppression but force. The subject cannot influence public affairs, but by convulsing the state. With us, rulers may be changed, without the horrors of a revolution. A republican government secures to its subjects this immense privilege, by confirming to them two most important rights—the right of suffrage, and the right of discussing with freedom the conduct of rulers. The value of these rights in affording a peaceful method of redressing public grievances, cannot be expressed, and the duty of maintaining them, of never surrendering them, cannot be too strongly urged. Resign either of these, and no way of escape from oppression will be left you, but civil commotion.

From the important place which these rights hold in a republican government, you should consider yourselves bound to support every citizen in the lawful exercise of them, especially when an attempt is made to wrest them from any by violent means. At the present time, it is particularly your duty to guard, with jealousy, the right of expressing with freedom your honest convictions respecting the measures of your rulers. Without this, the right of election is not worth possessing. If public abuses may not be exposed, their authors will never be driven from power. Freedom of opinion, of speech, and of the press, is our most valuable privilege, the very soul of republican institutions, the safeguard of all other rights. We may learn its value if we reflect that there is nothing which tyrants so much dread. They anxiously fetter the press; they scatter spies through society, that the murmurs, anguish, and indignation of their oppressed subjects may be smothered in their own breasts; that no generous sentiment may be nourished by sympathy and mutual confidence. Nothing awakens and improves men so much as free communication of thoughts and feelings. Nothing can give to public sentiment that correctness which is essential to the prosperity of a Commonwealth, but the free circulation of truth, from the lips and pens of the wise and good. If such men abandon the right of free discussion; if, awed by threats, they suppress their convictions; if rulers succeed in silencing every voice but that which approves them; if nothing reaches the people but what will lend support to men in power—farewell to liberty. The form of a free government may remain, but the life, the soul, the substance is fled.

If these remarks be just, nothing ought to excite greater indignation and alarm than the attempts which have lately been made, to destroy the freedom of the press. We have lived to hear the strange doctrine, that to expose the measures of rulers is treason; and we have lived to see this doctrine carried into practice. We have seen a savage populace excited and let loose on men whose crime consisted in bearing testimony against the present war; and let loose, not merely to waste their property, but to tear them from the refuge which the magistrate had afforded, and to shed their blood. In this, and in other events, there have been symptoms of a purpose to terrify into silence those who disapprove the calamitous war under which we suffer; to deprive us of the only method which is left, of obtaining a wiser and better government. The cry has been, that war is declared, and all opposition should therefore be hushed. A sentiment more unworthy of a free country can hardly be propagated. If this doctrine be admitted, rulers have only to declare war, and they are screened at once from scrutiny. At the very time when they have armies at command, when their patronage is most extended, and their power most formidable, not a word of warning, of censure, of alarm must be heard. The press, which is to expose inferior abuses, must not utter one rebuke, one indignant complaint, although our best interests and most valuable rights are put to hazard, by an unnecessary war! Admit this doctrine, let rulers once know, that, by placing the country in a state of war, they place themselves beyond the only power they dread, the power of free discussion, and we may expect war without end. Our peace and all our interests require, that a different sentiment should prevail. We should teach our present and all future rulers, that there is no measure for which they must render so solemn an account to their constituents, as for a declaration of war; that no measure will be so freely, so fully discussed; and that no ad-

ministration can succeed in persuading this people to exhaust
their treasure and blood in supporting war, unless it be palpably
necessary and just. In war, then, as in peace, assert the freedom
of speech and of the press. Cling to this as the bulwark of all
your rights and privileges.

But, my friends, I should not be faithful, were I only to call
you to hold fast this freedom. I would still more earnestly exhort
you not to abuse it. Its abuse may be as fatal to our country as its
relinquishment. If undirected, unrestrained by principle, the
press, instead of enlightening, depraves the public mind; and, by
its licentiousness, forges chains for itself and for the community.
The right of free discussion is not the right of uttering what we
please. Let nothing be spoken or written but truth. The influence
of the press is exceedingly diminished by its gross and frequent
misrepresentations. Each party listens with distrust to the statements of the other; and the consequence is, that the progress of
truth is slow, and sometimes wholly obstructed. Whilst we encourage the free expression of opinion, let us unite in fixing the
brand of infamy on falsehood and slander, wherever they originate, whatever be the cause they are designed to maintain.

But it is not enough that truth be told. It should be told for a
good end; not to irritate, but to convince; not to inflame the bad
passions, but to sway the judgment and to awaken sentiments of
patriotism. Unhappily the press seems now to be chiefly prized as
an instrument of exasperation. Those who have embraced error,
are hardened in their principles by the reproachful epithets
heaped on them by their adversaries. I do not mean by this, that
political discussion is to be conducted tamely, that no sensibility
is to be expressed, no indignation to be poured forth on wicked
men and wicked deeds. But this I mean,—that we shall deliberately inquire, whether indignation be deserved, before we express it; and the object of expressing it should ever be, not to
infuse ill will, rancor, and fury into the minds of men, but to
excite an enlightened and conscientious opposition to injurious
measures. . . .

2

THOMAS JEFFERSON:
"Like a Fire-Bell in the Night"

Revisionist opinion has become critical of Thomas Jefferson (1743–1826) for having withheld a full measure of concern for Negro emancipation as part of his faith in the Rights of Man. This fact reverses an earlier trend which presumed to imagine that Jefferson would have endorsed all revolutions against the American establishment. In fact the national government was Jefferson's major passion, and for it he had accepted the compromises which had secured slavery. Like Lincoln, later, Jefferson feared tampering with hard-won libertarian slogans and hopes in the interests of secessionist adventurers. The Missouri crisis of 1819–20 shocked and depressed him as the rock upon which the Union might be shattered and with it the Constitution as an arena in which otherwise dispersed sections could fight out and mature their differences. Thus his desperate measures, set down below, were offered not in defense of slavery but of a democratic forum which might nurture change without social disintegration. A few abolitionists later repudiated Jefferson. More found it helpful to call him as a witness to their crusade.

TO JOHN HOLMES

Monticello, April 22, 1820

I thank you, dear Sir, for the copy you have been so kind as to send me of the letter to your constituents on the Missouri question. It is a perfect justification to them. I had for a long time

SOURCE: Thomas Jefferson, *Works* (Washington, D.C.: Thomas Jefferson Memorial Association), vol. XV, pp. 248–250.

ceased to read newspapers, or pay any attention to public affairs, confident they were in good hands, and content to be a passenger in our bark to the shore from which I am not distant. But this momentous question, like a fire-bell in the night, awakened and filled me with terror. I considered it at once as the knell of the Union. It is hushed, indeed, for the moment. But this is a re-prieve only, not a final sentence. A geographical line, coinciding with a marked principle, moral and political, once conceived and held up to the angry passions of men, will never be obliterated; and every new irritation will mark it deeper and deeper. I can say, with conscious truth, that there is not a man on earth who would sacrifice more than I would to relieve us from this heavy reproach, in any *practicable* way. The cession of that kind of property, for so it is misnamed, is a bagatelle which would not cost me a second thought, if, in that way, a general emancipation and *expatriation* could be effected; and, gradually, and with due sacrifices, I think it might be. But as it is, we have the wolf by the ears, and we can neither hold him, nor safely let him go. Justice is in one scale, and self-preservation in the other. Of one thing I am certain, that as the passage of slaves from one State to an-other, would not make a slave of a single human being who would not be so without it, so their diffusion over a greater surface would make them individually happier, and proportion-ally facilitate the accomplishment of their emancipation, by dividing the burden on a greater number of coadjutors. An absti-nence too, from this act of power, would remove the jealousy excited by the undertaking of Congress to regulate the condition of the different descriptions of men composing a State. This certainly is the exclusive right of every State, which nothing in the Constitution has taken from them and given to the General Government. Could Congress, for example, say, that the non-freemen of Connecticut shall be freemen, or that they shall not emigrate into any other State?

I regret that I am now to die in the belief that the useless sacrifice of themselves by the generation of 1776 to acquire self-government and happiness to their country is to be thrown away by the unwise and unworthy passions of their sons, and that my only consolation is to be that I live not to weep over it. If they would but dispassionately weigh the blessings they will throw away against an abstract principle more likely to be effected by union than by scission, they would pause before they would perpetrate this act of suicide on themselves and of treason against the hopes of the world. To yourself, as the faithful advocate of the Union, I tender the offering of my high esteem and respect.

3.

JAMES FORTEN:
"Hoa, Negro, where is your Certificate!"

James Forten (1766–1842) was one of the most distinguished of all Negro leaders: a Philadelphian who served in the Revolutionary Navy and became a wealthy sailmaker and civic leader. During the War of 1812 he helped organize Negro volunteers to protect Philadelphia against British assaults. A pioneer abolitionist, he helped marshal Negro opinion against the colonization program. Forten helped subsidize William Lloyd Garrison's early efforts to establish the Liberator *and build an abolitionist movement. He also endorsed women's rights and other reform activities. The following protest appeared in published letters by Forten. It was one of many protests involving Negroes and white friends to prevent backsliding in northern states on civil rights. This continuing campaign—successful in the present instance—revealed aspects of northern tolerance and also of prejudice to both of which reformers would address their efforts.*

We hold this truth to be self-evident, that God created all men equal, is one of the most prominent features in the Declaration of Independence, and in that glorious fabric of collected wisdom, our noble Constitution. This idea embraces the Indian and the European, the savage and the Saint, the Peruvian and the Laplander, the white man and the African, and whatever measures are adopted subversive of this inestimable privilege, are in direct violation of the letter and spirit of our Constitution, and become

SOURCE: James Forten, *Letters from a Man of Colour on a Late Bill before the Senate of Pennsylvania* (Philadelphia, 1813).

subject to the animadversion of all, particularly those who are deeply interested in the measure.

These thoughts were suggested by the promulgation of a late bill, before the Senate of Pennsylvania, to prevent the emigration of people of color into this state. It was not passed into a law at this session, and must in consequence lay over until the next, before when we sincerely hope, the white men, whom we should look upon as our protectors, will have become convinced of the inhumanity and impolicy of such a measure, and forbear to deprive us of those inestimable treasures, liberty and independence. This is almost the only state in the Union wherein the African race have justly boasted of rational liberty and the protection of the laws, and shall it now be said they have been deprived of that liberty, and publicly exposed for sale to the highest bidder? Shall colonial inhumanity that has marked many of us with shameful stripes, become the practice of the people of Pennsylvania, while Mercy stands weeping at the miserable spectacle? People of Pennsylvania, descendants of the immortal Penn, doom us not to the unhappy fate of thousands of our countrymen in the Southern States and the West Indies; despise the traffic in blood, and the blessing of the African will forever be around you. Many of us are men of property, for the security of which we have hitherto looked to the laws of our blessed state, but should this become a law, our property is jeopardized, since the same power which can expose to sale an unfortunate fellow creature, can wrest from him those estates, which years of honest industry have accumulated. Where shall the poor African look for protection, should the people of Pennsylvania consent to oppress him? We grant there are a number of worthless men belonging to our color, but there are laws of sufficient rigor for their punishment, if properly and duly enforced. We wish not to screen the guilty from punishment, but with the guilty do not permit the innocent to suffer. If there are worthless men, there are also men of merit among the African race, who are useful members of Society. The truth of this let their benevolent institutions and the numbers clothed and fed by them witness. Punish the guilty man of color to the utmost limit of the laws, but sell him not to slavery! If he is in danger of becoming a public charge, prevent him! If he is too indolent to labor for his own subsistence, compel him to do so; but sell him not to slavery. By selling him you do not make him better, but commit a wrong, without benefiting the object of it or society at large. Many of our ancestors were brought here more than one hundred years ago; many of our fathers, many of ourselves, have fought and bled for the independence of our country. Do not then expose us to sale. Let not the spirit of the father behold the son robbed of that liberty which he died to establish, but let the motto of our legislature be: "The law knows no distinction. . . ."

Those patriotic citizens, who, after resting from the toils of an arduous war, which achieved our independence and laid the foundation of the only reasonable republic upon earth, associated together, and for the protection of those inestimable rights for the establishment of which they had exhausted their blood and treasure, framed the Constitution of Pennsylvania, have by the ninth article declared, that "All men are born equally free and independent, and have certain inherent and indefeasible rights, among which are those of enjoying life and liberty." Under the restraint of wise and well administered laws, we cordially unite in the above glorious sentiment, but by the bill upon which we have been remarking, it appears as if the committee who drew it up mistook the sentiment expressed in this article, and do not consider us as men, or that those enlightened statesmen who formed the Constitution upon the basis of experience, intended to exclude us from its blessings and protection. If the former, why are we not to be considered as men? Has the God who made the white man and the black left any record declaring us a different species? Are we not sustained by the same power, supported by the same food, hurt by the same wounds, wounded by the same wrongs, pleased with the same delights, and propagated by the same means? And should we not then enjoy the same liberty, and be protected by the same laws? We wish not to legislate, for our means of information and the acquisition of knowledge are, in the nature of things, so circumscribed, that we must consider ourselves incompetent to the task; but let us, in legislation be considered as men. It cannot be that the authors of our Constitution intended to exclude us from its benefits, for just emerging from unjust and cruel emancipation, their souls were too much affected with their own deprivations to commence the reign of terror over others. They knew we were deeper skinned than they were, but they acknowledged us as men, and found that many an honest heart beat beneath a dusky bosom. They felt that they had no more authority to enslave us, than England had to tyrannize over them. They were convinced that if amenable to the same laws in our actions we should be protected by the same laws in our rights and privileges. Actuated by these sentiments they adopted the glorious fabric of our liberties, and declaring "all men" free, they did not particularize white and black, because they never supposed it would be made a question whether *we were men or not*. Sacred be the ashes, and deathless be the memory of those heroes who are dead; and revered be the persons and the characters of those who still exist and lift the thunders of admonition against the traffic in blood. And here my brethren in color, let the tear of gratitude and the sigh of regret break forth for that great and good man, who lately fell a victim to the promiscuous fury of death, in whom you have lost a zealous friend, a powerful and herculean advocate; a sincere adviser, and one who spent many an hour of his life to break your fetters, and ameliorate your condition—I mean the ever to be lamented Dr. Benjamin Rush. . . .

Let us put a case, in which the law in question operates peculiarly hard and unjust.—I have a brother, perhaps, who resides in a distant part of the Union, and after a separation of years, actuated by the same fraternal affection which beats in the bosom of a white man, he comes to visit me. Unless that brother be registered in twenty-four hours after, and be able to produce a certificate of that effect, he is liable, according to the second and third sections of the bill, to a fine of twenty dollars, to arrest, imprisonment and sale. Let the unprejudiced mind ponder upon this, and then pronounce it the justifiable act of a free people, if he can. To this we trust our cause, without fear of the issue. The unprejudiced must pronounce any act tending to deprive a free man of his right, freedom and immunities, as not only cruel in the extreme, but decidedly unconstitutional both as regards the letter and spirit of that glorious instrument. The same power which protects the white man, should protect the black.

The evils arising from the bill before our Legislature, so fatal to the rights of freemen, and so characteristic of European despotism, are so numerous, that to consider them all would extend these numbers further than time or my talent will permit me to carry them. The concluding paragraph of my last utterance, states a case of peculiar hardship, arising from the second section of this bill, upon which I cannot refrain from making a few more remarks. The man of color receiving as a visitor any other person of color, is bound to turn informer, and rudely report to the Register, that a friend and brother has come to visit him for a few days, whose name he must take within twenty-four hours, or forfeit a sum which the iron hand of the law is authorized to rend from him, partly for the benefit of the Register. Who is this Register? A man, and exercising an office, where ten dollars is the fee for each delinquent, will probably be a cruel man and find delinquents where they really do not exist. The poor black is left to the merciless gripe of an avaricious Register, without an appeal, in the event, from his tyranny or oppression! O miserable race, born to the same hopes, created with the same feeling, and destined for the same goal, you are reduced by your fellow creatures below the brute. The dog is protected and pampered at the board of his master, while the poor African and his descendant, whether a Saint or a felon, is branded with infamy, registered as a slave, and we may expect shortly to find a law to prevent their increase, by taxing them according to numbers, and authorizing the constables to seize and confine every one who dare to walk the streets without a collar on his neck! . . .

For the honor and dignity of our native state, we wish not to see this bill pass into a law, as well as for its degrading tendency towards us; for although oppressed by those to whom we look for protection, our grievances are light compared with the load of reproach that must be heaped upon our commonwealth. The story will fly from the north to the south, and the advocates of slavery, the traders in human blood, will smile contemptuously at the once boasted moderation and humanity of Pennsylvania! What! That place, whose institutions for the prevention of slavery, are the admiration of surrounding states and of Europe, becomes the advocate of mancipation and wrong and the oppressor of the free and innocent!—Tell it not in Gath!

By the third section of this bill, which is its peculiar hardship, the police officers are authorized to apprehend any black, whether a vagrant or a man of reputable character, who cannot produce a certificate that he has been registered. He is to be arrayed before a justice, who is thereupon to commit him to prison!—The jailor is to advertise a Freeman, and at the expiration of six months, if no owner appear for this degraded black, he is to be *exposed to sale,* and if not sold to be confined at hard labor for seven years!!—Man of feeling, read this!—No matter who, no matter where. The constable, whose antipathy generally against the black is very great, will take every opportunity of hurting his feelings!—Perhaps he sees him at a distance, and having a mind to raise the boys in hue and cry against him, exclaims, "Halloa! Stop the Negro!" The boys, delighting in the sport, immediately begin to hunt him, and immediately from a hundred tongues is heard the cry—*"Hoa, Negro, where is your Certificate!"*—Can anything be done more shocking to the principles of civil liberty! A person arriving from another state, ignorant of the existence of such a law, may fall a victim to its cruel oppression. But he is to be advertised, and if no owner appear—how can an owner appear for a man who is free and belongs to no one!—if no owner appear, he is exposed for sale!—Oh, inhuman spectacle: found in no unjust act, convicted of no crime, he is barbarously sold, like the produce of the soil, to the highest bidder, or what is still worse, for no crimes, without the inestimable privilege of a trial by his peers, doomed to the dreary walls of a prison for the term of seven tedious years! . . .

The fifth section of this bill is also peculiarly hard, inasmuch as it prevents freemen from living where they please.—Pennsylvania has always been a refuge from slavery, and to this state the Southern black, when freed, has flown for safety. Why does he this? When masters in many of the Southern states, which they frequently do, free a particular black, unless the black leaves the state in so many hours, any person resident of the said state, can have him arrested and again sold to slavery:—The hunted black is obliged to flee, or remain and be again a slave. I have known persons of this description sold three times after being first emancipated. Where shall he go? Shut every state against him, and, like Pharaoh's kine, drive him into the sea.—Is there no spot on earth that will protect him! Against their inclination, his ancestors were forced from their homes by traders in human flesh, and even under such circumstances the wretched offspring are denied the protection you afford to brutes.

It is in vain that we are forming societies of different kinds to ameliorate the conditions of our unfortunate brethren, to correct their morals and to render them not only honest but useful members to society. All our efforts by this bill are despised, and we are doomed to feel the lash of oppression:—As well may we be outlawed, as well may the glorious privileges of the Gospel be denied us, and all endeavors used to cut us off from happiness hereafter as well as here! The case is similar, and I am much deceived if this bill does not destroy the morals it is intended to produce. . . .

4.

ROBERT OWEN:
New Harmony

Robert Owen (1771–1858), one of the founders of socialism, came to the United States with extraordinary credentials. His brilliant commercial success as an owner of cotton mills at New Lanark, Scotland, had involved experiments in labor relations, children's education and community living which suggested that industry need not threaten humanity but could emancipate it. Owen's A New View of Society *held character to be the product of circumstances. Given due conditions, labor would advance society rather than debase it. Owen's purchase of the Harmony settlement in Indiana from Rappites—a more successful community than Owen's, yet curiously forgotten—stirred interest. Owen's two lectures, February 25 and March 7, 1825, in the House of Representatives in Washington, from which passages are given below, were attended by President John Quincy Adams, former President James Monroe and numerous other dignitaries. New Harmony was conceived as a pilot plant to inspire the erection of others (one briefly materialized in Yellow Springs, Ohio), but the earnest efforts of Owen's excellent associates could not prevent New Harmony's rapid deterioration. Owen's own atheistic oration, July 4, 1826, announcing a Declaration of Mental Independence, was peculiarly unfortunate. For on that day Thomas Jefferson died at Monticello, his Virginia estate, and John Adams died at his home in Braintree, Massachusetts: the last of the signers of the Declaration of Independence. The pulpits rang with sermons alleging that the coincidence was manifestly supernatural.*

SOURCE: Robert Owen, *A Discourse on a New System of Society; As Delivered on the 25th of February, 1825* . . . (Washington, D.C.: Gales & Seaton, 1825), pp. 10 *et seq.*

Man, through ignorance, has been, hitherto, the tormentor of man.

He is *here,* in a nation deeming itself possessed of more privileges than all other nations, and which pretensions, in many respects, must be admitted to be true. Yet, even *here,* where the laws are the most mild, and consequently the least unjust and irrational, individuals are punished even to death, for actions which are the natural and necessary effects arising from the injurious circumstances which the government and society, to which they belong, unwisely permit to exist; while other individuals are almost as much injured by being as unjustly rewarded for performing actions for which, as soon as they shall become rational beings, they must be conscious they cannot be entitled to a particle of merit.

It is true that, from obvious causes, the great mass of the people, in all countries, have been so trained by the circumstances around them, that they have been forced, unknown to themselves, to receive notions which are opposed to the great and important truths which I have placed before you, and, in consequence, the most lamentable ignorance of human nature universally prevails, and poverty, and injustice, and vice, and misery, at this hour, everywhere superabound.

Vast numbers of men, and more particularly women, in all countries, have been forced, from generation to generation, to receive, in infancy, as true, various imaginary notions, long prevalent in those countries, and they have been taught that their happiness or misery depended upon their belief or disbelief in the truth of those notions. In various countries, these notions differ materially. In some, they are in direct opposition to others, and, as *all* are trained to think that the notions taught in their own country are so true that it is impossible they can be deceived, and that those in opposition to them are so false that none but the most ignorant and weak will be made to believe in them, and that such false and wicked notions must produce vicious conduct: In this manner, every imaginable bad feeling, that can be implanted in human nature, is generated and fostered. National, sectarian, and individual antipathies necessarily follow; division and counteraction, of every description, succeed, and the world is thus forced to become a chaotic scene of confusion, disorder, and misery.

It is so at this moment, and strange to say, it has been made to be so through those original qualities of our nature which, whenever they shall be rightly directed, and justice shall be done to them, will produce the fullness of charity, and kindness, and sincerity, from each to all, until we shall become, in fact and in reality, a new people, having but one common interest; and then all the benefits of the world will be freely open to every one, and, in consequence, all will be gainers, to an extent that no imagination has been yet trained to be competent to conceive. . . .

I have said, give liberty to America; but the natives of this empire have been taught to believe, that they already possess full liberty. I know it is *not* so; and, in proof of this denial, permit me to ask, how many present feel they possess the power to speak their real sentiments, freely and openly, on subjects the most important to themselves and to the well being of society? Until this can be done, and done without any disadvantage whatever to those who do it, liberty has not been attained, and you have yet to work out for yourselves this, the most precious and valuable part of liberty. Many must be now conscious that they are to a great extent under the despotism of weak minds, who are themselves the slaves of superstition and prejudice. Until human beings shall, without any inconvenience whatever, speak openly and frankly the genuine impression of their mind on all subjects, they must be considered to be in a state of mental bondage, and in that condition all men have ever yet been, and, to a greater extent, perhaps, than you suspect, you are so even now. By a hard struggle you have attained political liberty, but you have yet to acquire real mental liberty, and if you cannot possess yourselves of it, your political liberty will be precarious and of much less value. The attainment of political liberty is, however, a necessary step towards the acquirement of real mental liberty, and as you have obtained the former, I have come here to assist you to secure the latter. For, without mental liberty, there can be no sincerity; and, without sincerity, devoid of all deception, there can be no real virtue or happiness among mankind.

My desire now is, to introduce into these States, and through them, to the world at large, a new social system, formed in practice of an entire new combination of circumstances, all of them having a direct moral, intellectual, and beneficial tendency, fully adequate to effect the most important improvements throughout society. This system has been solely derived from the facts relative to our common nature, which I have previously explained.

In this new social arrangement, a much more perfect system of liberty and equality will be introduced than has yet anywhere existed, or been deemed attainable in practice. Within it, there will be no privileged thoughts or belief; everyone will be at full liberty to express the genuine impressions, which the circumstances around them have made on their minds, as well as their own undisguised reflections thereon, and then no motive will exist for deception or insincerity of any kind.

Everyone will be instructed in the outline of all the real knowledge which experience has yet discovered. This will be effected on a plan in unison with our nature, and by which the equality of the mental faculties will be rendered more perfect, and by which all will be elevated much above what any can attain under the existing despotism of mind; and by these arrangements the general intellect of society will be enabled to make greater advances in a year, than it has been hitherto allowed to attain in a century. The innumerable and incalculable evils and absurdities which have arisen from the inequality of wealth, will be effectually overcome and avoided throughout all the future. By arrangements, as simple and desirable as they will be beneficial for everyone, all will possess, at all times, a full supply of the best of everything for human nature, as far as present experience, on these matters, can direct our knowledge.

The degrading and pernicious practice in which we are now trained, of buying cheap and selling dear, will be rendered wholly unnecessary: for, so long as this principle shall govern the transactions of men, nothing really great or noble can be expected from mankind.

The whole trading system is one of deception; one by which each engaged in it is necessarily trained to endeavor to obtain advantages over others, and in which the interest of all is opposed to each, and, in consequence, not one can attain the advantages that, under another and a better system, might be, with far less labor, and without risk secured in perpetuity to all.

The consequence of this inferior trading system is to give a very injurious surplus of wealth and power to the few, and to inflict poverty and subjection on the many.

In the new system, union and co-operation will supersede individual interest, and the universal counteraction of each other's objects; and, by the change, the powers of one man will obtain for him the advantages of many, and all will become as rich as they will desire. The very imperfect experiments of the Moravians, Shakers, and Harmonites, give sure proof of the gigantic superiority of union over division, for the creation of wealth. But these associations have been hitherto subject to many disadvantages, and their progress and success have been materially counteracted by many obstacles which will not exist under a system, founded on a correct knowledge of the constitution of our nature.

We cannot fail to be alive to the superiority of combined over individual efforts, when applied to destroy. We all know the increased power acquired by a small army, united, and acting as one body, over the same number of men acting singly and alone—and if such advantages can be gained by union to destroy, why should it not be applied to our benefit for civil purposes?

During his second lecture, Owen discussed his plan for education which was to "comprise the first combination of circumstances . . . to do anything like justice to the physical and mental powers of any human being." He went on to explain a model of a community calculated to render extant communities obsolete:

The four buildings within the square, one of which projects from the centre of each of the sides, contain the culinary arrangements, the dining apartments, stores, washing, drying, brewing, and every other domestic accommodation, arranged in a superior manner, by men of great science and practical experience. The schools, lecture rooms, laboratories, chapels, ball and concert rooms, conversation rooms, committee and other public rooms, are in the centers and angles of the building. The private dwellings of the inhabitants are between the centers and angles, and occupy the first and second story. The third story contains the dormitories for the unmarried persons, and children above two years of age. There is a communication under cover, from each dwelling to every other, and to all the public rooms, throughout the whole extent of the square. Each apartment will be heated, cooled, ventilated, supplied with gas lights, and hot or cold water, at the will of the occupants, by merely turning a cock or moving a slide. All the apartments may be cooled in warm weather much below, and warmed in cold weather much above, the temperature of the atmosphere, and under these scientific domestic arrangements, one person, chiefly employed in an interesting direction of mechanical and chemical operations, will perform as much as twenty, under the separate individual system, can accomplish in the same time. By these new arrangements, two essential objects will be secured; the operative or producer will be better trained and educated than the working or any class has been heretofore, and they will be supported at a less expense than must be incurred under any individual system, which can afford but one-half of the advantages that these new arrangements will secure to everyone, even from the commencement. Under these circumstances, therefore, manual and mental power would be produced of a superior quality, and maintained at a less expenditure than under the separate or individual system; consequently, all other circumstances being supposed to be the same, whatever these united labors produce, whether from agriculture or manufactures, will be better and cheaper than similar productions can be brought to market by any individual, seeing that the cost of all productions consists in the value of the labor they contain. Upon this principle, now universally admitted, the present buildings in the country, in villages, towns, and cities, will as rapidly disappear as the new combinations before you can be introduced into practice.

This combination, however, will not only create a superior quality of labor, and support it, in more comfort, at a much less expense than any individual system, but it will place the parties under the most favorable circumstances for gardening, agricultural, and manufacturing operations, which will be so united as to enable each to assist the others, at the different seasons of the year, in such a manner as to secure seed and harvest operations with one-fourth of the favorable weather required in farms and gardens under the present system.

In short, the advantages of this new combination, for health, for forming a superior character, for producing, for consuming, for securing, free from all pecuniary anxieties, the chief benefits, without the disadvantages, of a country, city, and college life, and for enjoying the best society in the most convenient manner, will be discovered to offer such overwhelming temptations to human nature to change from the present system that I conclude it will be impracticable to provide these new abodes of rational improvement and enjoyment, as speedily as society will desire to possess them.

When these buildings, gardens, and pleasure grounds, shall be formed, the next important inquiry is, how are they to be governed?

To explain this part of the subject, I will, with your permission, now read some rules and regulations which were drawn up, two or three years ago, for an independent society, to be formed of the operative classes, upon the supposition that they borrowed all the capital. . . .

Such are the rules and regulations which are proposed and recommended for an association of the operative classes, on these new principles of union and co-operation, and I have no doubt, but the plain good sense and practical knowledge of many among those classes, will be found, with very little assistance, sufficient to understand the principles, and to carry them into practice upon borrowed capital, what security could be offered superior to that which they could give? Namely, land well chosen for their purpose, and bought at its present value; buildings erected, to be much more convenient, and, therefore, in the same proportion, more valuable than any existing buildings; the land annually improving, by an extensive and improved cultivation, and manufactures established under the latest improvements; these, added to the security of an association of from 1000 to 2000 industrious and temperate persons, each aiding and none opposing each other, would present such an aggregate of substantial security, continually improving, as is not to be found, perhaps, under any other circumstances. I hope the government of all the states composing the Union, will investigate the whole of this subject, in such a manner as to enable the citizens of each state to become fully satisfied that the principles on which it rests, are so true, that error cannot be found in them, and the practice so beneficial, that it will be evidently the interest of one and all to adopt it with the least delay, that not one day more of unnecessary anxiety and suffering should be experienced by the inhabitants of this country.

But, whatever others may do, my purpose is fixed—I mean to carry these measures of amelioration to the full extent of my means and influence, into immediate execution.

With this view, I have purchased from the Harmonite Society, the settlement and property of Harmony, in the states of Indiana and Illinois. The settlement, or town of Harmony, is upon the Wabash, in Indiana; it is composed of log, weather boarded, and brick dwelling houses; of infant manufactures, of wool, cotton, leather, hats, pottery, bricks, machinery, grain, distilleries, breweries, &c, &c., with granaries, and two large Churches, and other public buildings, laid out in regular squares like all the modern American towns. It does not, however, form such a combination as the model before you represents, and, therefore, it will serve only a temporary, but yet a useful temporary purpose, for the objects which I have in view. It will enable me to form immediately a preliminary society in which to receive a new population, and to collect, prepare, and arrange the materials for erecting several such combinations, as the model represents, and of forming several independent, yet united associations, having common property, and one common interest. These new establishments will be erected upon the high lands of Harmony, from two to four miles from the river, and its Island, of which the occupants will have a beautiful and interesting view, there being several thousand acres of well cultivated land, on a rich second bottom, lying between the highlands and the river. And here it is, in the heart of the United States, and almost the center of its unequalled internal navigation, that that power which directs and governs the universe and every action of man, has arranged circumstances which were far beyond my control, to permit me to commence a new empire of peace and good will to man, founded on other principles, and leading to other practices than those of the past or present, and which principles, in due season, and in the allotted time, will lead to that state of virtue, intelligence, enjoyment, and happiness, in practice, which has been foretold by the sages of past times, would, as some distant period, become the lot of the human race! Do not the dissatisfaction of all minds, in all countries, with the existing circumstances; the evident advance of just, kind, and benevolent feelings, and the universal expectation of some great change in human affairs, indicate and foretell this change? Do they not give assurance that the time is at hand, when evil shall give place to good—division to union—war to peace—anger to kindness—superstition to charity, and pure practical religion—prejudice to intelligence—and pain and misery to enjoyment and happiness? Assuredly they do, and it will be wise and prudent in us to be prepared for the event. . . .

The bright feature of our times is the existence of generous, hopeful, sympathizing spirits, intent on the melioration of their race.

William Ellery Channing

RESOLVED, that ten hours well and faithfully employed is as much as an employer ought to receive, or require, for a day's work; and that it is as much as any artisan, mechanic or laborer, ought to give. . . .

Resolutions passed at a meeting April 23, 1829, of "Mechanics and others, assembled . . . to consider the propriety of remonstrating against any further extension of the time of a day's work."

Elements of old social interests mingled with the new in transitional years between the War of 1812 and the 1830s. Thus Thomas H. Gallaudet was a pioneer in organizing educational schools for the deaf. He was also a minister earnestly concerned for disseminating the Scriptures among the young. Though no abolitionist, and only mildly antislavery in outlook, his eminent career lent respectability to more ardent spirits like Dr. Samuel Gridley Howe (1801–1876), who in the 1820s followed picturesque service with the Greeks in their battle against the Turks by dedicating himself to the blind and also, as the issue developed, to the Free Soil and abolitionist causes.

Many of the older generation were to serve the younger reformers, notably John Quincy Adams, who crowned his matchless career as United States Minister, Senator, Secretary of State and President by returning to the House of Representatives to become a fierce symbol of the fight for the right of petition. From 1836 to 1844 he resisted southern efforts to suppress Northerners who demanded their right, guaranteed by the First Amendment to the Constitution, to petition their congressmen for a redress of grievances. Those grievances included the presence of slaves in the District of Columbia (a district belonging to the entire nation), interference with freedom of the mails by postmasters reluctant to help circulate abolitionist newspapers and pamphlets and the attempt by partisans to bring Texas into the Union as slave territory. Since Texas's vast acres seemed destined to make perhaps six to eight slave states, such an accession threatened to destroy the balance of power in Congress between free and slave states.

Adams's fight for the right of petition—a varied and resourceful campaign which precipitated storms inside and out of the House of Representatives—underscored the dangers created by the slavery issue to the rights of free citizens as well as slaves and raised new defenders of those rights in Congress and throughout the North. When Adams was stricken at his desk in the House of Representatives in 1848, dying thereafter in the House chambers, it was as the true leader of a North which knew it could no longer afford Daniel Webster's prideful nationalistic rhetoric and vain hopes of sectional peace at the expense of its civil liberties.

Yet even Adams could not penetrate the troubled center of national unrest. President after President, in State of the Union messages, pointed to the continuing and expanding prosperity of the country. The economic depressions of 1815–1821 and after, including the severe panics of 1819 and 1837—products of short-sighted investments, suppression of labor organization and fiscal policies—could not dim the fact of America's awesome expanse of territory and untapped resources. Yet social unrest continued in good times and bad.

William Lloyd Garrison began his career not as an abolitionist but as a journalist and temperance advocate. Raised in a broken home and brother of a drunken seaman, Garrison saw in temperance a cause of primary social significance warranting his best talents. It also expressed his need for a simple, certain way of life, one of Christian rectitude. The moral assurance Garrison required could no more be satisfied by church ritual than it could satisfy Ralph Waldo Emerson, born in a family of ministers and graduate of the Divinity School of Harvard College. Emerson resigned his pastorate at the Second Church of Boston, where he was deemed popular and effective, because he could no longer sincerely administer the Lord's Supper. He needed a new faith, which introspection, travel and new associations matured. His invocations to nature, to self-reliance, to *oversoul* produced a minor scandal and contributed to a major social impulse toward self-expression at the expense of social forms. Garrison, too, in an era of individualists, had a career in journalism open to him which he put aside for more urgent matters.

Garrison in the late 1820s became associated with Lundy in Baltimore, helping him to issue the "gradualist" *Genius of Universal Emancipation*. There Garrison became convinced of the need for an "immediatist" approach to slavery. This meant not so much expecting an immediate end to the institution as treating it as infamous and refusing fellowship to slaveholders and those who cooperated with them. Garrison denounced in the *Genius* the owner of a slave ship who hailed from his own native Newburyport, Massachusetts. He thereby transgressed a tacit agreement which made it bad taste and libelous to criticize Northerners engaged in the domestic slave trade. As a result, he was sentenced to jail in Baltimore, but was released when his fine was paid by Arthur Tappan. Garrison then went north to consider how he might broaden his campaign against an institution he had inadvertently offended and which had disposed of him with such ease.

Even more indicative of the connection between the social unrest and spiritual unrest of the time was the career of Orestes A. Brownson (1803–1876), a strong-minded and learned seeker of religious truth. Having been raised on Congregationalist, Methodist and Presbyterian tenets, he became a Universalist preacher and later embraced the Working Men's Party of Robert Dale Owen and Frances Wright, along with its attendant atheism. It left Brownson in desperate need of spiritual solace, which a new enthusiasm for Transcendentalism and cooperative enterprises, notably Brook Farm, could not fill.

Meanwhile, he edited the well-esteemed *Boston Quarterly Review*, the *Democratic Review* and *Brownson's Quarterly Review*, which reflected his passionate hope that the Democratic party of Andrew Jackson might be a vehicle for heaven-sent justice. Its crashing failure in 1840—by which time the Whigs had learned the secret of Jacksonian demagoguery and had been able to deliver "Tippicanoe and Tyler Too" to a consenting public—drove Brownson to the Catholic Church where he served as acolyte and philosopher for the rest of his life. So summary a statement of Brownson's odyssey gives too little sense of his keen intelligence and hardy personal qualities. What Brownson felt, many felt but without his probing abilities and restless need for ultimate truth.

Others contributed to debates which brought differing groups closer to doubt and to a need for change. Thus women were solicited to aid temperance campaigns. Efforts by Horace Mann, Henry Barnard of Connecticut, Samuel Lewis in Ohio and many others to expand public facilities for educating the masses required the presence and support of women as teachers. Women of the Quaker persuasion, notably Lucretia Mott (1793–1880), served in meetings as ministers. Lundy gave place in his *Genius* to the compassionate verse and essays of young Elizabeth Chandler. It was only a matter of time before bolder women would demand more varied means to further these and related causes, and eventually to ask for places on platforms and equal suffrage.

So moral crusades and practical plans combined to reform a brash and competitive society. To an extent they were distinct and even antagonistic. *Moral* crusaders were concerned first of all for principles: tenets of religion, ideals of government, standards of human behavior. Garrison committed himself to hatred of slavery. He showed less awareness, however, of the "wage slavery" which shackled workers in the recently erected mill towns of New England and in such cities as New York and Philadelphia. He was little concerned for the cold reception and calculated exploitation which met Irish immigrants, despised for their rude manners and feared for their Catholicism. Emerson, too, rejected slavery, but his main thrust was toward individualism and exalted philosophic stances. Wars of liberation were to be fought, according to him, by individuals against their own weaker natures. As late as 1841, he thought of the Negroes, in their collective misery, as, in the most profound sense, slaves of themselves.[1] Emerson's inspirational writing could ultimately help individuals of all types and complexions, but their effect in the 1830s was mainly on people of his own kind: bold and free— but with Anglo-Saxon and Puritan expectations and with a sense of belonging which they did not share freely with strangers, ethnic or otherwise.

In contrast to such worthies were crusaders of the quality of Thomas Skidmore and Josiah Warren, also of English heritage, but with less regard for the ideal. Skidmore was a mechanic and early New York radical who joined the Working Men's Party of Robert Dale Owen and Frances Wright, but with more drastic goals in mind. Skidmore's *The Rights of Man in Property* (1829) demanded nothing less than an equal distribution of wealth, and he expected the wage earners to close ranks behind him to attain that end. His Poor People's Party—a banner rather than a program, an idea rather than an historical event—failed to attract supporters, and he himself died in 1832.

Josiah Warren was also a combination of ideals and material aims, but he was made of more enduring stuff. He was inspired by Robert Owen, more than by his son, and supported the New Harmony experiment in Indiana in 1825–1826. When it failed, he turned from the communal dream to the individual and set up in Cincinnati, Ohio, his "time store": an effort to determine the value of labor in the production of goods, rather than its scarcity or other conventional attributes. His plan for selling merchandise at cost, with charges for overhead, created a legend and a precedent.

Warren was an inventor as well as a formulator of philosophic anarchism. He later returned to the communal idea, but the village of Modern Times, which he created on Long Island, New

1. Ralph L. Rusk, *The Life of Ralph Waldo Emerson* (New York: Charles Scribner & Sons, 1949), p. 293.

York, in the 1830s, became more notorious for its "free love" experiments than for its philosophical content.

George Henry Evans (1805–1855) came as close to representing the antithesis of the moral reformer as any man of his era, though his labor publications, especially *The Working Man's Advocate* (1829–1845), exuded a moral fervor of its own. A transplanted Englishman, Evans was a freethinker and equalitarian. He favored an antimonopoly program, free land for willing workers, abolition of imprisonment for debt and delivery of mails on Sunday. Evans had little interest in Negroes, though his hatred of oppression caused him to denounce, in principle at least, all slavery, chattel or wage.

The two currents of reform, which both intermingled and separated in the 1820s and 1830s, were well illustrated by the contrast between Evans's career and that of his younger brother Frederick Williams Evans. The latter early favored Robert Owen's program, then joined his brother in New York as a labor advocate and freethinker. Frederick's life was abruptly changed by a visit to a Shaker community.

Shakers not only practiced community living, they also practiced celibacy: a mode of existence which shocked unthinking observers almost as much as did the "free love" experiments of the time. What critics of this version of social life failed to grasp was that, in the most principled exponents of "free love" or abstinence, the aim was neither euphoria nor repression, but grace. Their advocates yearned for contact with divinity. Their several modes of attaining it involved interpretations of scripture or of human destiny. Shakers were, in fact, a most cheerful and creative people. Shaker furniture, Shaker dances and Shaker spirituals were evidence that their inventors had found the psychic fulfillment they sought. Their most amazing achievement was to survive into the twentieth century without any natural increase.

Evans became one of the most distinguished of the Shakers, both as leader and spokesman. His books about Shaker doctrine and Shaker practice were read by contemporaries with respect, if only because of the patent prosperity and serenity of outlook which they heralded. Whether his brother's *History of the Origin and Program of the Working Man's Party* (1840) offered more to the future than the Shaker's own *Autobiography* (1869) is doubtless a matter of interpretation.

The goal of spiritual peace and communal living attracted some of the most vital spirits of the time. They appeared fairly tolerable, if bizarre, in such memorable experiments as Brook Farm, if only because the participants had unimpeachable credentials, as in the case of its organizer, Reverend George Ripley, and lived with decorum manifestly earning their keep through labor. Some experimenters appeared more scandalous, such as John Humphrey Noyes, who crowned a theological training at Andover Theological Seminary and the Divinity School of Yale College by announcing that he had attained perfection and was no longer subject to sin. Such views, and subsequent tenets which dissolved marital obligations, roused local outrage at Noyes's family home in Putney, Vermont. Noyes moved with his followers to Oneida, New York, to undertake the most momentous section of his career.

Although the experiments of Noyes, the Mormons and others such as Dr. Thomas L. Nichols, who sought to discover affinities proper to "free love," impressed skeptics as the work of outlaws they were not unique in their perspectives. The spiritual unrest drew respectable, conservative and unprobing social elements into its vortex, and sometimes ruined them. Such was the case with Robert Matthews, a country merchant of no consequence in upstate New York, who failed in business in 1816, professed to have been converted by Reverend Charles G. Finney, claimed revelations and came as "Father Matthias" to New York City wearing long hair and beard and a prophet's robe. He won the confidence of wealthy followers with a number of commandments denying the sanctity of marriage and the use of meat, made displays in an ornate carriage and robes, and was briefly worshipped as Christ on earth. The death, possibly from poisoning, of one of his patrons resulted in a trial during which he was acquitted, but he lost his following and left the scene. The development and spread of such enthusiasms indicated they had roots in American desires as well as in the creative imaginations of superior minds like those of Noyes and Ripley.

Conflicting goals and visions of the time met supremely in the career of Horace Greeley, a Vermont boy who rose in New York journalism of the 1830s to become a prominent Whig and in 1841 to launch his highly successful New York *Tribune*. Remarkably, though it was a party organ concerned with national events and opportunistic alliances, it also drew an impressive array of committed reformers as contributors and editors. Greeley brought to New York the Transcendentalists George Ripley and Margaret Fuller to express their ideas regularly in his *Tribune*. Charles A. Dana, also of Brook Farm, became a *Tribune* editor though he was in the radical portion of his career. He propounded not only the thoughts of the Frenchman Charles Fourier, who sought to organize society into "phalanxes," he also defended to the *Tribune* readers the anarchistic principles of another Frenchman, Pierre Joseph Proudhon, whose most famous dictum was: "Property is theft." Later Greeley also employed Karl Marx as a foreign correspondent.

Greeley's own causes were formidable in number and content. He was a strictly temperance man, antitobacco, anticapital punishment, in favor of woman suffrage, a vegetarian, a spiritualist and a believer in phrenology. He sponsored Fourierite experiments and cooperation in general. His *Hints toward Reforms* (1850) brought together in one volume his lectures, widely heard, expressing his sense of society in flux and in change.

Yet Greeley was a latecomer to abolitionism—one of the latest—and a political intriguer with a naïve but no less harmful greed for political power. He was no friend of labor organization, and he was a staunch defender of American industry, which he sought to shield with protective tariffs. The key to Greeley's reformist proclivities was that he reflected a society in ferment, rather than initiated reforms. That Greeley conducted a free forum of opinion did him honor and described the sturdy, resilient character of the America of his time. Reform itself, however, would have to wait for others who committed their lives and reputations to this enterprise.

The Indian, as a subject for reform, might most effectively have gained by being united with the fate of other minority and oppressed Americans. Different backgrounds, different ethnic circumstances and different human qualities ordained that the Indian problem should take a different course from that of other groups.

Indians had been pushed back upon the frontier, violently or by treaty, since earliest days of settlement. The process of removal was swifter in the North; by 1823 the Sacs and the Foxes of Illinois had been expelled by treaty across the Mississippi River. The Black Hawk War, a few years later, would make firm that treaty. The war enlisted Abraham Lincoln as a young captain of militia, though he was not required to engage in actual battle.

Meanwhile, the westward movement of the Indians further south proceeded more slowly. The Indian was a problem in statesmanship, but one which was to be submerged by bad faith and war. Indian reformers were sincere but fell between the two stools of philanthropy and Indian policy. Had the Indian been enslaved—enslavement had been unsuccessfully tried—he might have excited a unified agitation of the kind which was mounted in behalf of Negroes. But the Indian's quasi-independent status, coupled with the fact that in the South he presented an immediate threat of war, created a block to expansion. Hence northerners generally, and northern Whigs in particular, learned a glib sympathy for Indians and made of them a convenient tool for criticizing the southern leadership and despising the Jackson Administration, during which the Indian crisis came to a head.

There were sincere reformers who made an effort to maintain

Indian rights but they were unable to impede the tragedy of his fall. The Creeks had attempted to meet government savagery with savagery and were crushed. They were then, in devious ways, despoiled. The Seminoles during much of the 1830s waged a protracted war which largely disgraced the better-equipped regular Army troops. It was the Cherokees, however, pushed back for a century by wars and treaties into the mountain regions of Georgia, North Carolina, Tennessee and Alabama, who put United States integrity to its most severe test.

For the Cherokees accepted the white man's standards. They welcomed missionaries, attended their schools and studied Christian piety. They produced memorable leaders, first of all Sequoia, who created the Cherokee alphabet and enabled his people to reduce their language to written words. They sent their children to the white people to be trained for tribal service. Thus Galagina was placed in a mission school in Connecticut where he took the name of his Federalist benefactor, Elias Boudinot. In 1824 he began the famous *Cherokee Phoenix* which would carry the unhappy message of Cherokee dilemmas.

Boudinot was assisted by a young medical missionary, Reverend Samuel A. Worcester, who translated parts of the Bible into Cherokee. Another leader of the Cherokees was John Ross, who had with other of his people fought recklessly beside General Jackson in the latter's war on the Creeks; Ross had been praised by Jackson for his courage and loyalty.

It was all to no purpose so far as Cherokee rights to their tribal lands were concerned. The State of Georgia denounced all treaties, demanded that white coworkers of the Cherokees depart and took steps to force the removal of the Indians. Andrew Jackson, now President, ignoring this defiance of Federal power and authority, in 1830 asked Congress to prepare their removal. Theodore Frelinghuysen, a religious, conservative lawyer, president of the American Board of Commissioners for Foreign Missions and at that time a United States senator, made brave efforts—not unrelated to the strategy of anti-Jackson politicians—

to stop Congress in its work. His efforts were to no avail. Georgia whisked a number of the defiant missionaries off to prison. The Cherokees went to court and won the agreement of the Supreme Court that they were secure in their rights.

"John Marshall has made his decision, now let him enforce it." Jackson may not have uttered these precise words, but his deeds in connection with the Cherokees endorsed them. Georgia defied the court with impunity. Reverend Worcester tired of prison and petitioned for pardon. He abandoned efforts to maintain the Cherokee cause, and partly to make up for his surrender, perhaps, went west to continue his labors among those Indians who had given up the struggle. The mass sympathy of the North, which affected Lundy and Garrison as well as Frelinghuysen, lacked any element which might lead to action.

The turn came in 1835 when Major Ridge, a cousin of Boudinot, and like Ross a distinguished Cherokee and veteran of the Creek War, accepted a government treaty for removal. So was undertaken that "trail of tears" which was to carry the Cherokees westward to further trouble and other vicissitudes. In 1839 Ross led them to what became Oklahoma in no peaceful spirit. That same year both Boudinot and Major Ridge died by assassination. A remnant of the Cherokees remained in the eastern mountains as a memento of the failure of Indian reform.

5.

DAVID WALKER:

"I ask you, O Americans, I ask you . . .
can you deny these charges?"

David Walker (1785–1830) possessed talents which were crude but original. His Appeal . . . to the Coloured Citizens of the World, But, in Particular, and Very Expressly, to Those of the United States of America *marks an era in Negro expression and unrest. He was born in slavery in North Carolina, but freed by virtue of his mother's free condition. His personal sense of worth, fed by reading and experience, made him revolutionary in temperament. He left the South at about thirty years of age and lived in Boston, where he sold old clothes. Walker was active in the Negro community and emphasized its need for education and an abolitionist program. In 1829 his frustration finally produced the* Appeal, *which he successfully disseminated in the South, probably by way of sailors engaged in the coastal trade. It fell into the hands of southern authorities and editors who read it with alarm and indignation. Walker felt encouraged to issue a second and third edition of the* Appeal. *On June 28, 1830, he was found dead by the doorway of his shop, whether by natural or other causes is unknown. It is inaccurate to imagine that he gave birth to a militant antislavery movement. The reform era heard little of the* Appeal, *either from white crusaders or black, though Henry H. Garnet reprinted it in 1848 along with his own "Appeal to the Slaves of the United States of America." Walker undoubtedly voiced many thoughts present in the Negro community though*

SOURCE: *Walker's Appeal, with a Brief Sketch of His Life* (New York: J. H. Tobitt, 1848), p. 20 *et seq.*

*their effectiveness could not match those of such Negro spokes-
men as Forten, Frederick Douglass and William Wells Brown.*

But to prove farther that the condition of the Israelites was
better under the Egyptians than ours is under the whites. I call
upon the professing Christians, I call upon the philanthropist, I
call upon the very tyrant himself, to show me a page of history,
either sacred or profane, on which a verse can be found, which
maintains, that the Egyptians heaped the *insupportable insult*
upon the children of Israel, by telling them that they were not of
the *human family*. Can the whites deny this charge? Have they
not, after having reduced us to the deplorable condition of slaves
under their feet, held us up as descending originally from the
tribes of *Monkeys* or *Orang-Outangs?* O! my God! I appeal to
every man of feeling—is not this insupportable? Is it not heaping
the most gross insult upon our miseries, because they have got us
under their feet and we cannot help ourselves? Oh pity us we
pray thee, Lord Jesus, Master.—Has Mr. Jefferson declared to
the world, that we are inferior to the whites, both in the endowments of our bodies and our minds?[1] It is indeed surprising, that
a man of such great learning, combined with such excellent
natural parts, should speak so of a set of men in chains. I do not
know what to compare it to, unless, like putting one wild deer in
an iron cage, where it will be secured, and hold another by the
side of the same, then let it go, and expect the one in the cage to
run as fast as the one at liberty. So far, my brethren, were the
Egyptians from heaping these insults upon their slaves that
Pharaoh's daughter took Moses, a son of Israel for her own, as
will appear by the following.

"And Pharaoh's daughter said unto her, [Moses' mother] take
this child away, and nurse it for me, and I will pay thee thy
wages. And the woman took the child [Moses] and nursed it.

1. Walker's references, here and elsewhere, are to Jefferson's *Notes on
Virginia* (1785).

"And the child grew, and she brought him unto Pharaoh's daughter and he became her son. And she called his name Moses: and she said because I drew him out of the water."[2]

In all probability, Moses would have become Prince Regent to the throne, and no doubt, in process of time but he would have been seated on the throne of Egypt. But he had rather suffer shame, with the people of God, than to enjoy pleasures with that wicked people for a season. O! that the coloured people were long since of Moses' excellent disposition, instead of courting favour with, and telling news and lies to our *natural enemies,* against each other—aiding them to keep their hellish chains of slavery upon us. Would we not long before this time, have been respectable men, instead of such wretched victims of oppression as we are? Would they be able to drag our mothers, our fathers, our wives, our children and ourselves, around the world in chains and hand-cuffs as they do, to dig up gold and silver for them and theirs? This question, my brethren, I leave for you to digest; and may God Almighty force it home to your hearts. Remember that unless you are united, keeping your tongues within your teeth, you will be afraid to trust your secrets to each other, and thus perpetuate our miseries under the *Christians!!!!* ADDITION.— Remember, also to lay humble at the feet of our Lord and Master Jesus Christ, with prayers and fastings. Let our enemies go on with their butcheries, and at once fill up their cup. Never make an attempt to gain our freedom or *natural right,* from under our cruel oppressors and murderers, until you see your way clear[3]—

2. See Exodus, chap. ii. 9, 10. [Walker's note.]
3. It is not to be understood here, that I mean for us to wait until God shall take us by the hair of our heads and drag us out of abject wretchedness and slavery, nor do I mean to convey the idea for us to wait until our enemies shall make preparations, and call us to seize those preparations, take it away from them, and put every thing before us to death, in order to gain our freedom which God has given us. For you must remember that we are men as well as they. God has been pleased to give us two eyes, two hands, two feet, and some sense in our heads as well as they. They have no more right to hold us in slavery than we have to hold them, we have just as much right, in the sight of God, to hold them and their children in slavery and wretchedness, as they have to hold us, and no more. [Walker's note.]

when that hour arrives and you move, be not afraid or dismayed; for be you assured that Jesus Christ the King of heaven and of earth who is the God of justice and of armies, will surely go before you. And those enemies who have for hundreds of years stolen our *rights,* and kept us ignorant of Him and His divine worship, He will remove. Millions of whom, are this day, so ignorant and avaricious, that they cannot conceive how God can have an attribute of justice, and show mercy to us because it pleased Him to make us black—which colour, Mr. Jefferson calls unfortunate! ! ! ! ! ! As though we are not as thankful to our God, for having made us as it pleased Himself, as they, (the whites,) are for having made them white. They think because they hold us in their infernal chains of slavery, that we wish to be white, or of their color—but they are dreadfully deceived—we wish to be just as it pleased our Creator to have made us, and no avaricious and unmerciful wretches, have any business to make slaves of, or hold us in slavery. How would they like for us to make slaves of, and hold them in cruel slavery, and murder them as they do us?—But is Mr. Jefferson's assertion true? viz. "that it is unfortunate for us that our Creator has been pleased to make us *black.*" We will not take his say so, for the fact. The world will have an opportunity to see whether it is unfortunate for us, that our Creator *has made us* darker than the *whites.* . . .

The sufferings of the Helots among the Spartans, were some-what severe, it is true, but to say that theirs, were as severe as ours among the Americans, I do most strenuously deny—for instance, can any man show me an article on a page of ancient history which specifies, that, the Spartans chained, and hand-cuffed the Helots, and dragged them from their wives and children, children from their parents, mothers from their suckling babes, wives from their husbands, driving them from one end of the country to the other? Notice the Spartans were heathens, who lived long before our Divine Master made His appearance in the flesh. Can Christian Americans deny these barbarous cruelties? Have you not, Americans, having subjected us under you, added

to these miseries, by insulting us in telling us to our face, because
we are helpless, that we are not of the human family? I ask you,
O! Americans, I ask you, in the name of the Lord, can you deny
these charges? Some perhaps may deny, by saying, that they
never thought or said that we were not men. But do not actions
speak louder than words?—have they not made provisions for the
Greeks, and Irish? Nations who have never done the least thing
for them, while *we,* who have enriched their country with our
blood and tears—have dug up gold and silver for them and their
children, from generation to generation, and are in more miseries
than any other people under heaven, are not seen, but by comparatively, a handful of the American people? There are indeed,
more ways to kill a dog, besides choking it to death with butter.
Further—The Spartans or Lacedaemonians, had some frivolous
pretext, for enslaving the Helots, for they (Helots) while being
free inhabitants of Sparta, stirred up an intestine commotion, and
were, by the Spartans subdued, and made prisoners of war.
Consequently they and their children were condemned to perpetual slavery.[4]

I have been for years troubling the pages of historians, to find
out what our fathers have done to the *white Christians of
America,* to merit such condign punishment as they have inflicted
on them, and do continue to inflict on us their children. But I
must aver, that my researches have hitherto been to no effect. I
have therefore, come to the immoveable conclusion, that they
(Americans) have, and do continue to punish us for nothing else,
but for enriching them and their country. For I cannot conceive
of anything else. Nor will I ever believe otherwise, until the Lord
shall convince me.

The world knows, that slavery as it existed among the Romans,
(which was the primary cause of their destruction) was, comparatively speaking, no more than a *cypher,* when compared with

4. See Dr. Goldsmith's History of Greece—page 9. See also, Plutarch's
Lives. The Helots subdued by Agis, king of *Sparta.* [Walker's note.]

ours under the Americans. Indeed I should not have noticed the
Roman slaves, had not the very learned and penetrating Mr.
Jefferson said, "when a master was murdered, all his slaves in the
same house, or within hearing, were condemned to death."—
Here let me ask Mr. Jefferson, (but he is gone to answer at the
bar of God, for the deeds done in his body while living,) I
therefore ask the whole American people, had I not rather die, or
be put to death, than to be a slave to any tyrant, who takes not
only my own, but my wife and children's lives by the inches?
Yea, would I meet death with avidity far! far! ! in preference to
such *servile submission* to the murderous hands of tyrants. Mr.
Jefferson's very severe remarks on us have been so extensively
argued upon by men whose attainments in literature, I shall
never be able to reach, that I would not have meddled with it,
were it not to solicit each of my brethren, who has the spirit of a
man, to buy a copy of Mr. Jefferson's "Notes on Virginia," and
put it in the hand of his son. For let no one of us suppose that the
refutations which have been written by our white friends are
enough—they are *whites*—we are *blacks*. We, and the world
wish to see the charges of Mr. Jefferson refuted by the blacks
themselves, according to their chance; for we must remember
that what the whites have written respecting this subject, is other
men's labours, and did not emanate from the blacks. I know well,
that there are some talents and learning among the coloured
people of this country, which we have not a chance to develope,
in consequence of oppression; but our oppression ought not to
hinder us from acquiring all we can. For we will have a chance to
develope them by and by. God will not suffer us, always to be
oppressed. Our sufferings will come to an *end,* in spite of all the
Americans this side of *eternity.* Then we will want all the learning and talents among ourselves, and perhaps more, to govern
ourselves.—"Every dog must have its day," the American's is
coming to an end.

But let us review Mr. Jefferson's remarks respecting us some
further. Comparing our miserable fathers, with the learned phi-

losophers of Greece, he says: "Yet notwithstanding these and other discouraging circumstances among the Romans, their slaves were often their rarest artists. They excelled too, in science, insomuch as to be usually employed as tutors to their master's children; Epictetus, Terence and Phædrus, were slaves,—but they were of the race of whites. It is not their *condition* then, but *nature*, which has produced the distinction." See this, my brethren!! Do you believe that this assertion is swallowed by millions of the whites? Do you know that Mr. Jefferson was one of as great characters as ever lived among the whites? See his writings for the world, and public labours for the United States of America. Do you believe that the assertions of such a man, will pass away into oblivion unobserved by this people and the world? If you do you are much mistaken—See how the American people treat us—have we souls in our bodies? Are we men who have any spirits at all? I know that there are many *swell-bellied* fellows among us, whose greatest object is to fill their stomachs. Such I do not mean—I am after those who know and feel, that we are MEN, as well as other people; to them, I say, that unless we try to refute Mr. Jefferson's arguments respecting us, we will only establish them.

But the slaves among the Romans. Everybody who has read history, knows, that as soon as a slave among the Romans obtained his freedom, he could rise to the greatest eminence in the State, and there was no law instituted to hinder a slave from buying his freedom. Have not the Americans instituted laws to hinder us from obtaining our freedom? Do any deny this charge? Read the laws of Virginia, North Carolina, &c. Further: have not the Americans instituted laws to prohibit a man of colour from obtaining and holding any office whatever, under the government of the United States of America? Now, Mr. Jefferson tells us, that our condition is not so hard, as the slaves were under the Romans!!!!!!

It is time for me to bring this article to a close. But before I close it, I must observe to my brethren that at the close of the first Revolution in this country, with Great Britain, there were but thirteen States in the Union, now there are twenty-four, most of which are slave-holding States, and the whites are dragging us around in chains and in handcuffs, to their new States and Territories to work their mines and farms, to enrich them and their children—and millions of them believing firmly that we being a little darker than they, were made by our Creator to be an inheritance to them and their children for ever—the same as a parcel of *brutes*. . . .

6.

WILLIAM BIRNEY:
Gradual Emancipation

William Birney (1819–1907), worthy son of a worthy father, was an author and editor who rose to the rank of general during the Civil War as an organizer and leader of Negro troops. He sought to establish his father's priority and fame in James G. Birney and His Times: The Genesis of the Republican Party with Some Account of Abolition Movements in the South before 1828. *His major effort was to prove that Garrison had harmed a natural, responsible movement toward abolition, but that it had reorganized in a progression from Liberty Party (which offered his father as Presidential candidate in 1840 and again in 1844) to Free Soil Party to Republican Party, the latter consummating Emancipation. In the course of his account the younger Birney described some of the day to day workings of "gradualism."*

[A]n influential [por]tion of the slave-holders [of Virginia and Kentucky] themselves favored freedom. At its first annual meeting, held in 1830, the Kentucky Colonization Society had adopted the following statement in the manager's report: "The late disposition to voluntary emancipation is so increasing that no law is necessary to free us from slavery, provided there was an asylum accessible to all liberated. (See "African Repository," May, 1830.)

Such a movement was contemplated in 1821, under the leader-

SOURCE: William Birney, *James G. Birney and His Times: The Genesis of the Republican Party with Some Account of Abolition Movements in the South before 1828* (New York: D. Appleton and Company, 1890), p. 97 ff.

ship of Rufus King; but it was defeated by the non-concurrence of the friends of John Quincy Adams, who hoped to be made President in 1824, with a Southern man as Vice-President—General Jackson being the one considered as available.

Everything pointed to Henry Clay as the leader of such a movement in 1830. He was the favorite son of Kentucky, a popular man in his native State of Virginia, and the champion of the capitalists and manufacturers of the Northern and Eastern States. For his disastrous errors on the Arkansas and Missouri questions he had apologized in declarations, often repeated, against the "curse of slavery"; and, in his December speech in 1829, he had sketched a programme of operations for the final extinction of slavery which authorized all thinking men to believe him ready to join in them.

But Mr. Clay took a different view. For his expected candidacy in 1832 he was trimming his sails to catch the winds from both North and South, hoping to win General Jackson's friends, and work his way to the presidential chair by concessions to enemies, glittering but equivocal phrases, and waivers of his professed principles, which gained for him repeated defeats and the unenviable title of "the compromiser." He not only refused to participate personally in a gradual emancipation movement in Kentucky, but advised his friends not to do so; and it was chiefly through his influence that the efforts to set one on foot were chilled.

Before calling on Mr. Clay Mr. Birney had talked over the gradual emancipation project with the Rev. John C. Young, the eloquent President of Centre College; with Rev. J. D. Paxton, Judge John Green, Daniel Yeiser, P. G. Rice, Michael G. Yonce, and William Armstrong—all of Danville; with his wife's uncle James McDowell, and his long-time friends Thomas T. Skillman, bookseller and publisher, and the Rev. Robert J. Breckenridge—all of Lexington.

All these were ready to act, and thought many others would join them. The following paper was circulated for signatures.

Fourteen respectable citizens subscribed their names. At this point effort ceased until, at the instance of Mr. Birney, who wrote from Alabama, Mr. Skillman, the proprietor of the "Western Luminary," of Lexington, published the paper in that journal.

GRADUAL AND SAFE EMANCIPATION.

We, the undersigned, slave-holders, under a full conviction that there are insurmountable obstacles to the general emancipation of the present generation of slaves, but equally convinced of the necessity and practicability of emancipating their future offspring, have determined to form ourselves into a society for the purpose of investigating and impressing these truths upon the public mind, as well by example as by precept; by adopting among ourselves such a system for the gradual emancipation of our slaves as we would recommend to our fellow-citizens for their adoption as the law of the land; and by dispersing such writings as may be likely to contribute to so good an end. The society will not be called together until fifty subscribers are obtained.

Wm. R. Hines, Bardstown; Samuel K. Snead, Jefferson Co.; J. M. C. Irvin, R. J. Breckenridge, of Fayette Co.; A. J. Alexander, Charles Alexander, J. R. Alexander, Woodford Co.; James McCall, Rockcastle Co.; John Wallace, Fayette Co.; Norman Porter; Thomas T. Skillman, Lexington; George Clarke, Fayette Co.; James Blythe, Lexington; George W. Anderson, Fayette Co.; James G. McKinney, Lexington; James H. Allen, James McDowell, Fayette Co.

These gentlemen were among the most respected citizens of Kentucky. Within a few weeks thirty-four more slave-holders sent in their names as members, and, as received, they were published in the "Luminary." They were as follows:

Fayette Co.: J. S. Berryman, Rowland Chambers, Geo. M. Chambers, John C. Richardson, Hugh Foster, J. C. Harrison, Rev. Robert Stuart, James C. Todd, and John H. Bell; Mercer Co.: Thomas Cleland, Michael G. Yonce, P. G. Rice, President John C. Young, William Armstrong, Rev. John D. Paxton, and Daniel Yeiser; Lincoln Co.: Judge John Green, John L. Yantis, and Samuel Warren; Woodford C.: William E. Ashmore, Samuel Wingfield, Samuel V. Marshall, Robert Moffett, Dr. Louis Marshall, Colonel John Steele, and Dr. C.

Wallace; Franklin Co.: C. P. Bacon and Rev. J. T. Edgar; Hardin Co.:
David Weller; and Jefferson Co.: Warrick Miller.

Any native Kentuckian familiar with the old families of the
State will recognize the above list as remarkable for the intelligence, wealth, and influence of the persons named in it. Most of
them were Presbyterians, and at least six of them were Presbyterian preachers, three of these Reverends—Robert J. Breckenridge, John C. Young, and John D. Paxton—being men of
national reputation. Mr. Birney, not being a resident of the State
did not sign the paper; but he was alluded to as follows by his
friend Mr. Skillman, of the "Luminary":

In reply to a correspondent in Illinois, who wishes to know what
Presbyterians are doing in this cause, we remark that the first projector
of this emancipation scheme, as published in several of our last numbers, is a Presbyterian; and that, so far as we are informed, Presbyterians generally have taken a prominent part in promoting these
benevolent schemes, whose object is the amelioration of the condition
of our colored population.

But this well-considered scheme came to naught, for want of a
leader in Kentucky. Among its friends, this *rôle* might have been
taken by Judge Green, R. J. Breckenridge, or John C. Young; but
the Judge was absorbed in business, Mr. Breckenridge about that
time quit law for theology and had his hands full of controversies, and Mr. Young was the president of a college. Mr. Clay's
friends were begging for postponement, until after the next
presidential election, of a movement likely to compromise him
either with the South or the North; and they were full of promises. The opportune moment was lost, and the Gradual Emancipation Society was not organized when it might have accomplished something. It was postponed to a more convenient
season. . . .

7.

FRANCES WRIGHT:
"The People at War"

One of the outstanding women of the nineteenth century, Frances Wright (1795–1852) opened subjects of inquiry rather than advanced them. She early acquired rationalistic and equalitarian views, visited the United States as author and libertarian in 1818–1820 and again in 1824, when she met Jefferson and Madison and discussed Negro emancipation projects. Her Nashoba, Tennessee, colony attracted Negroes and whites (1825–1828) but deteriorated as a working venture. Under Robert Dale Owen's influence she edited with him The New-Harmony Gazette. *When their perspectives shifted, they transferred to New York, where they issued the* Free Enquirer, *and helped promote the Working Men's Party. She herself scandalized the nation with public lectures which derogated religion and conventions and spoke for equality of the sexes and the equal distribution of wealth. More an individual than an organizer, she instituted campaigns which differed from those of other women, who worked within the main body of society and sought to win over public opinion rather than defy it.*

The People at War. What a season of deep interest is the present. . . .

What distinguishes the present from every other struggle in which the human race has been engaged, is, that the present is, evidently, openly and acknowledgedly, a war of class, and that

SOURCE: John R. Commons et al., *A Documentary History of American Industrial Society* (Cleveland: Arthur H. Clark Co., 1910), vol. V, pp. 180–181.

this war is universal. It is no longer nation pitched against nation for the good pleasure and sport of Kings and great Captains, nor sect cutting the throats and roasting the carcasses of sect for the glory of God and satisfaction of priests, nor is it one army butchering another to promote the fortunes of their leaders—to pass from a James to a George or a Charles to a Louis Philip the privilege of coining laws, money and peers, and dividing the good things of the land among his followers. No; it is now every where the oppressed millions who are making common cause against oppression; it is the ridden people of the earth who are struggling to throw from their backs the "booted and spurred" riders whose legitimate title to starve as well as to work them to death will no longer pass current; it is labor rising up against idleness, industry against money, justice against law and against privilege. And truly the struggle hath not come too soon. Truly there hath been oppression and outrage enough on the one side, and suffering and endurance enough on the other, to render the millions rather chargeable with excess of patience and over abundance of good nature than with too eager a spirit for the redress of injury, not to speak of recourse to vengeance.

It has been long clear to me that in every country the best feelings and the best sense are found with the laboring and useful classes, and the worst feelings and the worst sense with the idle and the useless. Until all classes shall be merged into one however by gradual but fundamental changes in the whole organization of society, much bad feeling must prevail every where. . . .

8.

BLACK HAWK:
"How different is our situation now!"

Numerous records detailed the sorrows of white men and women who survived Indian massacres and other by-products of settlement. Yet throughout the unfolding of racial conflict a strain of inquiry could be perceived looking toward a just version of its meaning. This process was illustrated in the career of Black Hawk (1767–1838), a Sauk war chief resentful of a treaty drawn up in 1804 which ceded to the United States the whole of their country east of the Mississippi River. In 1832, believing he had formed an Indian confederation, Black Hawk attempted to regain control of his old tribal lands. The short, sharp war which followed left him a prisoner who, briefly, won the attention of the country. In turn he was sufficiently inspired by its sights and personalities to wish to explain himself and his people. His Autobiography *was dictated to an American interpreter and prepared for publication by a journalist and accepted almost at once as an American classic.*

The great chief [William Clark] at St. Louis having sent word for us to go down and confirm the treaty of peace, we did not hesitate, but started immediately, that we might smoke the *peace-pipe* with him. On our arrival, we met the great chiefs in council. They explained to us the words of our Great Father at Washington, accusing us of heinous crimes and divers misdemeanors, particularly in not coming down when first invited. We

SOURCE: Milo Milton Quaife, ed., *Life of Black Hawk* (Chicago: R. R. Donnelley & Sons Company, 1916), pp. 85 ff.

knew very well that *our Great Father had deceived us,* and thereby *forced* us to join the British and could not believe that he had put this speech into the mouths of these chiefs to deliver to us. I was not a civil chief, and consequently made no reply: but our chiefs told the commissioners that "what they had said was a *lie!*—that our Great Father had sent no such speech, he knowing the situation in which we had been placed had been *caused by him!*" The white chiefs appeared very angry at this reply, and said they "would break off the treaty with us, and *go to war,* as they would not be insulted."

Our chiefs had no intention of insulting them, and told them so—"that they merely wished to explain to them that *they had told a lie,* without making them angry; in the same manner that the whites do, when they do not believe what is told them!" The council then proceeded, and the pipe of peace was smoked.

Here, for the first time, I touched the goose quill to the treaty—not knowing, however, that, by that act, I consented to give away my village. Had that been explained to me, I should have opposed it, and never would have signed their treaty, as my recent conduct will clearly prove.

What do we know of the manner of the laws and customs of the white people? They might buy our bodies for dissection, and we would touch the goose quill to confirm it, without knowing what we are doing. This was the case with myself and people in touching the goose quill the first time.

We can only judge of what is proper and right by our standard of right and wrong, which differs widely from the whites, if I have been correctly informed. The whites *may do bad* all their lives, and then, if they are *sorry for it* when about to die, *all is well!* But with us it is different: we must continue throughout our lives to do what we conceive to be good. If we have corn and meat, and know of a family that have none, we divide with them. If we have more blankets than sufficient, and others have not enough, we must give to them that want. But I will presently explain our customs, and the manner we live.

We were friendly treated by the white chiefs, and started back to our village on Rock river. Here we found that troops had arrived to build a fort at Rock island. This, in our opinion, was a contradiction to what we had done—"to prepare for war in time of peace." We did not, however, object to their building the fort on the island, but we were very sorry, as this was the best island on the Mississippi, and had long been the resort of our young people during the summer. It was our garden (like the white people have near to their big villages) which supplied us with strawberries, blackberries, gooseberries, plums, apples, and nuts of different kinds; and its waters supplied us with fine fish, being situated in the rapids of the river. In my early life, I spent many happy days on this island. A good spirit had care of it, who lived in a cave in the rocks immediately under the place where the fort now stands, and has often been seen by our people. He was white, with large wings like a *swan's,* but ten times larger. We were particular not to make much noise in that part of the island which he inhabited, for fear of disturbing him. But the noise of the fort has since driven him away, and no doubt a *bad spirit* has taken his place!

Our village was situated on the north side of Rock river, at the foot of its rapids, and on the point of land between Rock river and the Mississippi. In its front, a prairie extended to the bank of the Mississippi; and in our rear, a continued bluff, gently ascending from the prairie. On the side of this bluff we had our corn-fields, extending about two miles up, running parallel with the Mississippi; where we joined those of the Foxes whose village was on the bank of the Mississippi, opposite the lower end of Rock island, and three miles distant from ours. We had about eight hundred acres in cultivation, including what we had on the islands of Rock river. The land around our village, uncultivated, was covered with blue-grass, which made excellent pasture for our horses. Several fine springs broke out of the bluff, near by, from which we were supplied with good water. The rapids of Rock river furnished us with an abundance of excellent fish, and the land, being good, never failed to produce good crops of corn, beans, pumpkins, and squashes. We always had plenty—our children never cried with hunger, nor our people were never in want. Here our village had stood for more than a hundred years, during all which time we were the undisputed possessors of the valley of the Mississippi, from the Ouisconsin to the Portage des Sioux, near the mouth of the Missouri, being about seven hundred miles in length.

At this time we had very little intercourse with the whites, except our traders. Our village was healthy, and there was no place in the country possessing such advantages, nor no hunting grounds better than those we had in possession. If another prophet had come to our village in those days, and told us what has since taken place, none of our people would have believed him. What! to be driven from our village and hunting grounds, and not even permitted to visit the graves of our forefathers, our relations, and friends?

This hardship is not known to the whites. With us it is a custom to visit the graves of our friends, and keep them in repair for many years. The mother will go alone to weep over the grave of her child! The brave, with pleasure, visits the grave of his father, after he has been successful in war, and re-paints the post that shows where he lies! There is no place like that where the bones of our forefathers lie, to go to when in grief. Here the Great Spirit will take pity on us!

But, how different is our situation now, from what it was in those days! Then we were as happy as the buffalo on the plains—but now, we are as miserable as the hungry, howling wolf in the prairie! But I am digressing from my story. Bitter reflection crowds upon my mind, and must find utterance.

When we returned to our village in the spring, from our wintering grounds, we would finish trading with our traders, who always followed us to our village. We purposely kept some of our fine furs for this trade; and, as there was great opposition among them, who should get these skins, we always got our goods cheap. After this trade was over, the traders would give us a few kegs of rum, which was generally promised in the fall, to encourage us to make a good hunt, and not go to war. They would then start with their furs and peltries for their homes. Our old men would take a frolic (at this time our young men never drank.) When this was ended, the next thing to be done was to bury our dead (such as had died during the year.) This is a great *medicine feast*. The relations of those who have died, give all the goods they have purchased, as presents to their friends—thereby reducing themselves to poverty, to show the Great Spirit that they are humble, so that he will take pity on them. We would next open the cashes, and take out corn and other provisions, which had been put up in the fall,—and then commence repairing our lodges. As soon as this is accomplished, we repair the fences around our fields, and clean them off, ready for planting corn. This work is done by our women. The men, during this time, are feasting on dried venison, bear's meat, wild fowl, and corn, prepared in different ways; and recounting to each other what took place during the winter.

Our women plant the corn, and as soon as they get done, we make a feast, and dance the *crane* dance, in which they join us, dressed in their best, and decorated with feathers. At this feast our young braves select the young woman they wish to have for a wife. He then informs his mother, who calls on the mother of the girl, when the arrangement is made, and the time appointed for him to come. He goes to the lodge when all are asleep (or pretend to be) lights his matches, which have been provided for the purpose, and soon finds where his intended sleeps. He then awakens her, and holds the light to his face that she may know him—after which he places the light close to her. If she blows it out, the ceremony is ended, and he appears in the lodge the next morning, as one of the family. If she does not blow out the light, but leaves it to burn out, he retires from the lodge. The next day he places himself in full view of it, and plays his flute. The young women go out, one by one, to see who he is playing for. The tune changes, to let them know that he is not playing for them. When his intended makes her appearance at the door, he continues his *courting* tune, until she returns to the lodge. He then gives over playing, and makes another trial at night, which generally turns out favorable. During the first year they ascertain whether they can agree with each other, and can be happy—if not, they part, and each looks out again. If we were to live together and disagree, we should be as foolish as the whites. No indiscretion can banish a woman from her parental lodge—no difference how many children she may bring home, she is always welcome—the kettle is over the fire to feed them.

The crane dance often lasts two or three days. When this is over, we feast again, and have our *national* dance. The large square in the village is swept and prepared for the purpose. The chiefs and old warriors, take seats on mats which have been spread at the upper end of the square—the drummers and singers come next, and the braves and women form the sides, leaving a large space in the middle. The drums beat, and the singers commence. A warrior enters the square, keeping time with the music. He shows the manner he started on a war party—how he approached the enemy—he strikes, and describes the way he killed him. All join in applause. He then leaves the square, and another enters and takes his place. Such of our young men as have not been out in war parties, and killed an enemy, stand back ashamed—not being able to enter the square. I remember that I was ashamed to look where our young women stood, before I could take my stand in the square as a warrior.

What pleasure it is to an old warrior, to see his son come forward and relate his exploits—it makes him feel young, and induces him to enter the square, and "fight his battles o'er again."

This national dance makes our warriors. When I was travelling last summer, on a steam boat, on a large river, going from New York to Albany, I was shown the place where the Americans dance their national dance [West Point]; where the old warriors recount to their young men, what they have done, to stimulate them to go and do likewise. This surprised me, as I did not think the whites understood our way of making braves.

When our national dance is over—our corn-fields hoed, and every weed dug up, and our corn about knee-high, all our young men would start in a direction towards sun-down, to hunt deer and buffalo—being prepared, also, to kill Sioux, if any are found on our hunting grounds—a part of our old men and women to the lead mines to make lead—and the remainder of our people start to fish, and get mat stuff. Every one leaves the village, and remains about forty days. They then return: the hunting party bringing in dried buffalo and deer meat, and sometimes *Sioux scalps,* when they are found trespassing on our hunting grounds. At other times they are met by a party of Sioux too strong for them, and are driven in. If the Sioux have killed the Sacs last, they expect to be retaliated upon, and will fly before them, and vice versa. Each party knows that the other has a right to retaliate, which induces those who have killed last, to give way before their enemy—as neither wish to strike, except to avenge the death of their relatives. All our wars are predicated by the relatives of those killed; or by aggressions upon our hunting grounds. . . .

I will here relate the manner in which corn first came. According to tradition, handed down to our people, a beautiful woman was seen to descend from the clouds, and alight upon the earth, by two of our ancestors, who had killed a deer, and were sitting by a fire, roasting a part of it to eat. They were astonished at seeing her, and concluded that she must be hungry, and had smelt the meat—and immediately went to her, taking with them a piece of the roasted venison. They presented it to her, and she eat—and told them to return to the spot where she was sitting, at the end of one year, and they would find a reward for their kindness and generosity. She then ascended to the clouds, and disappeared. The two men returned to their village, and explained to the nation what they had seen, done, and heard—but were laughed at by their people. When the period arrived, for them to visit this consecrated ground, where they were to find a reward for their attention to the beautiful woman of the clouds, they went with a large party, and found, where her right hand had rested on the ground, *corn* growing—and where the left hand had rested, *beans*—and immediately where she had been seated, *tobacco*.

The two first have, ever since, been cultivated by our people, as our principal provisions—and the last used for smoking. The white people have since found out the latter, and seem to relish it as much as we do—as they use it in different ways, viz. smoking, snuffing and eating!

We thank the Great Spirit for all the benefits he has conferred upon us. For myself, I never take a drink of water from a spring, without being mindful of his goodness.

We next have our great ball play—from three to five hundred on a side, play this game. We play for horses, guns, blankets, or any other kind of property we have. The successful party take the stakes, and all retire to our lodges in peace and friendship.

We next commence horse-racing, and continue our sport and feasting, until the corn is all secured. We then prepare to leave our village for our hunting grounds. The traders arrive, and give us credit for such articles as we want to clothe our families, and enable us to hunt. We first, however, hold a council with them, to ascertain the price they will give us for our skins, and what they will charge us for goods. We inform them where we intend hunting—and tell them where to build their houses. At this place, we deposit part of our corn, and leave our old people. The traders have always been kind to them, and relieved them when in want. They were always much respected by our people—and never since we have been a nation, has one of them been killed by any of our people.

We disperse, in small parties, to make our hunt, and as soon as it is over, we return to our traders' establishment, with our skins, and remain feasting, playing cards and other pastimes, until near the close of the winter. Our young men then start on the beaver hunt; others to hunt raccoons and muskrats—and the remainder of our people go to the sugar camps to make sugar. All leave our encampment, and appoint a place to meet on the Mississippi, so that we may return to our village together, in the spring. We always spent our time pleasantly at the sugar camp. It being the season for wild fowl, we lived well, and always had plenty, when the hunters came in, that we might make a feast for them. After this is over, we return to our village, accompanied, sometimes, by our traders. In this way, the year rolled round happily. But these are times that were! . . .

The Sioux having committed depredations on our people, we sent out war parties that summer, who succeeded in killing *fourteen*. I paid several visits to fort Armstrong during the summer, and was always well treated. We were not as happy then in our village as formerly. Our people got more liquor than customary. I used all my influence to prevent drunkenness, but without effect. As the settlements progressed towards us, we became worse off, and more unhappy. Many of our people, instead of going to their old hunting grounds, where game was plenty, would go near to the settlements to hunt—and, instead of saving their skins to pay the trader for goods furnished them in the fall, would sell them to the settlers for whisky! and return in the spring with their families, almost naked, and without the means of getting any thing for them.

About this time my eldest son was taken sick and died. He had always been a dutiful child, and had just grown to manhood. Soon after, my youngest daughter, an interesting and affectionate child, died also. This was a hard stroke, because I loved my children. In my distress, I left the noise of the village, and built my lodge on a mound in my corn-field, and enclosed it with a fence, around which I planted corn and beans. Here I was with my family alone. I gave every thing I had away, and reduced myself to poverty. The only covering I retained, was a piece of buffalo robe. I resolved on blacking my face and fasting, for two years, for the loss of my two children—drinking only of water in the middle of the day, and eating sparingly of boiled corn at sunset. I fulfilled my promise, hoping that the Great Spirit would take pity on me.

My nation had now some difficulty with the Ioways, with whom we wished to be at peace. Our young men had repeatedly killed some of the Ioways; and these breaches had always been made up by giving presents to the relations of those killed. But the last council we had with them, we promised that, in case any more of their people were killed by ours, instead of presents, we would give up the person, or persons, that had done the injury. We made this determination known to our people; but, notwithstanding, one of our young men killed an Ioway the following winter.

A party of our people were about starting for the Ioway village to give the young man up. I agreed to accompany them. When we were ready to start, I called at the lodge for the young man to go with us. He was sick, but willing to go. His brother, however, prevented him, and insisted on going to die in his place, as he was unable to travel. We started, and on the seventh day arrived in sight of the Ioway village, and when within a short distance of it, halted and dismounted. We all bid farewell to our young brave, who entered the village alone, singing his *death-song*, and sat down in the square in the middle of the village. One of the Ioway chiefs came out to us. We told him that we had fulfilled our promise—that we had brought the brother of the young man who had killed one of their people—that he had volunteered to come in his place, in consequence of his brother being unable to travel from sickness. We had no further conversation, but mounted our horses and rode off. As we started, I cast my eye towards the village, and observed the Ioways coming out of their lodges with spears and war clubs. We took our trail back, and travelled until dark—then encamped and made a fire. We had not been here long, before we heard the sound of horses coming towards us. We seized our arms; but instead of an enemy, it was our young brave with two horses. He told me that after we had left him, they menaced him with death for some time—then gave him something to eat—smoked the pipe with him—and made him a present of the two horses and some goods, and started him after us. When we arrived at our village, our people were much pleased; and for the noble and generous conduct of the Ioways, on this occasion, not one of their people has been killed since by any of our nation. . . .

9.

ORESTES A. BROWNSON:
"The Laboring Classes"

Although Orestes A. Brownson's mind was fixed on spiritual certitude during his years of fame as a Transcendentalist, it had a remarkable pertinacity which distinguished it from that of the more abstract idealist of his time. The two essays in his Boston Quarterly Review *represented a highwater mark of radical thinking respecting the rights and wrongs of labor. Widely denounced by Whig orators as the voice of unbridled Jacksonianism, the essays in fact had as little to do with the latter's election promises as with the former's. They did, however, reflect genuine working-men's dissatisfaction with their portion of the nation's wealth in more material terms than Brownson intended. Brownson joined many Jackson idealogues by derogating slavery as a priority issue as compared with the plight of the white workers or in bluntly defending slavery as preferable to "wage slavery" or appropriate to the governance of Negroes. Brownson's disillusionment with the vagaries of American democracy drove him, in a sensational turn-about, out of politics and into Catholicism and a career as a philosopher.*

No one can observe the signs of the times with much care, without perceiving that a crisis as to the relation of wealth and labor is approaching. It is useless to shut our eyes to the fact, and like the ostrich fancy ourselves secure because we have so concealed our heads that we see not the danger. We or our children

SOURCE: *Boston Quarterly Review* (July 1840), pp. 366 *et seq.;* (October 1840), pp. 460 *et seq.*

will have to meet this crisis. The old war between the King and the Barons is well nigh ended, and so is that between the Barons and the Merchants and Manufacturers,—landed capital and commercial capital. The business man has become the peer of my Lord. And now commences the new struggle between the operative and his employer, between wealth and labor. Every day does this struggle extend further and wax stronger and fiercer; what or when the end will be God only knows. . . .

What, we would ask, is, throughout the Christian world, the actual condition of the laboring classes, viewed simply and exclusively in their capacity of laborers? They constitute at least a moiety of the human race. . . . In any contest they will be as two to one, because the large class of proprietors who are not employers, but laborers on their own lands or in their own shops will make common cause with them.

Now we will not so belie our acquaintance with political economy, as to allege that these alone perform all that is necessary to the production of wealth. We are not ignorant of the fact, that the merchant, who is literally the common carrier and exchange dealer, performs a useful service, and is therefore entitled to a portion of the proceeds of labor. But make all necessary deductions on his account, and then ask what portion of the remainder is retained, either in kind or in its equivalent, in the hands of the original producer, the workingman? All over the world this fact stares us in the face, the workingman is poor and depressed, while a large portion of the nonworkingmen, in the sense we now use the term, are wealthy. It may be laid down as a general rule, with but few exceptions, that men are rewarded in an inverse ratio to the amount of actual service they perform. Under every government on earth the largest salaries are annexed to those offices, which demand of their incumbents the least amount of actual labor either mental or manual. And this is in perfect harmony with the whole system of repartition of the fruits of industry, which obtain in every department of society. Now here is the system which prevails, and here is its result. The whole class of simple laborers are poor, and in general unable to procure anything beyond the bare necessaries of life. . . .

In our own country this condition has existed under its most favorable aspects, and has been made as good as it can be. It has reached all the excellence of which it is susceptible. It is now not improving but growing worse. The actual condition of the workingman today, viewed in all its bearings, is not so good as it was fifty years ago. If we have not been altogether misinformed, fifty years ago, health and industrious habits, constituted no mean stock in trade, and with them almost any man might aspire to competence and independence. But it is so no longer. The wilderness has receded, and already the new lands are beyond the reach of the mere laborer, and the employer has him at his mercy. If the present relation subsist, we see nothing better for him in reserve than what he now possesses, but something altogether worse. . . .

Now the great work for this age and the coming, is to raise up the laborer, and to realize in our own social arrangements and in the actual condition of all men, that equality between man and man, which God has established between the rights of one and those of another. In other words, our business is to emancipate the proletaries, as the past has emancipated the slaves. This is our work. There must be no class of our fellow men doomed to toil through life as mere workmen at wages. If wages are tolerated it must be, in the case of the individual operative, only under such conditions that by the time he is of a proper age to settle in life, he shall have accumulated enough to be an independent laborer on his own capital,—on his own farm or in his own shop. Here is our work. How is it to be done? . . .

For our part, we yield to none in our reverence for science and religion; but we confess that we look not for the regeneration of the race from priests and pedagogues. They have had a fair trial. They cannot construct the temple of God. They cannot conceive its plan, and they know not how to build. They daub with untempered mortar, and the walls they erect tumble down if so

much as a fox attempt to go up thereon. In a word they always
league with the people's masters, and seek to reform without
disturbing the social arrangements which render reform necessary. They would change the consequents without changing the
antecedents, secure to men the rewards of holiness, while they
continue their allegiance to the devil. We have no faith in priests
and pedagogues. They merely cry peace, peace, and that too
when there is no peace, and can be none. . . .

The truth is, the evil we have pointed out is not merely individual in its character. It is not, in the case of any single
individual, of any one man's procuring, nor can the efforts of any
one man, directed solely to his own moral and religious perfection, do aught to remove it. What is purely individual in its
nature, efforts of individuals to perfect themselves, may remove.
But the evil we speak of is inherent in all our social arrangements, and cannot be cured without a radical change of those
arrangements. Could we convert all men to Christianity in both
theory and practice, as held by the most enlightened sect of
Christians among us, the evils of the social state would remain
untouched. Continue our present system of trade, and all its
present evil consequences will follow, whether it be carried on by
your best men or your worst. Put your best men, your wisest,
most moral, and most religious men, at the head of your paper
money banks, and the evils of the present banking system will
remain scarcely diminished. The only way to get rid of its evils is
to change the system, not its managers. The evils of slavery do
not result from the personal characters of slave masters. They are
inseparable from the system, let who will be masters. Make all
your rich men good Christians, and you have lessened not the
evils of existing inequality in wealth. The mischievous effects of
this inequality, do not result from the personal character of either
rich or poor, but from itself, and they will continue, just so long
as there are rich men and poor men in the same community. You
must abolish the system or accept its consequences. No man can
serve both God and Mammon. If you will serve the devil, you

must look to the devil for your wages; we know no other way. . . .

But what shall government do? Its first doing must be an *un-*doing. There has been thus far quite too much government, as well as government of the wrong kind. The first act of government we want, is a still further limitation of itself. It must begin by circumscribing within narrower limits its powers. And then it must proceed to repeal all laws which bear against the laboring classes, and then to enact such laws as are necessary to enable them to maintain their equality. We have no faith in those systems of elevating the working classes, which propose to elevate them without calling in the aid of the government. We must have government, and legislation expressly directed to this end.

But again what legislation do we want so far as this country is concerned? We want first the legislation which shall free government, whether State or Federal, from the control of the Banks. The Banks represent the interest of the employer, and therefore of necessity interests adverse to those of the employed; that is, they represent the interests of the business community in opposition to the laboring community. So long as the government remains under the control of the Banks, so long it must be in the hands of the natural enemies of the laboring classes, and may be made, nay, will be made, an instrument of depressing them yet lower. . . . Uncompromising hostility to the whole banking system should therefore be the motto of every workingman, and of every friend of Humanity. The system must be destroyed. On this point there must be no misgiving, no subterfuge, no palliation. The system is at war with the rights and interest of labor, and it must go. Every friend of the system must be marked as an enemy to his race, to his country, and especially to the laborer. No matter who he is, in what party he is found, or what name he bears, he is, in our judgment, no true democrat, as he can be no true Christian.

Following the destruction of the Banks, must come that of all monopolies, of all PRIVILEGE. There are many of these. . . . We only say now, that as we have abolished hereditary monarchy and hereditary nobility, we must complete the work by abolishing hereditary property. A man shall have all he honestly acquires, so long as he himself belongs to the world in which he acquires it. But his power over his property must cease with his life, and his property must then become the property of the state, to be disposed of by some equitable law for the use of the generation which takes his place. Here is the principle without any of its details, and this is the grand legislative measure to which we look forward. We see no means of elevating the laboring classes which can be effectual without this. And is this a measure to be easily carried? Not at all. It will cost infinitely more than it cost to abolish either hereditary monarchy or hereditary nobility. It is a great measure, and a startling. The rich, the business community, will never voluntarily consent to it, and we think we know too much of human nature to believe that it will ever be effected peaceably. It will be effected only by the strong arm of physical force. It will come, if it ever come at all, only at the conclusion of war, the like of which the world as yet has never witnessed, and from which, however inevitable it may seem to the eye of philosophy, the heart of Humanity recoils with horror. . . .

Our account of the condition of the laboring classes, we have been told, is exaggerated and false. This objection would have some weight with us, were it not urged exclusively by those who live by availing themselves of the labors of the workingmen, and who, therefore, have a direct interest in keeping them as they are. . . .

The class of persons, who have been loudest in their condemnation of us, are the *Nouveaux riches, parvenus*, upstarts, men who have themselves come up from the class of proletaries, and who have made it a virtue to forget "the rock whence they were hewn." Standing now on the shoulders of their brethren, they are too elevated to see what is going on at the base of the social organization. Would you know what is going on down there, you must interrogate those who dwell there, and feel the pressure that is on them. One would not interrogate the rider in order to ascertain the sensations the horse has in being ridden. . . .

"But *we* have risen and so may others." Yes, doubtless; *some* others; but *all* others? How have you risen? By the productive industry of your own hands? By hard work. Aye, but by what kind of hard work? Has it not been by hard work in studying how you could turn the labors of others to your own profit; that is, transfer the proceeds of labor from the pockets of the laborer to your own? If you had had no laboring class, dependent entirely on its labor for the means of living, whose industry you could lay under contribution, would you ever have risen to your present wealth? Of course not. Of course, then, only a certain number of individuals of the laboring classes could, even with your talents, skill, and matchless virtues, rise as you have done. One rises from the class of proletaries only by making those, he leaves behind, the lever of his elevation. This, therefore, necessarily implies that there must always be a laboring class, and of course that the means, which this or that laborer uses for his individual elevation, cannot in the nature of things be used by all of his class. . . .

"But what would you that we should do? Do we not pay the market price for labor?" Aye, the market price; but who fixes the market price; you, or the laborer? Why do you employ him? Is it not that you may grow rich? Why does he seek employment? Is it not that he may not die of hunger, he, his wife, and little ones? Which is the more urgent necessity, that of growing rich, or that of guarding against hunger? You can live, though you do not employ the laborer; but, if he find not employment, he must die. He is then at your mercy. You have over him the power of life and death. It is then of his necessity that you avail yourselves, and by taking advantage of that you reduce the price of labor to the minimum of human subsistence, and then grow rich by pur-chasing it. Would you be willing to labor through life as he does, and live on the income he receives? Not at all. You would regard, as the greatest of calamities which could befall you, that of losing your property, and being reduced to the necessity of supporting yourselves and families on the wages you could receive as common laborers. Do you not then see that you condemn in the most positive terms the condition of the proletary, that you de-clare plainer than any words we can use, that you look upon that condition as a serious calamity? What right have you then to maintain that a condition, which you regard with horror so far as concerns yourself, is good enough for your brethren? . . . And why complain of us for calling upon you to do all in your power, so to arrange matters, that no one shall be doomed to that condi-tion? Why do you not, as the Christian law, of doing unto others as you would be done by, commands you, set yourselves at work in earnest to remodel the institution of property, so that all shall be proprietors, and you be relieved from paying wages, and the proletary from the necessity of receiving them? This is what we would have you do; what we hold you bound to do, and which you must do, or the wrongs and sufferings of the laborer will lie at your door, and his cries will ascend to the ears of an avenging God against you,—a God who espouses the cause of the poor and needy, and has sworn to avenge them on their oppressors. . . .

With regard to physical force, we have not much to say. We see an immense system of wrong everywhere established, and everywhere upheld. This system is the growth of a hundred ages, and is venerable in the eyes of many; but it must be overthrown. Man must be free, and SHALL be free,—free to develop his lofty and deathless nature, and prove himself a child of God. This is in his destiny. But how can he become thus free? How can the huge system of accumulated wrongs, under which he now groans, be overthrown, and a new and better system introduced and estab-lished? Peaceably? We would fain hope so; but we fear not. We are well assured of one thing; that the reform party will not be the first to take up arms. It will proceed calmly and peaceably, but energetically to its work. It will use no arms but those of the intellect and the heart. It fixes its eye on Justice, and marches steadily towards its realization. Will the conservatives yield up peaceably their exclusive privileges? Will they consent that justice shall be realized? If so, there will be no war. But we think we know the conservatives too well to believe this. A party that could collect together in this city, by hundreds, to mob a poor itinerant lecturer, and by thousands to consult on demolishing the post-office, because the postmaster insisted on obeying the laws, we do not believe will suffer the reform party to proceed quietly to the realization of its hopes. The proletaries will never resort to physical forces; but that the masters may, for the purpose of keeping the proletaries in their present condition, we must believe, till we have some evidence to the contrary. They have already threatened it here. Distinguished members of Congress have said publicly, that they would resort to force, if necessary, to effect a change in the policy of the Federal Administration, in case they should fail in their efforts to elect General Harrison to the Presidency. And what in England, in France, throughout all Europe, but armed soldiery, sustains the existing order of things? We know the conservative spirit. It fights against all reforms; it would hold the human race back to the past, and never suffer it to take a single step forward. Hitherto, it has been only on the battlefield; a Marathon, a Plataea, a Marston Moor, a Naseby, a Bunker's Hill, a Saratoga, or a Yorktown, that Humanity has conquered her power to advance. The Past has always stood in the gate, and forbid the Future to enter; and it has been only in mortal encounter, that the Future has as yet ever been able to force its entrance. . . .

10.

WILLIAM LEGGETT:
An Antislavery Jacksonian

William Leggett (1801–1839) was one of the most attractive of Jackson's followers. A mercurial journalist, he joined William Cullen Bryant in 1829 as assistant editor and part owner of the New York Evening Post. *There he denounced the Second Bank of the United States and spoke for workers' rights. He helped organize in New York the "Loco-Foco" faction of the Democratic party, radical in outlook. He also expressed himself vigorously, first against the suppression of abolitionists by riot and mail censorship then more directly against slavery itself: a position which cooled enthusiasm for him among some associates though others admired his courage. Fighting sickness, Leggett left the* Post *in 1836 and then issued the* Plaindealer *for more forthright statements of position. His death was mourned by frustrated antislavery Democrats and also by such others as John Greenleaf Whittier, who celebrated Leggett in prose and verse. A fellow Jacksonian, Theodore Sedgwick, Jr., issued* A Collection of the Political Writings of William Leggett.*

It will be seen by the report of the proceedings of the Board of Aldermen last evening [July 21, 1834], published in another column, that the communication of the Executive Committee of the Anti-Slavery Association was treated with great contempt by that body. As the communication has been inserted, as an advertisement, in nearly all the newspapers, the public generally are

SOURCE: Theodore Sedgwick, Jr., *A Collection of the Political Writings of William Leggett* (New York: Taylor & Dodd, 1840), vol. I, pp. 37 ff.

probably pretty well apprized of its contents. It is a perfectly respectful document, prepared with the purpose of showing that the association above named had transcended none of those rights which are guarantied to its members, in common with all their fellow-citizens, by the Constitution of the United States; and that the objects of the society are not incompatible with the duties of its members as citizens under the existing institutions of this country.

With all due respect for the motives which actuated the Board of Aldermen in unanimously refusing to entertain this document, we must take the liberty to say that we think they did not act wisely in casting it out. An occasion was presented them for the expression of a calm and temperate opinion on the conduct of the abolitionists, as it affects the peace and order of society, which, properly embraced, might have been productive of much good, both on the minds of the enthusiasts in the cause of negro emancipation, and those, more especially, of the community at large. We would not have the Common Council throw itself in as a disputant in the fierce and inflammatory discussion which has already engaged so many fiery antagonists; but we should have been glad to see it treat the subject as a legislative body—as a body of municipal magistrates, charged with the framing and the enforcing of the laws. We should have been glad if this letter of Arthur Tappan and his associates had been referred to a discreet and intelligent committee, to the end that they might draw up a report, not controverting the abstract notions of the abolitionists on the subject of the emancipation and equal rights of the blacks, but proving by mild and judicious arguments, that even if the end they aim at is in itself proper, the time is ill chosen, and the means employed calculated, not merely to defeat their object, but to plunge the negroes into a far worse condition than that which they are now taught by their deluded guides to repine at.

The report might further have shown, that, even allowing the time to be well chosen for the work, and the means adapted to the end, they pursue a radically erroneous course in addressing their doctrines to the negroes themselves, whom they thus render discontented and wretched, but whose condition they cannot meliorate. To effect their object the minds of the whites must be convinced of its propriety; and all discourses addressed to the blacks meanwhile, to show them the degradation of their situation, and their natural right to an equal footing with the race of white men, must inevitably tend, at the best, to make them unhappy, and may lead to scenes of outrage which the mind shudders to contemplate.

In a report such as we are supposing, the committee might also have taken occasion to speak words of salutary counsel to those classes of the community most likely to be stirred up to acts of violence by the fanatical conduct of the abolitionists. They might have shown them that any insurrectionary movement, instead of effecting the object desired, would, by an invariable law of human nature, be followed by a very contrary result. They might have shown, that persecution is the very fuel that feeds the fire of fanaticism; that such men as the abolitionists are but fixed more firmly in their faith by the opposition that seeks to prostrate them; that like the waves of the ocean, which swell from billows into mountains as the gale rages against them, their spirits but rise the higher when assailed by a storm of popular fury, nor subside again till the tempest is overpast. Fanaticism has ever flourished most exuberantly in the most intolerant countries; nor are there many minds in this community so ignorant of the history of nations as not to know, that, whether in religion or politics, enthusiasm gains strength and numbers the more its dogmas are opposed. The effort to put down the Roman Catholic religion by persecution has been tried, and with what result? The attempt to destroy the heresy, as it was deemed, of the Covenanters in Scotland, by hunting down its professors, was also thoroughly tried; but though the devoted peasantry were driven to caves and dens, and forced to subsist on the roots of the earth, the storm of religious persecution, instead of extinguishing, only fanned the fire of zeal into a fiercer flame.

These are views which, if the Common Council had embraced the opportunity of the letter of Arthur Tappan and his associates to put them before the community, in a report drawn up with ability and judgment, might, we think, have been productive of very considerable good. The Anti-Slavery Society, as the reader probably remarked, after stating that nothing had occurred to change their views on those subjects in relation to which they are associated, declare their determination not "to recant or relinquish any principle or measure they have adopted," but on the contrary, avow their readiness "to live and die" by the principles they have espoused. In this—however mistaken, however mad, we may consider their opinions in relation to the blacks—what honest, independent mind can blame them? Where is the man so poor of soul, so white-livered, so base, that he would do less, in relation to any important doctrine in which he religiously believed? Where is the man who would have his tenets drubbed into him by the clubs of ruffians, or would hold his conscience at the dictation of a mob?

There is no man in this community more sincerely and strongly opposed to the views and proceedings of the abolitionists than this journal is, and always has been. Our opposition was commenced long before that of those prints which now utter the most intemperate declamation on the subject, nor have we omitted to express it on any proper occasion since. But in doing this temperately, in employing argument and reasoning, instead of calling on the populace "to arm and strike a blow for liberty"—instead of painting disgusting portraits of the "blubber lips and sooty blood of negroes"—we think we are more effectually advancing the desired end, than we possibly could, by the most furious and inflammatory appeals to the angry passions of the multitude. Indeed, one of the reasons why we lamented the late violations of public order and private right, was, that the effect of such outrages would be to increase, instead of abating, the zeal of abolition fanaticism, and warm many minds perhaps, which were before only moderately inclined to those doctrines, to a pitch of

11.

JOHN GREENLEAF WHITTIER:
"The Prisoner for Debt"

John Greenleaf Whittier (1807–1892) made so formidable a reputation as a poet in later years that his distinction as an abolitionist writer and editor was lost. He was first discovered by Garrison, who published his early verses and turned him from an interest in local New England lore to themes of social justice. He served in the Massachusetts legislature, edited the Pennsylvania Freeman *(1838–1840) and other papers, helped found the Liberty party and wrote verse on crises and incidents of reform. They were influential in molding northern opinion and made Whittier a mediating figure between northern radicals and moderates. Later he helped edit the* National Era *in Washington, D.C., and contributed to its pages. The following verse, "The Prisoner for Debt," appeared in 1835 and was one of the writings he collected in his several volumes of abolitionist and reform verses. It was suggested by the case of a Revolutionary soldier, "confined in Charleston [Massachusetts] jail for a debt of fourteen dollars, and [who] on the fourth of July was seen waving a handkerchief from the bars of his cell in honor of the day."*

> Look on him! through his dungeon grate,
>   Feebly and cold, the morning light
> Comes stealing round him, dim and late,
>   As if it loathed the sight.
> Reclining on his strawy bed,
> His hand upholds his drooping head;

SOURCE: *The Poetical Works of John Greenleaf Whittier* (Boston: Houghton, Mifflin and Co., 1888), pp. 99–100.

His bloodless cheek is seamed and hard,
Unshorn his gray, neglected beard;
And o'er his bony fingers flow
His long, dishevelled locks of snow. . . .

What has the gray-haired prisoner done?
   Has murder stained his hands with gore?
Not so; his crime's a fouler one;
   God made the old man poor!
For this he shares a felon's cell,
The fittest earthly type of hell!
For this, the boon for which he poured
His young blood on the invader's sword,
And counted light the fearful cost,
His blood-gained liberty is lost!

And so, for such a place of rest,
   Old prisoner, dropped thy blood as rain
On Concord's field, and Bunker's crest,
   And Saratoga's plain?
Look forth, thou man of many scars,
Through thy dim dungeon's iron bars;
It must be joy, in sooth, to see
Yon monument upreared to thee;
Piled granite and a prison cell,—
The land repays thy service well!

Go, ring the bells and fire the guns,
   And fling the starry banner out;
Shout "Freedom!" till your lisping ones
   Give back their cradle-shout;
Let boastful eloquence declaim
Of honor, liberty, and fame;
Still let the poet's strain be heard,
With glory for each second word,
And everything with breath agree
To praise "our glorious liberty"! . . .

Down with the law that binds him thus!
   Unworthy freemen, let it find
No refuge from the withering curse

Of god and human-kind!
Open the prison's living-tomb,
And usher from its brooding gloom
The victims of your savage code
To the free sun and air of God;
No longer dare as crime to brand
The chastening of the Almighty's hand.

About once in every six months, the abolitionists are scattered to the winds of heaven by their spasmodic opponents, who rush upon them like a hurricane, fill the air with feathers, brickbats, and all sorts of argumentative missiles, and burn and destroy all before them! Semiannually, too, the Constitution is triumphant! Still, the ghost of murdered Banquo "will not down." In a short time, the abolitionists are seen in multitudinous array every where, marching from village to village, from city to city, from State to State, augmenting their number at every step, and evidently invigorated by the respite from their labors which the storm enabled them to take. Once more, however, they have been utterly annihilated—and again has the Constitution been rescued from the hand of treason! It is more than probable, that the world will soon witness another miracle of restoration. . . . Nay, even the Courier and Enquirer begins already to despond! Hear it—"It is dreadful to contemplate the short period of time which has elapsed since these abolitionists were a mere handful, to the MULTITUDE they have since become." So, then we derive from our opponents these instructive but paradoxical facts—that without numbers, we are multitudinous; without power, we are sapping the foundation of the confederacy; without a plan, we are hastening the abolition of slavery; and without wealth or talent, we are rapidly converting the nation!

William Lloyd Garrison

The only true courage is that which impels us to do right without regard to consequences. To fear a populace is as servile as to fear an emperor. The only salutary restraint is the fear of doing wrong.

Lydia Maria Child

General William Birney's biography of his father James G. Birney made earnest and informed efforts to prove that Birney, and men of Birney's outlook, had been strategic in the campaign to turn the North against slavery. His endeavor included allegations that William Lloyd Garrison, far from having been the leader of the abolitionist forces, had been a futile fanatic who had done more to antagonize Northerners anxious to oppose social wrong in America than to win them to abolition.

It was a curious fact that in 1896 when Birney published his memoirs, Garrison was esteemed in the North as an immortal who had rung the tocsin of abolition and held the North accountable to its duty until abolition had finally been achieved. By then, the elder Birney had been all but forgotten in popular lore. Evidently, honor and indifference were distributed according to the spirit of the times, rather than as a result of judicious inquiry.

Birney was certainly correct in asserting and displaying evidence that there were upright personalities and even groups favoring and working for abolition before the advent of Garrison. It was equally certain that none of them other than Benjamin Lundy had taken a position which either carried beyond his local or other circumstances or was capable of rousing the nation. For example, the Reverend George Bourne, author of *The Book and Slavery Irreconcilable* (1816), had spoken out in Virginia against slavery in words which required him to leave his pulpit and migrate north. The Reverend John Rankin left Kentucky with his congregation to obtain ease of spirit in antislavery Ohio. In Ripley, Ohio, overlooking the Ohio River, Rankin pursued his antislavery work in 1826 publishing his pioneer *Letters on Slavery,* which developed rude but effective arguments pointing to a more active, more demanding abolitionist viewpoint.

But neither Bourne nor Rankin nor a dozen other wilderness breakers of abolition who could be named nor even Lundy challenged the nation to confront slavery as a system. Their hope lay in widening appeal to the social conscience. Their program proposed meliorating work of various kinds, none of which directly threatened slavery or even the individual self-esteem of slaveholders. Assuredly, the reformers did worthy work in appealing to state legislatures to secure the rights of free Negroes. They gave secret aid to runaways. They provided some schooling for Negro children. And, in many cases, they struggled sincerely to make of colonization a positive instrument, helpful to Negroes as individuals and as groups.

Yet all their efforts together added up to little compared to the overwhelming power of the slave states. Birney's own career in the South, as has been seen, no more than demonstrated that the section of his birth, upbringing and career was impervious to the appeals of one of its distinguished sons. There was no abolitionist career for Birney in the South.

Garrison drew direct or indirect sustenance from all of the efforts of his predecessors and contemporaries. Nor was the program he so dramatically unfolded original with him. A British Quaker, Elizabeth Heyrick, had in 1824 caused comment with her pamphlet, *Immediate, Not Graduate Emancipation.* But Garrison, a seasoned young journalist, early took an ardent stance which displayed itself first in the temperance cause, then more generally in moral reform and gradual abolition mixed with Whiggism and other contemporary matters. He then became an aide to Lundy in Baltimore, editing the *Genius of Universal Emancipation,* while his chief pursued antislavery organizing missions elsewhere.

Following his practical expulsion from Baltimore, Garrison went north. Subsequent events acquainted him personally with

the Tappans in New York, James Fo?cert
Reverend Lyman Beecher in Boston, ₐPhiladelphia and the
some encouraged him to promote his caᵤ others. Although
Beecher, feared his unbending sternness, none gₐnd others, like
tial. His *Liberator,* as first issued January 1, 1831, wₐ ᵈ his poten-
ᵢᵣculated
to a small, almost trifling readership. His New-Englanᵥ Anti-
Slavery Society began its meetings late that year by attracting ten
persons.

They were, to be sure, of astonishing quality, including individuals like Ellis Gray Loring from Boston's elite. But then, as
later, Garrison possessed neither funds nor constituency. His
appeal was nothing if not moral.

Garrison was made notorious by two equally undistinguished
events. One was the 1829 Boston publication of David Walker's
violent denunciation of white America, which furnished in the
South a pretext for setting new curbs on the education and free
movement of slaves. In August of 1831, an uprising of some
seventy slaves in one of the southern-most counties of Virginia
was led by Nat Turner, a brooding and religious Negro who had
pondered the Bible and interpreted signs. The insurrectionary
effort resulted in local atrocities on both sides and bared Virginia
as a thoroughly frightened and concerned state. A momentous
debate in its legislature on the issue of freeing or removing the
Negroes from Virginia resulted in the total victory of the proslavery forces: the forces of simple suppression.

Although the *Liberator* attracted few readers, it circulated to
editors everywhere, and its "incendiary" character was angrily
noted in the southern press. It proceeded to make Garrison a
symbol of all the things it feared the North capable of tolerating.
In passionately demanding Garrison's suppression, it stirred the
feelings of numerous men and women in the free states. Some of
these were roused to actions which quickly made abolition a
major public issue.

Abolitionists were of every type and concern. They included

John Greenleaf W̶ ʳ, born of humble people in Massachusetts and Willi of New York, son of the late Chief Justice of
the United s John Jay. The abolitionists included Lydia
Maria Cl who, as a young woman, had made a name as a
story-t and composer of juvenilia and other welcome literary
far Garrison drew her and her husband David Lee Child, a
promising lawyer and editor, out of their respectable orbits and
into antislavery work. Mrs. Child's *An Appeal in Favor of That
Class of Americans Called Africans* (1833) narrowed her circle
of friends but influenced such vital personalities as the eloquent
Wendell Phillips and the rising "scholar in politics," Charles
Sumner.

The Quakers contributed many abolitionists, from the conservative Philadelphian Roberts Vaux to the uncompromising
Isaac T. Hopper, whom the Quakers finally disowned. A figure of
great, if unspectacular, consequence was Dr. Gamaliel Bailey,
who came from the East to Cincinnati where he helped Birney
issue his moderately abolitionist *The Philanthropist* and succeeded him as editor. Bailey dreamed of an abolitionist movement which would enlist armies of voters of all political
persuasions. In 1847 he left Cincinnati for Washington, D.C.
where he would publish the *National Era* and continue to pursue
his hope of a national antislavery party.

Thus, some abolitionists followed the lead of Garrison who
demanded that slavery be regarded as sinful and slaveholders as
steeped in sin. Others held with Birney, Bailey, the Tappans and
others to greater or lesser degree that slavery was an unfortunate
condition which afflicted the country and was to be expunged by
a majority of the nation's voters. All abolitionists, however, were
surrounded by religious imperatives which drove them, sometimes reluctantly, to non-conformist thought. Abolitionism was
outstandingly—unlike the reform impulse which had directed
Owenites—a religiously-motivated development.

This drive toward a more vital church produced a host of
extraordinary talents. One of the most remarkable in the 1830s

was Theodore Dwight Weld, a young man of inspiring mien and eloquence, who began with temperance and a plan for building "manual labor" schools combining religious fervor with the discipline of work. Weld found himself in Lane Seminary, Cincinnati, then under the rule of Lyman Beecher. The school's mission was to produce Congregational ministers to combat Catholicism in the West. But there, in 1834, Weld engineered the great debate over slavery which drew in the entire student body and most of the faculty. Nine days of controversy turned the majority into abolitionists. When the school's trustees concluded that contemporary issues ought not to concern students—many of whom were in their late twenties and even thirties—the "Lane rebels" left, some to infuse life into struggling young Oberlin College in northern Ohio.

Later, in New York, Weld became a vital force in the new American Anti-Slavery Society founded in Philadelphia in 1833. He organized the famous "Seventy": evangelical abolitionist agents whom he sent out to stir up the countryside. In 1839 he issued, under title of *American Slavery as It Is,* a powerful collection of items, mostly culled from southern sources, revealing the darker workings of the slavery system. It aggravated the feelings of thousands of otherwise neutral northern citizens and directly influenced writings by Harriet Beecher Stowe and Charles Dickens.

Thus abolition flourished in the North during the 1830s, while it withered in the South, foretelling a different career from that which the British were experiencing. They, too, had raised crusaders to fight the foreign slave trade and had put it outside the law—but there were no slaves in the British Isles. There the struggle was between Parliamentary factions free to deal as they pleased with their Caribbean islands, containing three-quarters of a million slaves. In London humanitarian debate on the slave trade practically foredoomed legal slavery. In the United States the states-rights compact permitted southern leaders to stand tall and thereby destroyed the middle ground of compromise which helped the British to ease their way through an awkward tangle of social and economic interests.

Between 1832 and 1838 Parliamentary rhetoric and petitions brought about the legal emancipation of slaves in the British islands at the resounding price of 20 million pounds. Abolitionists in America made every effort to impress this example upon their countrymen, with relatively little result. Whether British emancipation was successful or unsuccessful, and in what sense, remained unresolved in American debates. Whether it was or was not "at the expense" of the suffering British poor was an open question. Abolitionists sought British support and financial aid. They raised the patriotic ire of Democrats and slaveholders who read malice and meddling in American affairs into such donations and who profited from domestic memories of the two wars the nation had fought to be free of British influence.

Meanwhile, the years 1834 and 1835 were the abolitionists' time in America for sensational organization in the face of angry agitation.[1] Riots punctuated their meetings, and the lives of abolitionists were threatened. In New York Lewis Tappan's home was gutted by mobsters. In Boston on a lurid occasion Garrison was led through the streets with the rope encircling him entering into legend as a prelude to his hanging. Birney escaped a Cincinnati mob by mere accident. And so with others. In 1837 Reverend Elijah P. Lovejoy died by gunfire at Alton, Illinois, defending his fourth press from determined antiabolitionists who had already done away with three others. The next year in Philadelphia, Pennsylvania Hall, built by reformers to be a center for their friends and activities, was burned to the ground during dedication ceremonies.

The eternal question was whether these and other heroics

---

1. Leonard L. Richards, *"Gentlemen of Property and Standing": Anti-Abolition Mobs in Jacksonian America* (New York: Oxford University Press, 1970); see also Harriet Martineau, *The Martyr Age of the United States* (Boston: Weeks, Jordan & Co., 1839).

dragged the nation forward toward emancipation in spite of itself or interfered with a slower, sounder growth of abolitionist sentiment, and, instead, created an angry, divided nation. That was the force of Birney's critique of Garrison. The question haunted reform activities throughout the decade. By its end many abolitionists, who had originally acknowledged Garrison's demand for an "immediatist" approach, were ready to repudiate his "aberrations." They repudiated his sweeping condemnation of the church as a proslavery institution. They saw no virtue in his condemnation of the government and the Constitution as instruments of evil. They wrote off as intolerable his millenarian acceptance of "universal reform" as disruptive of their abolitionist cause. This last tenet of Garrisonianism took its most acute form in the sect's approval of women's participation on the most active levels of abolitionism. Garrisonians believed that women merited places not merely in audiences or even merely prior places at Anti-Slavery Fairs but also on platforms and in policy-making committees.

The turmoil caused by Garrisonian agitation involved a vast spectrum of experimental personalities, entirely in the North, including Margaret Fuller, raised by her father to be a prodigy of learning, Abby Kelley, taken from the schoolroom to add spirit and eloquence to antislavery meetings and Maria Weston Chapman, of wealthy upbringing. The key sensation of the decade, so far as women's participation in public issues went, was provided by two carefully raised young women from one of the most distinguished of South Carolina families, Sarah and Angelina Grimké.

Their peculiarity lay in having been raised in a household proud of its Revolutionary past and progressive present; their brother, Thomas Smith Grimké (1786–1834) was a highly esteemed civic leader well-known in educational and moral reform circles. Yet their lives and traditions centered about slave and slave relations. (They were later to discover that another brother had fathered children by a slave and to acknowledge as nephews Archibald Henry and Francis James Grimké, both became outstanding leaders of the Negro community.)

Pious and searching, the young women joined the Philadelphia Quakers and were caught up in abolitionist talk and enterprises. Angelina, the younger and more vibrant of the two, in 1836 published her epochal *Appeal to the Christian Women of the South,* causing a scandal below the Mason-Dixon line and a sensation farther north. Soon, the Grimkés, determined to testify against slavery, offered semipublic addresses in churches under abolitionist auspices. The unprecedented nature of their exposure—as distinguished from that of "Fanny Wright" women and men— even under controlled conditions, drew them into the Garrisonian orbit. More conservative abolitionists feared the Grimkés might not only disgrace themselves but their cause.

They became more radical still; concerned with women's rights as well as slavery, they alienated women as well as men. One example was Catherine E. Beecher, one of Lyman Beecher's extraordinary children and an outstanding educator. Her *Essay on Slavery and Abolitionism, with Reference to the Duty of American Females* (1837) directly reproved the Grimkés for mixing into matters not in their province and drew Sarah's retort in her *Letters on the Equality of the Sexes* (1838). Sarah J. Hale, whose distinguished editorial services sadly interested posterity less than her creation of the verse beginning "Mary had a little lamb," also derogated women's entrance into men's sphere at the expense of moral influence.

By 1838 the North seethed with abolitionist societies to some 250,000 in number and with many more friends and sympathizers. They divided roughly into sections. In New England Garrisonians generally dominated. They ranged from Nathaniel P. Rogers of New Hampshire, editor of the *Herald of Freedom,* whom even Garrison could not control, to Henry C. Wright, who persuaded Garrison to initiate a succession of radical innovations. The New York abolitionists sought to colonize New England with a more decorous group of abolitionists who would be less antagonistic to churches and less interested in women's participation. The moderates sent men of substance north, including Henry B. Stanton, one of the "Lane rebels" and husband of Elizabeth Cady Stanton, later a leader of the suffragists. Their movement failed. New Englanders, far removed from slavery, preferred to divide into evangelical abolitionists and skeptics.

New York and Pennsylvania activists tended to be more practical in their approach, if only because they were opposed by more powerful and varied interests. New York merchants, for example, had a heavy stake in the southern economy, and a greater number of Negroes resided among them than could be found farther north. Ohio had perhaps the best-balanced antislavery enterprise, drawing dedicated extremists of the stamp of John Brown of the Western Reserve and Salmon P. Chase of Cincinnati, who was reluctant to be termed an abolitionist at all. He clung to the Democratic party, but his actions in behalf of runaway slaves earned him the gratitude of the Negro community.

The abolitionists accomplished much during the 1830s. They won the right to free speech and press, and revealed southern inability to defend either. They raised the issue of slavery in the District of Columbia. Their persistent scrutiny of Texas developments ensured that it might make one slave state but not more than one. Their visits to Great Britain created a strong and informed auxiliary there.

More important, abolitionists multiplied their aid to runaways and raised constitutional questions respecting slave catching in free states which pierced to American democratic expectations. Since laws undermining slave rights might eat at the civil defences of whites (there were recorded cases of *white* persons seized and transported into slavery), partisans could elicit sympathy for Personal Liberty laws which impeded the work of professional slavers. Such laws created bonds between abolitionists and others in free states, including even antiabolitionists.

A major hero of what became known as the "underground

railroad" was Thomas Garrett (1789–1871) of Delaware, a slave state strategically lying between slave Maryland and free Pennsylvania and New Jersey. In some thirty years of underground work this fearless Quaker was said to have aided more than 2,700 fugitive slaves to freedom. Numerous others beside Garrett risked prison, reputation and life itself to aid individual Negroes and to deny the sanctity of slave property. They also created indispensable liaison relations with Negro communities which sought without pause to help their own.

Yet all these victories excited still greater ambitions to advance antislavery beyond individuals and the subversion of laws helpful to the slavery system. Political abolition could gain no foothold in the 1830s, but moderates were increasingly determined to silence the troublesome Garrisonians. Differences reached a head in their Society's 1840 annual meeting in New York where Garrisonians pressed for women on committees. The antifeminist wing, outmaneuvered, left to set up the rival American and Foreign Anti-Slavery Society. Thus abolitionism entered the 1840s with two organizations claiming to represent it. A third political group moved to advance beyond the appeals of moderates or extremists.

12.

WILLIAM LLOYD GARRISON:
"Exciting the Minds of the People"

William Lloyd Garrison (1805–1879) cut so deep a niche into his time as to raise the question of what his peculiar genius had been. Others bested him in social status, eccentricity and dramatic involvements. Garrison was mild-mannered, regular in habits and with no distinctions in performance. The secret of his presence was hidden deep in his heritage and experiences. His detractors raged at his vanity, his lack of charity, his myopia respecting practical problems of abolition. They failed to perceive his unblinking concentration on the wrong *of slavery. His followers honored his unswerving nature. His contemporaries, though they ridiculed, threatened and ignored him, expressed their gratitude for his faithfulness to the key principle by remembering him above all others. The following, addressed "To the Public," appeared on the first page of the first issue of the* Liberator.

In the month of August, I issued proposals for publishing "THE LIBERATOR" in Washington City; but the enterprise, though hailed in different sections of the country, was palsied by public indifference. Since that time, the removal of the *Genius of Universal Emancipation* to the Seat of Government has rendered less imperious the establishment of a similar periodical in that quarter.

During my recent tour for the purpose of exciting the minds of the people by a series of discourses on the subject of slavery,

SOURCE: William Lloyd Garrison, "To the Public," *Liberator,* January 1, 1831.

every place that I visited gave fresh evidence of the fact, that a greater revolution in public sentiment was to be effected in the free States—*and particularly in New-England*—than at the South. I found contempt more bitter, opposition more active, detraction more relentless, prejudice more stubborn, and apathy more frozen, than among slave-owners themselves. Of course, there were individual exceptions to the contrary. This state of things afflicted, but did not dishearten me. I determined, at every hazard, to lift up the standard of emancipation in the eyes of the nation, *within sight of Bunker Hill and in the birthplace of liberty*. That standard is now unfurled; and long may it float, unhurt by the spoliations of time or the missiles of a desperate foe—yea, till every chain be broken, and every bondman set free! Let Southern oppressors tremble—let their secret abettors tremble—let their Northern apologists tremble—let all the enemies of the persecuted blacks tremble.

I deem the publication of my original Prospectus unnecessary, as it has obtained a wide circulation. The principles therein inculcated will be steadily pursued in this paper, excepting that I shall not array myself as the political partisan of any man. In defending the great cause of human rights, I wish to derive the assistance of all religions and of all parties.

Assenting to the "self-evident truth" maintained in the American Declaration of Independence, "that all men are created equal, and endowed by their Creator with certain inalienable rights—among which are life, liberty and the pursuit of happiness," I shall strenuously contend for the immediate enfranchisement of our slave population. In Park-Street Church, on the Fourth of July, 1829, in an address on slavery, I unreflectingly assented to the popular but pernicious doctrine of *gradual* abolition. I seize this opportunity to make a full and unequivocal recantation, and thus publicly to ask pardon of my God, of my country, and of my brethren the poor slaves, for having uttered a sentiment so full of timidity, injustice, and absurdity. A similar recantation, from my pen, was published in the *Genius of Uni-*

versal Emancipation at Baltimore, in September, 1829. My conscience is now satisfied.

I am aware that many object to the severity of my language;
but is there not cause for severity? I *will be* as harsh as truth, and
as uncompromising as justice. In this subject, I do not wish to
think, or speak, or write, with moderation. No! no! Tell a man
whose house is on fire to give a moderate alarm; tell him to
moderately rescue his wife from the hands of the ravisher; tell
the mother to gradually extricate her babe from the fire into
which it has fallen;—but urge me not to use moderation in a
cause like the present. I am in earnest—I will not equivocate—I
will not excuse—I will not retreat a single inch—AND I WILL BE
HEARD. The apathy of the people is enough to make every statue
leap from its pedestal, and to hasten the resurrection of the dead.

It is pretended, that I am retarding the cause of emancipation
by the coarseness of my invective and the precipitancy of my
measures. *The charge is not true.* On this question my influence,—humble as it is,—is felt at this moment to a considerable
extent, and shall be felt in coming years—not perniciously, but
beneficially—not as a curse, but as a blessing; and posterity will
bear testimony that I was right. I desire to thank God, that he
enables me to disregard "the fear of man which bringeth a
snare," and to speak his truth in its simplicity and power. . . .

13.

WILLIAM JAY:
Colonization and Abolition

William Jay (1789–1858) was too much the gentleman, the judge, the patriot and the evangelical Episcopalian to be widely remembered. Yet he was one of the most important of abolitionists. He gave them the benefit of his name when they needed it most. His conscientious writings advanced reform even while he wondered uneasily whether he was not helping to unleash an irresponsible democracy. Jay also disturbed his fellow-aristocrats by aiding in 1826 in the succor of a free Negro, Gilbert Horton, who had been arrested as a fugitive slave in Washington. He disturbed his peers by sponsoring a petition for the abolition of slavery in the District of Columbia. He was a judge of Westchester County, New York, until 1843 when antiabolitionists succeeded in preventing his reappointment. Meanwhile, his Inquiry into the Character and Tendency of the American Colonization and American Anti-Slavery Societies *had all but destroyed the colonization movement, at least as a factor in current affairs. His books opposing war, and especially the Mexican War, sharpened principles which were directly recalled during the Hague Peace Conference of 1899 and in the aftermath of World War I.*

On the 23d December, 1816, the Legislature of Virginia passed a resolution requesting the Governor to correspond with the President of the United States, "for the purpose of obtaining a territory on the coast of Africa, or at some other place not within any of the States, or territorial governments of the United States,

SOURCE: William Jay, *Inquiry into the Character and Tendency of the American Colonization and American Anti-Slavery Societies* (New York: Leavitt, Lord & Co., 1834), pp. 11 ff., 30 ff.

to serve as an asylum for such persons of colour as are now free, and may desire the same, and for those who may hereafter be emancipated within this commonwealth."

Within a few days of the date of this resolution, a meeting was held at Washington to take this very subject into consideration. It was composed almost entirely of southern gentlemen. Judge Washington presided; Mr. Clay, Mr. Randolph, and others, took part in the discussions which ensued, and which resulted in the organization of the American Colonization Society. Judge Washington was chosen President, and of the seventeen Vice Presidents, only five were selected from the free States, while the twelve managers were, it is believed, without one exception, slaveholders.

The first two articles of the constitution, are the only ones relating to the object of the Society. They are as follows:

Art I. This Society shall be called the American Society for colonizing the free people of color of the United States.

Art II. The object to which its attention is to be *exclusively* directed, is to promote and execute a plan for colonizing (with their consent) the free people of color residing in our country in Africa, or such other place as Congress shall deem most expedient. And the Society shall act to effect this object in co-operation with the general government and such of the States as may adopt regulations on the subject. . . .

The omission of all avowal of *motives* was, probably, not without design, and has not been without effect. It has secured the co-operation of three distinct classes. First, such as sincerely desire to afford the free blacks an asylum from the oppression they suffer here and by their means to extend to Africa the blessings of Christianity and civilization, and who at the same time flatter themselves that colonization will have a salutary influence in accelerating the abolition of slavery: Secondly, such as expect to enhance the value and security of slave property, by removing the free blacks: And, thirdly, such as seek relief from a bad population, without the trouble and expense of improving it.

The doors of the Society being thrown open to all, a heterogeneous multitude has entered, and within its portals men are brought into contact, who, in the ordinary walks of life, are separated by a common repulsion. The devoted missionary, ready to pour out his life on the sands of Africa, is jostled by the trafficker in human flesh; the humble, self-denying Christian, listens to the praises of the Society from the unblushing profligate; and the friend of human rights and human happiness greets as his fellowlaborer the man whose very contribution to the cause is extorted from the unrequited labor of his fellow-men. This anomalous amalgamation of characters and motives, has necessarily led to a lamentable compromise of principle. Whatever may be the object each member proposes to himself, he is conscious it can be effected only by the harmonious co-operation of all the other members. Hence it is all important to avoid giving and taking offence; and never was the maxim, "bear and forbear," more scrupulously obeyed. Certain irreconcileable opinions, but regarded by their holders as fundamental, are, by common consent, wholly suppressed; while in matters of less importance, the expression of opposite sentiments is freely allowed and borne with commendable patience. . . .

The simplicity of the object of the Society as stated in its constitution, tends in a powerful degree to encourage and enforce this compromise of principle. The constitution, in fact, vests a discretionary veto in every member on the expression of unpalatable opinions. The attention of the Society is to be "exclusively" directed to the colonization of persons of color, and the constitution contains no allusion to slavery. Hence any denunciation of slavery as sinful,[1] any arguments addressed to slave

---

1. Candor requires the admission that there is at least one exception to this remark. At the annual meeting of the Society in 1834, the Rev. Mr. Breckenridge in his speech insisted on the sinfulness of slavery. A distinguished lay member of the Society, who was present, complained to the author of Mr. B.'s unconstitutional conduct, and declared that he was strongly tempted publicly to call him to order. [Jay's note.]

holders to induce them to manumit their slaves, would be unconstitutional, and are therefore carefully avoided. But the free blacks cannot be transported without money, and much money cannot be had, without the aid of the enemies of slavery. It is therefore permitted to represent the Society as an antidote to slavery, as tending to effect its abolition, any thing in the constitution to the contrary notwithstanding. But then this abolition is to be brought about at some future indefinite period. True it is, that the constitution is as silent, with respect to manumission, as it is to slavery; but by common consent, this silence is not permitted to interpose the slightest obstacle to a unanimous, vigorous, and persevering opposition to present manumission. Were the American Bible Society to deprecate the emancipation of slaves, and to censure all who proposed it, the outrage would excite the indignation of the whole community. But what would be a perversion of its avowed object in a Bible Society, is perfectly lawful in a Colonization Society, not because it is authorized by the constitution, but because it is *expedient* to conciliate the slave holders.

Many of the supporters of the Society are interested in the *American* slave trade—a trade replete with cruelty and injustice. To condemn *this* trade, or to labor for its suppression, would be unconstitutional. The *African* slave trade rather interferes with, than promotes the interests of the slave owners, and the Society deem it unnecessary to seek for any constitutional warrant to justify the most violent denunciation of the *foreign* traffic; or an application to foreign powers to declare it piratical. . . .

The constitution indeed, forbids the transportation of the free blacks without "their consent"; but it is very constitutional to justify and encourage such oppression of them, as shall compel them to seek in the wilds of Africa, a refuge from American cruelty.

The natural result of this compromise of principle, this suppression of truth, this sacrifice to unanimity, has been the adoption of *expediency* as the standard of right and wrong, in the place of the revealed will of God. Unmindful of the poet's precept,

> Be virtuous ends pursued by virtuous means,
> Nor think the intention sanctifies the deed,

good men, and good Christians, have been tempted by their zeal for the Society, to countenance opinions and practices inconsistent with justice and humanity. Confident that their motives were good, and their object important, they have been too little scrupulous of the means they employed; and hence the Society has actually exerted a demoralizing influence over its own members, by leading them occasionally to advance in its behalf opinions at variance with truth and Christianity. Unhappily the evil influence of the Society has not been confined to its own members. It has to a lamentable extent, vitiated the moral sense of the community, by reconciling public opinion to the continuance of slavery, and by aggravating those sinful prejudices against the free blacks, which are subjecting them to insult and persecution, and denying them the blessings of education and religious instruction. . . .

Miss Crandall, a communicant in the Baptist church, and, as we believe, a lady of irreproachable character, had for some time been at the head of a female boarding school, in the town of Canterbury, Connecticut, when in the autumn of 1832, a pious colored female applied to her for admission into her school, stating that she wanted "to get a little more learning—enough if possible to teach colored children." After some hesitation, Miss Crandall consented to admit her, but was soon informed that this intruder must be dismissed, or that the school would be greatly injured. This threat turned her attention to the cruel prejudices and disadvantages under which the blacks are suffering, and she resolved to open a school *exclusively* for colored girls. It has been thought expedient to doubt the philanthropy of this resolution, and to attribute it to pecuniary motives. Whatever may have been her motives, and pecuniary ones would not have been unlawful, she had a perfect right to open a school for pupils of any color whatever, and had not the moral sense of the community been perverted, this attempt to instruct the poor, the friendless, and the ignorant, would have met with applause instead of contumely. She discontinued her school, and in February, 1833, gave public notice of her intention to open one for colored girls. This notice excited prodigious commotion in the town of Canterbury. That *black* girls should presume to learn reading, and writing, and music, and geography, was past all bearing. Committee after committee waited on Miss Crandall, to remonstrate against the intended school but to no purpose. More efficient means were found necessary to avert the impending calamity, and a legal town meeting was summoned to consider the awful crisis. At this meeting resolutions were passed, expressing the strongest disapprobation of the proposed school, and the preamble declared that "the obvious tendency of this school would be to collect within the town of Canterbury, large numbers of persons from other States, whose characters and habits might be various and unknown to us, thereby rendering insecure the *persons, property, and reputations* of our citizens." Had this extreme nervous apprehension of danger, been excited in the good people of Canterbury, by the introduction of some hundreds of Irish laborers into their village to construct a rail road or canal, we should still have thought their temperament very peculiar; but when we find them thus affecting to tremble not merely for their property, but for their *persons* and *reputations*, at the approach of fifteen or twenty "young ladies and little misses of color," we confess we are astonished that the collected wisdom of these people was not able to frame an argument against the school, less disgraceful to themselves.

Andrew T. Judson, Esq. acted as clerk to this meeting, and supported the resolutions in a speech, in which he is reported to have said, "that should the school go into operation, their sons and daughters would be forever ruined, and property no longer safe." For his part, he was not willing for the honor and welfare of the town, that even *one corner* of it should be appropriated to such a purpose. After the example which New Haven had set, he continued, "shall it be said that *we* cannot, that we dare not resist?" Mr. Judson farther stated, that they had "A LAW which should prevent that school from going into operation."

The resolutions of the town meeting, as became so grave a matter, were communicated to Miss Crandall by the "civil authority and selectmen," but strange as it may seem, that lady stood less in dread of them, than they did of the "young ladies of color," for she refused to retreat from the ground she had taken. . . .

Mr. Judson had indeed a certain LAW in reserve, but it was necessary that *certain influences* should be previously brought into action, before a civilized and Christian people could be induced to tolerate the application of that law. Colonization, as already remarked, had taken a deep hold on the affections of the people of Connecticut. Their most eminent men had enrolled themselves in the ranks of the Society. To this powerful association recourse was now had. On the 22d March, 1833, the "civil authority and selectmen" of Canterbury made their "APPEAL TO THE AMERICAN COLONIZATION SOCIETY." In this most extraordinary paper, they expatiate on the *benevolence* of the Society towards the colored population, and deplore the opposition it encounters from certain individuals who have formed "the Anti-Slavery Society." These men, they assert, wish to admit the blacks "into the bosom of our society," and would "justify intermarriages with the white people." They then recite their own grievances, detail the proceedings of their town-meeting, dwell on Miss Crandall's pertinacity in pursuing her own plans, express their horror of abolition principles, and state that Mr. Garrison had said that the excitement in Canterbury "is one of the genuine flowers of the Colonization garden"; and they add, "Be it so, we APPEAL *to the*

American Colonization Society, to which our statement is addressed—we appeal to every philanthropist and to every Christian!" Mr. Judson's name appears at the head of the signers to the
appeal. . . .

Having thus identified their cause with that of the Colonization
Society, and secured the sympathy of its numerous and powerful
friends in Connecticut, Mr. Judson and his associates proceeded
to further operations. Foiled in their attempts to persuade or
intimidate, they now resolved on coercion. On the first April,
another town-meeting was convened, at which it was "Voted that
a petition in behalf of the town of Canterbury, to the next
General Assembly, be drawn up in suitable language, deprecat-
ing the evil consequences of bringing from *other towns* and other
States people of color for *any* purpose, and more especially for
the purpose of disseminating the principles and doctrines opposed to THE BENEVOLENT COLONIZATION SYSTEM, praying said
assembly to pass and enact such laws as in their wisdom will
prevent *the evil."* Mr. Judson, with others, was appointed a
Committee to prepare the petition, and to request other towns to
forward similar petitions. The malignity of this vote is equalled
only by its absurdity. The desired law is to prevent the evil of
blacks passing not only from other States, but *other towns.* Every
black citizen of Connecticut is to be imprisoned in the town in
which the law happens to find him, and he may not travel into
the adjoining town for "any purpose," and all this especially to
prevent interference with "the *benevolent* Colonization system."

Did the Colonization Society protest against such an outrage
being committed in its behalf—did it indignantly disclaim all
connexion, all sympathy with men, who in its name, were striving
to perpetrate such abominable tyranny? It is not known, that in
any way whatever, it has ever expressed its disapprobation of
these proceedings. Certain it is, that the effect of the "appeal"
and of this vote, was not such as to induce the Canterbury
gentlemen to falter in their career—we have seen that Mr. Judson

had a LAW, which was to arrest the school. When the "appeal" had been before the public just one month, the selectmen resolved to avail themselves of this law.

Among the pupils of Miss Crandall, was a colored girl about seventeen years of age, who had come from Rhode Island to enjoy the advantages of the school. The pursuit of knowledge under discouraging difficulties has rarely failed to excite applause; and the virtuous struggles of the poor and obscure to improve and elevate themselves, claim the sympathy of Christian benevolence. In the present instance we behold a youthful female, of a despised and depressed race, attempting to emerge from the ignorance and degradation into which she had been cast by birth; and abandoning her home and friends, and travelling to another State, applying for instruction to the only seminary in the whole country open to receive her. And now let us see what sympathy this poor and defenceless, but innocent and praiseworthy girl, experienced from the admirers of "the benevolent Colonization system." In the day after her arrival, she was ordered by the selectmen to leave the town. This order, as illegal as it was inhumane, was disregarded; and on the 22nd April, Mr. Judson and his fellow functionaries instituted on behalf of the town, a suit against her under an old vagrant act of Connecticut, and a writ was issued to the sheriff, to require her appearance before a Justice of the Peace. The writ recited, that according to the statute she had forfeited to the town $1.62 for each day she had remained in it, since she was ordered to depart; and that in default of payment, she WAS TO BE WHIPPED ON THE NAKED BODY NOT EXCEEDING TEN STRIPES, unless she departed within ten days after conviction. The barbarous and obsolete law under which this suit was brought was intended to protect towns from the intrusion of paupers who might become chargeable. The friends of the school had offered to give the selectmen bonds to any amount, to secure the town from all cost on account of the pupils; and of course this suit was a wicked perversion of the law, and the plaintiffs ought to have been indicted, for a malicious prosecution under color of office. With equal propriety might the civil authority of New Haven warn a student in Yale College from New York to leave the city, and on his refusal, order him to be whipped on the naked body as a vagrant pauper.

About the time of the return of this writ, the Legislature of Connecticut assembled, and so successfully had the Canterbury persecution been identified with Colonization, that a law was passed to suppress the school, and all others of a similar character. Its preamble declared that "attempts have been made to establish literary institutions in this State for the instruction of colored persons belonging to other States and countries, which would tend to the *great increase* of the colored population of this State, and thereby to the *injury* of the people." The act provides, that every person, who shall set up or establish any school, academy, or literary institution, for the instruction or education of colored persons who are not inhabitants of Connecticut; or who shall teach in such school, or who shall board any colored pupil of such school, not an inhabitant of the State, shall forfeit one hundred dollars for the first offence, two hundred dollars for the second, and so on, doubling for each succeeding offence, unless the consent of the civil authority, and select men of the town, be previously obtained.

Mr. Judson's late attempt to enforce the whipping law, reminded the Legislature of the propriety of abolishing that relic of barbarism, and it was accordingly revealed, and thus were the backs of Miss Crandall's pupils saved from the threatened laceration.

It is painful and mortifying to reflect on the law obtained by Mr. Judson and his associates, for the suppression of the school, and which has very generally received the title of "the Connecticut Black Act." It is an act alien to the habits, the character, the religion of Connecticut. It is an act which neither policy nor duty can vindicate. It is an act which will afford its authors no consolation in the prospect of their final account, and which their children will blush to remember.

14.

LYDIA MARIA CHILD:
The Mind of an Abolitionist

Although not a partisan of women's rights such as later materialized, Lydia Maria Child (1802–1880) did much to create conditions from which the women's cause profited. Widely read and sensitive to social trends, she was felicitous and informative rather than deep. Her Appeal in Favor of That Class of Americans Called Africans *(1833) sacrificed her prestige with the respectable but pioneered discussion of the Negroes' human rights. She was a Garrisonian editor but left the group when she concluded that they acted in petty, sectarian fashion. Her pen continued to be that of a reformer. She stirred the country once more when John Brown was lodged in prison following his Harpers Ferry raid, and she exchanged views with proslavery defenders. Her* Letters *illustrates her courage and growth during the abolitionist era and beyond.*

TO E. CARPENTER

March 20, 1838

I thought of you several times while Angelina [Grimké] was addressing the committee of the Legislature. I knew you would have enjoyed it so much. I think it was a spectacle of the greatest moral sublimity I ever witnessed. The house was full to overflowing. For a moment a sense of the immense responsibility resting on her seemed almost to overwhelm her. She trembled and grew pale. But this passed quickly, and she went on to speak gloriously, strong in utter forgetfulness of herself, and in her own

SOURCE: Lydia Maria Child, *Letters* (Boston: Houghton, Mifflin and Company, 1882), pp. 26 ff.

earnest faith in every word she uttered. "Whatsoever comes from the heart goes to the heart." I believe she made a very powerful impression on the audience. Boston, like other cities, is very far behind the country towns on this subject; so much so that it is getting to be Boston *versus* Massachusetts, as the lawyers say. The Boston members of the legislature tried hard to prevent her having a hearing on the second day. Among other things, they said that such a crowd were attracted by curiosity the galleries were in danger of being broken down; though in fact they are constructed with remarkable strength. A member from Salem, perceiving their drift, wittily proposed that a "committee be appointed to examine the foundations of the State House of Massachusetts, to see whether it will bear another lecture from Miss Grimké."

One sign that her influence is felt is that the "sound part of the community" (as they consider themselves) seek to give vent to their vexation by calling her Devil-ina instead of Angel-ina, and Miss Grimalkin instead of Miss Grimké. Another sign is that we have succeeded in obtaining the Odeon, one of the largest and most central halls, for her to speak in; and it is the first time such a place has been obtained for anti-slavery in this city.

Angelina and Sarah have been spending the winter at the house of Mr. P——, about five miles from here. The family were formerly of the Society of Friends—are now, I believe, a little Swedenborgian, but more Quaker, and swinging loose from any regular society; just as I and so many hundred others are doing at the present day. I should like earnestly and truly to believe with some large sect, because religious sympathy is so delightful; but I now think that if I were to live my life over again I should not inwardly join any society, there is such a tendency to spiritual domination, such an interfering with individual freedom.

Have you read a little pamphlet called "George Fox and his First Disciples"? I was charmed with it. Don't you remember I told you I was sure that the *thou* and *thee* of Friends originated in a principle of Christian [e]quality? This pamphlet confirms my conjecture. In the English language of George Fox's time, and in most European languages now, *thou* was used only to familiars and equals.

Kings say *we,* and nobles are addressed as *you.* The Germans carry this worshipful plurality to an absurd extent. The prince being missed by his companions on a hunting excursion, one of the noblemen asked a peasant, "Hast thou seen the prince pass this way?" "No, my lord," replied the peasant, "but their dog have passed." It was this distinction of language addressed to superiors, and to inferiors or equals, that the early Friends resisted. The custom had life in it then, for it was merely the outward expression or form of a vital principle. What is it now? An inherited formality, of which few stop to inquire the meaning. Thus have all human forms the seed of death within them; but luckily when the body becomes dead, the inward soul or principle seeks a new form and lives again. The Friends as a society may become extinct; but not in vain did they cast forth their great principles into everlasting time. No truth they uttered shall ever die; neither shall any truth that you or I may speak, or express in our lives. Two centuries after William Penn brought indignation upon himself by saying "thou" to the Duke of York, the French revolutionists, in order to show that they were friends of equality, wrote in their window, "In this house we 'thou' it." And this idea, dug up by the Friends from the ashes of early Christianity, has in fact given rise to the doctrine of "spiritual brotherhood," echoed and reëchoed from Priestley to Channing.

15.

THEODORE DWIGHT WELD:
Disturber of the Peace

Theodore Dwight Weld (1803–1895) was an agitator like Garrison but an organizer beyond Garrison's capacities. Striking in appearance, emotional in presentation, Weld stirred country audiences and founded local societies. He instructed others, particularly in the ministry, in tactics of rousing and enlisting members, especially after 1836 when his voice was permanently affected. He then labored between New York and Washington to create stratagems for advancing antislavery sentiments in and out of government. In 1838 he married Angelina Grimké. His loss of a voice for public speaking, the 1840 schism in antislavery ranks and introspection regarding his life purposes appear to have diminished Weld's faith in social campaigns, and he left the field early in the 1840s for the private life of a farmer and educator. The following appeared in the New York Emancipator, *an organ of the American Anti-Slavery Society. It was addressed to Elizur Wright, Jr.*

Elyria, Ohio, October 6, 1835

My dear Brother: When I wrote you last, I think I was in Cleveland. Before I finished my lectures there, I was obliged to leave, in order to fulfill some appointments in Geauga county, made some weeks before. Went the first day to Chester; audience large; lectured on the safety of emancipation. At the close of the lecture, between forty and fifty persons joined the Chester Anti-Slavery society; making the whole number of the society 100.

SOURCE: New York *Emancipator,* October 20, 1835.

Next day, went to Chardon, the county seat, and attended the annual meeting of the Geauga county Anti-Slavery Society. While speaking to a resolution before the society, a gentleman arose and insisted upon being heard.

President. "There is a gentleman on the floor."

"Very well sir, I insist upon being heard."

Pres. "Order, sir, please not to interrupt the meeting." The man continued.

"The abolitionists are always clamoring about free discussion. I wish to discuss, and you refuse to hear."

Pres. "We are unwilling to hear two speaking *at once,* sir; wait until the gentleman on the floor has completed his remarks." We then informed the gentleman that if he was anxious for *discussion,* he should certainly be accommodated; that as soon as the business of the meeting was concluded, which would not occupy more than an hour, I would join with him in the choice of a moderator, and we would discuss the question *just as long as he pleased;* that he refused to do—but insisted upon reading the Boston [antiabolitionist] resolutions, and began to scream them out at the top of a stentorian voice. He was encouraged to proceed by a considerable number of men, who had come from different parts of the county, on purpose, as it appeared, to disturb the meeting. The society finding it impossible to proceed with the meeting, adjourned to a large school house across the street, and left the disturbers in possession of the Court House. I had hardly begun to speak again, when a mob gathered with tin horns, sleigh bells, drums, etc., and ding dong'd like bedlam broke loose; valorously pelted the *ladies* with rotten *eggs,* and performed divers other feats, all strictly in keeping. But enough; at the close of the meeting, we received thirty or forty additional signatures to the anti-slavery society. Went same evening to Painesville; a mob assembled, stoned the house, and made other patriotic developments quite characteristic. The sheriff and one of the judges of the court, however, succeeded in quieting them. The next day a great meeting was called, of all the citizens of

Painesville, to express their views of the abolitionists; the mayor in the chair. Flaming resolutions were passed, much like those in the large cities, against the abolitionists; among the rest, one requesting me to leave the place; and the mayor and another were appointed a committee to inform me of the resolutions.

The next day I lectured again in the afternoon, as the members of the church were not willing to risk it at *night*. After the fourth lecture, the Common Council of the village finding that I had not departed out of their coasts, called a special meeting, and passed resolutions against my lectures, calling me a disturber of the peace, etc.

At the fifth lecture, Gen. C. C. Paine, the leader of the opposition, came in at the head of a number of his party—broke in upon me while I was speaking—charging me with treason against the government—violation of the constitution, etc., and closed by saying, "I take it upon me to say there *shall not be another lecture* delivered upon abolition in this place." I replied to his charges, went on and finished my lecture, and appointed another for the next day. The next day the meeting went off without the least disturbance of any sort. According to previous arrangements, I discussed the question publicly with a lawyer of the village, from one o'clock till four, and then lectured till six.

Had no interruption after this, and at the close of the course, read a constitution previously prepared for an anti-slavery society, and *fifty* of the audience gave in their names on the spot. Shortly after I left, they met and organized with nearly one hundred members, as I am since informed. From Painesville I went to Madison, where an anti-slavery society had existed about a year, with sixty members. Staid there 5 days; lectured ten times; about fifty additions were made to the society, embodying a large amount of influence in the township. . . .

16.

ANGELINA E. GRIMKÉ:
"The Bible is my ultimate appeal"

Angelina Grimké Weld (1805–1879), as she became, forced a breach in contemporary thinking by the facts of her distinguished birth, ardent religiosity and female nature. Her impeccable credentials made it impossible for foes to write her off as bizarre in the fashion of "Fanny Wright" or meanly motivated. Her brief evangel revealed a situation already manifest in numerous avenues of social relationship: that a modernization of women's roles in society had to be recognized and accepted, in commerce, religious pursuits, education, marriage relations and frontier circumstances. She herself, following marriage, retired from the public scene.

It is because I feel a deep and tender interest in your present and eternal welfare that I am willing thus publicly to address you. Some of you have loved me as a relative, and some have felt bound to me in Christian sympathy, and Gospel fellowship; and even when compelled by a strong sense of duty, to break those outward bonds of union which bound us together as members of the same community, and members of the same religious denomination, you were generous enough to give me credit, for sincerity as a Christian, though you believed I had been most strangely deceived. I thanked you then for your kindness, and I ask you *now*, for the sake of former confidence, and former friendship, to read the following pages in the spirit of calm

SOURCE: Angelina E. Grimké, "Appeal to the Christian Women of the South, *Anti-Slavery Examiner* (New York: American Anti-Slavery Society, 1836), pp. 1 ff.

investigation and fervent prayer. It is because you have known me, that I write thus unto you.

But there are other Christian women scattered over the Southern States, of whom a very large number have never seen me, and never heard my name, and feel *no* personal interest whatever in *me*. But I feel an interest in *you*, as branches of the same vine from whose root I daily draw the principle of spiritual vitality—Yes! Sisters in Christ I feel an interest in *you*, and often has the secret prayer arisen on your behalf, Lord "open thou their eyes that they may see wondrous things out of thy Law"—It is then, because I *do feel* and *do pray* for you, that I thus address you upon a subject about which of all others, perhaps you would rather not hear any thing; but, "would to God ye could bear with me a little in my folly, and indeed bear with me, for I am jealous over you with godly jealousy." Be not afraid then to read my appeal; it is *not* written in the heat of passion or prejudice, but in that solemn calmness which is the result of conviction and duty. . . .

It has been urged that the patriarchs held slaves, and therefore, slavery is right. Do you really believe that patriarchal servitude was like American slavery? Can you believe it? If so, read the history of these primitive fathers of the church and be undeceived. Look at Abraham, though so great a man, going to the herd himself and fetching a calf from thence and serving it up with his own hands, for the entertainment of his guests. Look at Sarah, that princess as her name signifies, baking cakes upon the hearth. If the servants they had were like Southern slaves, would they have performed such comparatively menial offices for themselves? Hear too the plaintive lamentation of Abraham when he feared he should have no son to bear his name down to posterity. "Behold thou hast given me no seed, &c, one born in my house *is mine* heir." From this it appears that one of his *servants* was to inherit his immense estate. Is this like Southern slavery? I leave it to your own good sense and candor to decide. Besides, such was the footing upon which Abraham was with *his* servants, that he trusted them with arms. Are slaveholders willing to put swords and pistols into the hands of their slaves? He was as a father among his servants; what are planters and masters generally among theirs? When the institution of circumcision was established, Abraham was commanded thus; "He that is eight days old shall be circumcised among you, *every* man-child in your generations; he that is born in the house, or bought with money of any stranger which is not of thy seed." And to render this command with regard to his *servants* still more impressive it is repeated in the very next verse; and herein we may perceive the great care which was taken by God to guard the *rights of servants* even under this "dark dispensation." What too was the testimony given to the faithfulness of this eminent patriarch. "For I know him that he will command his children and his *household* after him, and they shall keep the way of the Lord to do justice and judgment." Now my dear friends many of you believe that circumcision has been superseded by baptism in the Church; *Are you* careful to have *all* that are born in your house or bought with money of any stranger, baptized? Are *you* as faithful as Abraham to command *your household to keep the way of the Lord?* I leave it to your own consciences to decide. Was patriarchal servitude then like American Slavery? . . .

We have seen that the code of laws framed by Moses with regard to servants was designed to *protect them as men and women,* to secure to them their *rights* as *human beings,* to guard them from oppression and defend them from violence of every kind. Let us now turn to the Slave laws of the South and West and examine them too. I will give you the substance only, because I fear I shall tresspass too much on your time, were I to quote them at length.

1. *Slavery* is hereditary and perpetual, to the last moment of the slave's earthly existence, and to all his descendants to the latest posterity.

2. The labor of the slave is compulsory and uncompensated; while the kind of labor, the amount of toil, the time allowed for

rest, are dictated solely by the master. No bargain is made, no wages given. A pure despotism governs the human brute; and even his covering and provender, both as to quantity and quality, depend entirely on the master's discretion.

3. The slave being considered a personal chattel may be sold or pledged, or leased at the will of his master. He may be exchanged for marketable commodities, or taken in execution for the debts or taxes either of a living or dead master. Sold at auction, either individually, or in lots to suit the purchaser, he may remain with his family, or be separated from them for ever.

4. Slaves can make no contracts and have no *legal* right to any property, real or personal. Their own honest earnings and the legacies of friends belong in point of law to their masters.

5. Neither a slave nor a free colored person can be a witness against any *white*, or free person, in a court of justice, however atrocious may have been the crimes they have seen him commit, if such testimony would be for the benefit of a *slave;* but they may give testimony *against a fellow slave*, or free colored man, even in cases affecting life, if the *master* is to reap the advantage of it. . . .

Shall I ask you now my friends, to draw the *parallel* between Jewish *servitude* and American *slavery?* No! For there is *no likeness* in the two systems; I ask you rather to mark the contrast. The laws of Moses *protected servants* in their *rights* as *men and women,* guarded them from oppression and defended them from wrong. The Code Noir of the South *robs the slave of all his rights* as a *man,* reduces him to a chattel personal, and defends the *master* in the exercise of the most unnatural and unwarrantable power over his slave. . . .

But perhaps you will be ready to query, why appeal to *women* on this subject? *We* do not make the laws which perpetuate slavery. *No* legislative power is vested in *us; we* can do nothing to overthrow the system, even if we wished to do so. To this I reply, I know you do not make the laws, but I also know that *you*

*are the wives and mothers, the sisters and daughters of those
who do;* and if you really suppose *you* can do nothing to overthrow slavery, you are greatly mistaken. You can do much in
every way: four things I will name. 1st. You can read on this
subject. 2d. You can pray over this subject. 3d. You can speak on
this subject. 4th. You can *act* on this subject. I have not placed
reading before praying because I regard it more important, but
because, in order to pray aright, we must understand what we
are praying for; it is only then we can "pray with the understanding and the spirit also." . . .

But you may say we are *women,* how can *our* hearts endure
persecution? And why not? Have not *women* arisen in all the
dignity and strength of moral courage to be the leaders of the
people, and to bear a faithful testimony for the truth whenever
the providence of God has called them to do so? Are there no
women in that noble army of martyrs who are now singing the
song of Moses and the Lamb? Who led out the women of Israel
from the house of bondage, striking the timbrel, and singing the
song of deliverance on the banks of that sea whose waters stood
up like walls of crystal to open a passage for their escape? It was
a *woman;* Miriam, the prophetess, the sister of Moses and
Aaron. . . .

But this is not all. Roman *women* were burnt at the stake, *their*
delicate limbs were torn joint from joint by the ferocious beasts
of the Amphitheatre, and tossed by the wild bull in his fury, for
the diversion of that idolatrous, warlike, and slaveholding people.
Yes, *women* suffered under the ten persecutions of heathen
Rome, with the most unshrinking constancy and fortitude; not all
the entreaties of friends, nor the claims of new born infancy, nor
the cruel threats of enemies could make *them* sprinkle one grain
of incense upon the altars of Roman idols. Come now with me to
the beautiful valleys of Piedmont. Whose blood stains the green
sward, and decks the wild flowers with colors not their own, and
smokes on the sword of persecuting France? It is *woman's,* as
well as man's? Yes, *women* were accounted as sheep for the

slaughter, and were cut down as the tender saplings of the wood. . . .

And what, I would ask in conclusion, have *women* done for the great and glorious cause of Emancipation? Who wrote that pamphlet which moved the heart of Wilberforce to pray over the wrongs, and his tongue to plead the cause of the oppressed African? It was a *woman*, Elizabeth Heyrick. Who labored assiduously to keep the sufferings of the slave continually before the British public? They were *women*. And how did they do it? By their needles, paint brushes and pens, by speaking the truth, and petitioning Parliament for the abolition of slavery. And what was the effect of their labors? Read it in the Emancipation bill of Great Britain. Read it, in the present state of her West India Colonies. Read it, in the impulse which has been given to the cause of freedom, in the United States of America. Have English women then done so much for the negro, and shall American women do nothing? Oh no! Already are there sixty female Anti-Slavery Societies in operation. These are doing just what the English women did, telling the story of the colored man's wrongs, praying for his deliverance, and presenting his kneeling image constantly before the public eye on bags and needle-books, card-racks, pen-wipers, pin-cushions, &c. Even the children of the north are inscribing on their handy work, "May the points of our needles prick the slaveholder's conscience." Some of the reports of these Societies exhibit not only considerable talent, but a deep sense of religious duty, and a determination to persevere through evil as well as good report, until every scourge, and every shackle, is buried under the feet of the manumitted slave. . . .

17.

ELIJAH P. LOVEJOY:
"I dare not abandon my sentiments"

An extraordinary aspect of the abolitionist crusade was the fact that, despite violent differences of public opinion, few individuals in the free states lost their lives by violence. Property was often damaged and meetings closed by riot. But when, as with Elijah P. Lovejoy, death actually resulted, a thrill over the state of democratic privileges disturbed the nation. Lovejoy (1802–1837) was a sensitive young man and a brilliant student at Princeton's theological school. He went to St. Louis to help oppose the spread of Catholic doctrine. His weekly Observer *stirred resentment which turned to riot when he turned to abolitionism: a step which lost him supporters who might have approved his attacks on "Popery." Lovejoy was clear on his constitutional rights and fearless toward mobs. He crossed the river to Alton, Illinois, on promises of support and because of worry over his young wife, then pregnant. In Alton he endured mob violence without flinching and finally concluded to defend his press with arms.*

[A meeting at Alton shortly before the final tragedy drew citizens who feared Lovejoy was bringing unrest to their town, and who approved resolutions to that effect. Lovejoy rose to defend himself:]

Mr. Chairman—it is not true, as has been charged upon me, that I hold in contempt the feelings and sentiments of this community, in reference to the question which is now agitating it. I respect and appreciate the feelings and opinions of my fellow-

SOURCE: Joseph C. and Owen Lovejoy, *The Memoir of the Rev. Elijah P. Lovejoy; Who Was Murdered in Defence of Liberty of the Press,* . . . *Nov. 7, 1837* (New York: John S. Taylor, 1838), pp. 278–281.

citizens, and it is one of the most painful and unpleasant duties of my life, that I am called upon to act in opposition to them. If you suppose, sir, that I have published sentiments contrary to those generally held in this community, because I delighted in differing from them, or in occasioning a disturbance, you have entirely misapprehended me. But, sir, while I value the good opinion of my fellow-citizens, as highly as any one, I may be permitted to say, that I am governed by higher considerations than either the favour or the fear of man. I am impelled to the course I have taken, because I fear God. As I shall answer it to my God in the great day, I dare not abandon my sentiments, or cease in all proper ways to propagate them.

I, Mr. Chairman, have not desired, or asked any *compromise*. I have asked for nothing but to be protected in my rights as a citizen—rights which God has given me, and which are guaranteed to me by the constitution of my country. Have I, sir, been guilty of any infraction of the laws? Whose good name have I injured? When and where have I published any thing injurious to the reputation of Alton? Have I not, on the other hand, laboured, in common, with the rest of my fellow-citizens, to promote the reputation and interests of this city? What, sir, I ask, has been my offence? Put your finger upon it—define it—and I stand ready to answer for it. If I have committed any crime, you can easily convict me. You have public sentiment in your favour. You have your juries, and you have your attorney, (looking at the Attorney-General,) and I have *no doubt* you can *convict* me. But if I have been guilty of no violation of law, why am I hunted up and down continually like a partridge upon the mountains? Why am I threatened with the *tar-barrel?* Why am I waylaid every day, and from night to night, and my life in jeopardy every hour?

You have, sir, made up, as the lawyers say, a false issue; there are not two parties between whom there can be a *compromise*. I plant myself, sir, down on my unquestionable *rights*, and the question to be decided is, whether I shall be protected in the exercise, and enjoyment of those rights—*that is the question, sir;*—whether my property shall be protected, whether I shall be suffered to go home to my family at night without being assailed, and threatened with tar and feathers, and assassination; whether my afflicted wife, whose life has been in jeopardy, from continued alarm and excitement, shall night after night be driven from a sick bed into the garret to save her life from the brickbats and violence of the mobs; *that sir, is the question.* [Here, much affected and overcome by his feelings, he burst into tears. Many, not excepting even his enemies, wept—several sobbed aloud, and the sympathies of the whole meeting were deeply excited. He continued.] Forgive me, sir, that I have thus betrayed my weakness. It was the allusion to my family that overcame my feelings. Not, sir, I assure you, from any fears on my part. I have no personal fears. Not that I feel able to contest the matter with the whole community, I know perfectly well I am not. I know, sir, that you can tar and feather me, hang me up, or put me into the Mississippi, without the least difficulty. But what then? Where shall I go? I have been made to feel that if I am not safe at Alton, I shall not be safe any where. I recently visited St. Charles to bring home my family, and was torn from their frantic embrace by a mob. I have been beset night and day at Alton. And now if I leave here and go elsewhere, violence may overtake me in my retreat, and I have no more claim upon the protection of any other community than I have upon this; and I have concluded, after consultation with my friends, and earnestly seeking counsel of God, to *remain at Alton,* and here to insist on protection in the exercise of my rights. If the civil authorities refuse to protect me, I must look to God; and if I die, I have determined to make my grave in Alton.

A writer who was present, after giving the substance of these remarks, observes:

His *manner*—but I cannot attempt to describe it. He was calm and serious, but firm and decided. Not an epithet or unkind allusion escaped his lips, notwithstanding he knew he was in the midst of those who were seeking his blood, and notwithstanding he was well aware of the influence that that meeting, if it should not take the right turn, would have in infuriating the mob to do their work. He and his friends had prayed earnestly that God would overrule the deliberations of that meeting for good. He had been all day communing with God. His countenance, the subdued tones of his voice, and whole appearance indicated a mind in a peculiarly heavenly frame, and ready to acquiesce in the will of God, whatever that might be. I confess to you, sir, that I regarded him at the time, in view of all the circumstances, as presenting a spectacle of moral sublimity, such as I had never before witnessed, and such as the world seldom affords. It reminded me of Paul before Festus, and of Luther at Worms.

18.

WENDELL PHILLIPS:
"Men begin, as in 1776 and 1640,
to discuss principles"

The murder of Lovejoy inspired the greatest extemporaneous speech since Patrick Henry's in Richmond, Virginia, March 23, 1775, calling for liberty or death. Wendell Phillips in 1837 was a young man of distinguished family developing a law career. The meeting called in Boston to memorialize Lovejoy brought together friends and foes of abolition. Thereafter Phillips took his place beside Garrison, and until his death in 1884, was the organ voice not only of abolition but of women's rights and associated causes. Unlike many of his colleagues, he refused to retire from reform following Emancipation.

MR. CHAIRMAN:—We have met for the freest discussion of these resolutions, and the events which gave rise to them. [Cries of "Question," "Hear him," "Go on," "No gagging," etc.] I hope I shall be permitted to express my surprise at the sentiments of the last speaker,—surprise not only at such sentiments from such a man, but at the applause they have received within these walls. A comparison has been drawn between the events of the Revolution and the tragedy at Alton. We have heard it asserted here, in Faneuil Hall, that Great Britain had a right to tax the Colonies, and we have heard the mob at Alton, the drunken murderers of Lovejoy, compared to those patriot fathers who threw the tea overboard! [Great applause.] Fellow-citizens, is this Faneuil

SOURCE: Louis Filler, ed., *Wendell Phillips on Civil Rights and Freedom* (New York: Hill and Wang, 1965), pp. 2 ff.

Hall doctrine? ["No, no."] The mob at Alton were met to wrest from a citizen his just rights,—met to resist the laws. We have been told that our fathers did the same; and the glorious mantle of Revolutionary precedent has been thrown over the mobs of our day. To make out their title to such defence, the gentleman says that the British Parliament had a *right* to tax these Colonies. It is manifest that, without this, his parallel falls to the ground; for Lovejoy had stationed himself within constitutional bulwarks. He was not only defending the freedom of the press, but he was under his own roof, in arms with the sanction of the civil authority. The men who assailed him went against and over the laws. The *mob,* as the gentleman terms it,—mob, forsooth! certainly we sons of the tea-spillers are a marvellously patient generation!— the "orderly mob" which assembled in the Old South to destroy the tea were met to resist, not the laws, but illegal exactions. Shame on the American who calls the tea-tax and stamp-act *laws!* Our fathers resisted, not the King's prerogative, but the King's usurpation. To find any other account, you must read our Revolutionary history upside down. Our State archives are loaded with arguments of John Adams to prove the taxes laid by the British Parliament unconstitutional,—beyond its power. It was not till this was made out that the men of New England rushed to arms. The arguments of the Council Chamber and the House of Representatives preceded and sanctioned the contest. To draw the conduct of our ancestors into a precedent for mobs, for a right to resist laws we ourselves have enacted, is an insult to their memory. The difference between the excitements of those days and our own, which the gentleman in kindness to the latter has overlooked, is simply this: the men of that day went for the right, as secured by the laws. They were the people rising to sustain the laws and constitution of the Province. The rioters of our day go for their own wills, right or wrong. Sir, when I heard the gentleman lay down principles which place the murderers of Alton side by side with Otis and Hancock, with Quincy and Adams, I thought those pictured lips [pointing to the portraits in the Hall] would have broken into voice to rebuke the recreant American, —the slanderer of the dead. [Great applause and counter applause.] The gentleman said that he should sink into insignificance if he dared to gainsay the principles of these resolutions. Sir, for the sentiments he has uttered, on soil consecrated by the prayers of Puritans and the blood of patriots, the earth should have yawned and swallowed him up.

Applause and hisses, with cries of "Take that back." The uproar became so great that for a long time no one could be heard. At length G. Bond, Esq., and Hon. W. Sturgis came to Mr. Phillips's side at the front of the platform. They were met with cries of "Phillips or nobody." "Make him take back 'recreant.'" "He sha'n't go on till he takes it back." When it was understood they meant to sustain, not to interrupt, Mr. Phillips, Mr. Sturgis was listened to, and said: "I did not come here to take any part in this discussion, nor do I intend to; but I do entreat you, fellow-citizens, by everything you hold sacred,—I conjure you by every association connected with this Hall consecrated by our fathers to freedom of discussion,—that you listen to every man who addresses you in a decorous manner." Mr. Phillips resumed.

Fellow-citizens, I cannot take back my words. Surely the Attorney-General, so long and well known here, needs not the aid of your hisses against one so young as I am,—my voice never before heard within these walls!

Another ground has been taken to excuse the mob, and throw doubt and discredit on the conduct of Lovejoy and his associates. Allusion has been made to what lawyers understand very well,— the "conflict of laws." We are told that nothing but the Mississippi River rolls between St. Louis and Alton; and the conflict of laws somehow or other gives the citizens of the former a right to find fault with the defender of the press for publishing his opinions so near their limits. Will the gentleman venture that argument before lawyers? How the laws of the two States could be said to come into conflict in such circumstances I question whether any lawyer in this audience can explain or understand. No matter whether the line that divides one sovereign State from another be an imaginary one or ocean-wide, the moment you cross it the State you leave is blotted out of existence, so far as you are concerned. The Czar might as well claim to control the deliberations of Faneuil Hall, as the laws of Missouri demand reverence, or the shadow of obedience, from an inhabitant of Illinois.

I must find some fault with the statement which has been made of the events at Alton. It has been asked why Lovejoy and his friends did not appeal to the executive,—trust their defence to the police of the city. It has been hinted that, from hasty and ill-judged excitement, the men within the building provoked a quarrel, and that he fell in the course of it, one mob resisting another. Recollect, Sir, that they did act with the approbation and sanction of the Mayor. In strict truth, there was no executive to appeal to for protection. The Mayor acknowledged that he could not protect them. They asked him if it was lawful for them to defend themselves. He told them it was, and sanctioned their assembling in arms to do so. They were not, then, a mob; they were not merely citizens defending their own property; they were in some sense the *posse comitatus,* adopted for the occasion into the police of the city, acting under the order of a magistrate. It was civil authority resisting lawless violence. Where, then, was the imprudence? Is the doctrine to be sustained here, that it is *imprudent* for men to aid magistrates in executing the laws?

Men are continually asking each other, Had Lovejoy a right to resist? Sir, I protest against the question, instead of answering it. Lovejoy did not resist, in the sense they mean. He did not throw himself back on the natural right of self-defence. He did not cry anarchy, and let slip the dogs of civil war, careless of the horrors which would follow.

Sir, as I understand this affair, it was not an individual protecting his property; it was not one body of armed men resisting another, and making the streets of a peaceful city run blood with their contentions. It did not bring back the scenes in some old Italian cities, where family met family and faction met faction, and mutually trampled the laws under foot. No; the men in that house were regularly *enrolled*, under the sanction of the Mayor. There being no militia in Alton, about seventy men were enrolled with the approbation of the Mayor. These relieved each other every other night. About thirty men were in arms on the night of the sixth, when the press was landed. The next evening, it was not thought necessary to summon more than half that number; among these was Lovejoy. It was, therefore, you perceive, Sir, the police of the city resisting rioters,—civil government breasting itself to the shock of lawless men.

Here is no question about the right of self-defence. It is in fact simply this: Has the civil magistrate a right to put down a riot?

Some persons seem to imagine that anarchy existed at Alton from the commencement of these disputes. Not at all. "No one of us," says an eyewitness and a comrade of Lovejoy, "has taken up arms during these disturbances but at the command of the Mayor." Anarchy did not settle down on that devoted city till Lovejoy breathed his last. Till then the law, represented in his person, sustained itself against its foes. When he fell, civil authority was trampled under foot. He had "planted himself on his constitutional rights,"—appealed to the laws,—claimed the protection of the civil authority,—taken refuge under "the broad shield of the Constitution. When through that he was pierced and fell, he fell but one sufferer in a common catastrophe." He took refuge under the banner of liberty,—amid its folds; and when he fell, its glorious stars and stripes, the emblem of free institutions, around which cluster so many heart-stirring memories, were blotted out in the martyr's blood.

It has been stated, perhaps inadvertently, that Lovejoy or his comrades fired first. This is denied by those who have the best means of knowing. Guns were first fired by the mob. After being twice fired on, those within the building consulted together and deliberately returned the fire. But suppose they did fire first. They had a right so to do; not only the right which every citizen has to defend himself, but the further right which every civil officer has to resist violence. Even if Lovejoy fired the first gun, it would not lessen his claim to our sympathy, or destroy his title to be considered a martyr in defence of a free press. The question now is, Did he act within the Constitution and the laws? The men who fell in State Street on the 5th of March, 1770, did more than Lovejoy is charged with. They were the *first* assailants. Upon some slight quarrel they pelted the troops with every missile within reach. Did this bate one jot of the eulogy with which Hancock and Warren hallowed their memory, hailing them as the first martyrs in the cause of American liberty? . . .

Imprudent to defend the liberty of the press! Why? Because the defence was unsuccessful? Does success gild crime into patriotism, and the want of it change heroic self-devotion to imprudence? Was Hampden imprudent when he drew the sword and threw away the scabbard? Yet he, judged by that single hour, was unsuccessful. After a short exile, the race he hated sat again upon the throne. . . .

Mr. Chairman, from the bottom of my heart I thank that brave little band at Alton for resisting. . . . Does not the event show they judged rightly? Absorbed in a thousand trifles, how has the nation all at once come to a stand? Men begin, as in 1776 and 1640, to discuss principles, to weigh characters, to find out where they are. Haply we may awake before we are borne over the precipice.

I am glad, Sir, to see this crowded house. It is good for us to be here. When Liberty is in danger, Faneuil Hall has the right, it is her duty, to strike the key-note for these United States. I am glad, for one reason, that remarks such as those to which I have alluded have been uttered here. The passage of these resolutions, in spite of this opposition, led by the Attorney-General of the Commonwealth, will show more clearly, more decisively, the deep indignation with which Boston regards this outrage.

19.

SOJOURNER TRUTH:
"A'n't I a woman?"

*Sojourner Truth was born Isabelle, of slave parents belonging
to a Dutch New York farmer, about 1797, and freed by the general
emancipation law in 1727 but ungraciously maintained in
slavery by another owner beyond an agreed date. She also suffered
pangs in separation from her children, being sustained only
by a passionate religiosity. Her name was her own invention. Her
mystic search misled her into association with the imposter
Matthias but also to more fruitful contacts. Her Narrative of Sojourner
Truth, a Northern Slave (1850), prepared with the aid of
a white friend and published with the encouragement of abolitionists,
was one of the notable documents of slavery. Travelling
throughout the North, addressing abolitionist and other gatherings
and selling her book, she was recognized as a living testament
against slavery. Her speech at the Woman's Rights Convention
at Akron, Ohio, in May 1851, was one of the great expressions
of folk eloquence. It appears in the reminiscences of
the suffragette Frances D. Gage.*

The cause was unpopular then. The leaders of the movement
trembled on seeing a tall, gaunt black woman, in a gray dress
and white turban, surmounted by an uncouth sun-bonnet, march
deliberately into the church, walk with the air of a queen up the
aisle, and take her seat upon the pulpit steps. A buzz of disapprobation
was heard all over the house, and such words as
these fell upon listening ears:—

SOURCE: Elizabeth Cady Stanton et al., *History of Woman Suffrage* (New
York: Fowler & Wells, 1881), vol. I, pp. 115–117.

"An abolition affair!" "Woman's rights and niggers!" "We told you so!" "Go it, old darkey!"

I chanced upon that occasion to wear my first laurels in public life as president of the meeting. At my request, order was restored and the business of the hour went on. The morning session was held; the evening exercises came and went. Old Sojourner, quiet and reticent as the "Libyan Statue," sat crouched against the wall on the corner of the pulpit stairs, her sun-bonnet shading her eyes, her elbows on her knees, and her chin resting upon her broad, hard palm. At intermission she was busy, selling "The Life of Sojourner Truth," a narrative of her own strange and adventurous life. Again and again timorous and trembling ones came to me and said with earnestness, "Don't let her speak, Mrs. Gage, it will ruin us. Every newspaper in the land will have our cause mixed with abolition and niggers, and we shall be utterly denounced." My only answer was, "We shall see when the time comes."

The second day the work waxed warm. Methodist, Baptist, Episcopal, Presbyterian, and Universalist ministers came in to hear and discuss the resolutions presented. One claimed superior rights and privileges for man on the ground of superior intellect; another, because of the manhood of Christ. "If God had desired the equality of woman, he would have given some token of his will through the birth, life, and death of the Saviour." Another gave us a theological view of the sin of our first mother. There were few women in those days that dared to "speak in meeting," and the august teachers of the people were seeming to get the better of us, while the boys in the galleries and the sneerers among the pews were hugely enjoying the discomfiture, as they supposed, of the "strong minded." Some of the tender-skinned friends were on the point of losing dignity, and the atmosphere of the convention betokened a storm.

Slowly from her seat in the corner rose Sojourner Truth, who, till now, had scarcely lifted her head. "Don't let her speak!" gasped half a dozen in my ear. She moved slowly and solemnly to the front, laid her old bonnet at her feet, and turned her great, speaking eyes to me. There was a hissing sound of disapprobation above and below. I rose and announced "Sojourner Truth," and begged the audience to keep silence for a few moments. The tumult subsided at once, and every eye was fixed on this almost Amazon form, which stood nearly six feet high, head erect, and eye piercing the upper air, like one in a dream. At her first word, there was a profound hush. She spoke in deep tones, which, though not loud, reached every ear in the house, and away through the throng at the doors and windows:—

"Well, chilern, whar dar is so much racket dar must be something out o' kilter. I tink dat 'twixt de niggers of de Souf and de women at de Norf all a talkin' 'bout rights, de white men will be in a fix pretty soon. But what's all dis here talkin' 'bout? Dat man ober dar say dat women needs to be helped into carriages, and lifted ober ditches, and to have de best place every whar. Nobody eber help me into carriages, or ober mud puddles, or gives me any best place [and raising herself to her full hight and her voice to a pitch like rolling thunder, she asked], and a'n't I a woman? Look at me! Look at my arm! [And she bared her right arm to the shoulder, showing her tremendous muscular power.] I have plowed, and planted, and gathered into barns, and no man could head me—and a'n't I a woman? I could work as much and eat as much as a man (when I could get it), and bear de lash as well—and a'n't I a woman? I have borne thirteen chilern and seen 'em mos' all sold off into slavery, and when I cried out with a mother's grief, none but Jesus heard—and a'n't I a woman? Den dey talks 'bout dis ting in de head—what dis dey call it?" "Intellect," whispered some one near. "Dat's it honey. What's dat got to do with women's rights or niggers' rights? If my cup won't hold but a pint and yourn holds a quart, wouldn't ye be mean not to let me have my little half-measure full?" And she pointed her significant finger and sent a keen glance at the minister who had made the argument. The cheering was long and loud.

"Den dat little man in black dar, he say women can't have as much rights as man, cause Christ want a woman. Whar did your Christ come from?" Rolling thunder could not have stilled that crowd as did those deep, wonderful tones, as she stood there with outstretched arms and eye of fire. Raising her voice still louder, she repeated, "Whar did your Christ come from? From God and a woman. Man had nothing to do with him." Oh! what a rebuke she gave the little man.

Turning again to another objector, she took up the defense of mother Eve. I cannot follow her through it all. It was pointed, and witty, and solemn, eliciting at almost every sentence deafening applause; and she ended by asserting that "if de fust woman God ever made was strong enough to turn the world upside down, all 'lone, dese togedder [and she glanced her eye over us], ought to be able to turn it back and get it right side up again, and now dey is asking to do it, de men better let em." Long-continued cheering. "Bleeged to ye for hearin' on me, and now ole Sojourner ha'n't got nothing more to say."

Amid roars of applause, she turned to her corner, leaving more than one of us with streaming eyes and hearts beating with gratitude. She had taken us up in her strong arms and carried us safely over the slough of difficulty, turning the whole tide in our favor. I have never in my life seen anything like the magical influence that subdued the mobbish spirit of the day and turned the jibes and sneers of an excited crowd into notes of respect and admiration. Hundreds rushed up to shake hands, and congratulate the glorious old mother and bid her God speed on her mission of "testifying again concerning the wickedness of this 'ere people."

20.

THE HUTCHINSONS:

"Ho! The car emancipation"

The Hutchinsons were a phenomenon of popular music and reform. Beginning in their "Old Granite State" of New Hampshire, they sang for temperance and then, amid stormy approbation, for antislavery. These songs they varied with religious, sentimental and humorous ditties in individual, quartet and chorus formations. The eldest son Jesse, organizer of the troupe, fitted new words to old airs on "Old Granite State," "Good Old Days of Yore," "The Slave Mother," and most stirringly, "Emancipation Song." Abby, their much-beloved sister, sang contralto and Asa sang basso. Judson was the humorist and moody one; he later committed suicide. John, best endowed in voice, later detailed their extraordinary careers in his Story of the Hutchinsons *(1896). They became one symbol of popular feeling in their ability to make audiences laugh and cry, and also respond with increasing enthusiasm to their antislavery lyrics as northern feeling turned decisively in that direction. They offended abolitionists by singing for Henry Clay and dedicating a song to "Brave Harry of the West." Debarred from Federal lines by General George B. McClellan once the Civil War was on for singing antislavery songs, they were readmitted to the soldiers' camps by order of President Lincoln.*

Ho! the car Emancipation
Rides majestic thro' our Nation,

source: John Wallace Hutchinson, *Story of the Hutchinsons*, ed. and comp., Charles E. Mann (Boston, 1896), pp. 115–116, 259–260.

Bearing on its train the story,
Liberty! a nation's glory.

Roll it along,
Roll it along,
Roll it along,
Thro' the Nation Freedom's Car,
    Emancipation.
Roll it along,
Roll it along,
Roll it along,
Thro' the Nation Freedom's Car,
    Emancipation.

Men of various predilections,
Frightened, run in all directions;
Merchants, Editors, Physicians,
Lawyers, Priests and Politicians.
    Get out of the way! every station,
    Clear the track! Emancipation.
Rail Roads to Emancipation
Cannot rest on *Clay* foundation.

And the *tracks* of "The Magician"
Are but *Rail Roads* to perdition.
    Pull up the Rails! Emancipation
    Cannot rest on such foundation.

All true friends of Emancipation,
Haste to Freedom's Rail Road Station;
Quick into the Cars get seated,
All is ready and completed.
    Put on the Steam! All are crying,
    And the Liberty Flags are flying.

Hear the mighty car wheels humming!
Now look out! *The Engine's coming!*
Church and Statesmen! hear the thunder!
Clear the track! or you'll fall under.
    Get off the track! all are singing,
    While the *Liberty Bell* is ringing.

On triumphant, see them bearing,
Through sectarian rubbish tearing;
The' Bell and Whistle and the Steaming,
Startles thousands from their dreaming.
    Look out for the cars! while the Bell rings,
    Ere the sound your funeral knell rings.

See the people run to meet us;
At the Depots thousands greet us;
All take seats with exultation,
In the car Emancipation.
    Huzza! Huzza! Emancipation
    Soon will bless our happy nation.
        Huzza! Huzza!! Huzza!!!

I looked to the South, and I looked to the West,
    And I saw old slavery a comin'
With four Northern doughfaces hitched up in front,
    Driving Freedom to the other side of Jordan.
        Then take off coats, boys, roll up sleeves,
        Slavery is a hard foe to battle, I believe.

Slavery and Freedom, they both had a fight,
    And the whole North came up behind 'em,
Hit Slavery a few knocks, with a free ballot-box,
    Sent it staggering to the other side of Jordan.
        Take off, etc.

If I was the Legislature of these United States,
    I'd settle this great question accordin';
I'd let every slave go free, over land and on the sea,
    Let 'em have a little hope this side of Jordan.
        Then rouse up, ye freemen, the sword unsheathe;
        Freedom is the best road to travel, I believe.

The South have their school, where the masters learn to rule,
    And they lord it o'er the Free States accordin';
But sure they'd better quit, ere they rouse the Yankee grit,
    And we tumble 'em over t'other side of Jordan.
        Take off, etc.

Pennsylvania and Vermont have surely come to want,
  To raise such scamps as Buck and Stephen,
And they'd better hire John [Mitchel] with shillalah, club and switchel,
  Drive 'em down to Alabama, and leave 'em.
      Take off, etc.

Edward Everett oped his mouth for the votes of the South,
  But his whishy-washy speech was so rotten,
That it struck to his spine, and he took a bee-line
  Lodged in State Street behind a bag of cotton.
      Take off coats, boys, roll up your sleeves,
        Cotton bags are hard things to battle, I believe.

But the day is drawing nigh that Slavery must die,
  And every one must do his part accordin';
Then let us all unite, to give every man his right,
  And we'll get our pay the other side of Jordan.
        Rouse up, ye freemen, the sword unsheathe,
        Freedom is the best road to travel, I believe.

21.

JOHN QUINCY ADAMS:
Old Man Eloquent

The rise of John Quincy Adams (1767–1848) to a position representing northern feeling was unparalleled. No man was better prepared for the presidency in training, intellect or love of country. His national program was frustrated by the Jacksonian alliance which nullified internal improvements, a Pan-American Union and other administration measures. Adams returned to Congress in 1831 as a Massachusetts representative. There he resisted the annexation of Texas and the extension of slavery. He won his special crown with his battle against the "gag rule," intended to stop discussion of slavery in Congress by ignoring petitions on the subject thereby abrogating the First Amendment to the Constitution. Many in the North wrote Adams down as cantankerous, but his death in 1848 silenced them. The following reminiscences are by "an Old Colony Man."

On the 7th of February, 1837, after Mr. Adams had offered some two hundred or more abolition petitions, he came to a halt; and, without yielding the floor, employed himself in packing up his budget. He was about resuming his seat, when he took up a paper, and hastily glancing at it, exclaimed, in a shrill tone—

"Mr. Speaker, I have in my possession a petition of a somewhat extraordinary character; and I wish to inquire of the chair if it be in order to present it."

"If the gentleman from Massachusetts," said the Speaker, "will

SOURCE: William Henry Seward, *Life and Public Services of John Quincy Adams* (Auburn, New York: Derby, Miller and Company, 1849), pp. 286 ff.

inform the chair what the character of the petition is, it will probably be able to decide on the subject."

"Sir," ejaculated Mr. Adams, "the petition is signed by eleven slaves of the town of Fredericksburgh, in the county of Culpepper, in the state of Virginia. It is one of those petitions which, it has occurred to my mind, are not what they purport to be. It is signed partly by persons who cannot write, by making their marks, and partly by persons whose handwriting would manifest that they have received the education of slaves. The petition declares itself to be from slaves, and I am requested to present it. I will send it to the chair."

The Speaker (Mr. Polk,) who habitually extended to Mr. Adams every courtesy and kindness imaginable, was taken by surprise, and found himself involved in a dilemma. Giving his chair one of those *hitches* which ever denoted his excitement, he said that a petition from slaves was a novelty, and involved a question that he did not feel called upon to decide. He would like to take time to consider it; and, in the meantime, would refer it to the House.

The House was very thin at the time, and little attention was paid to what was going on, till the excitement of the Speaker attracted the attention of Mr. Dixon H. Lewis, of Alabama, who impatiently, and under great excitement, rose and inquired what the petition was.

Mr. Speaker afforded the required information. Mr. Lewis, forgetting all discretion, whilst he frothed at the mouth, turned towards Mr. Adams, and ejaculated at the top of his voice, "By G–d, sir this is not to be endured any longer!"

"Treason! treason!" screamed a half dozen other members. "Expel the old scoundrel; put him out; do not let him disgrace the House any longer!"

"Get up a resolution to meet the case," exclaimed a member from North Carolina.

Mr. George C. Dromgoole, who had acquired a very favorable reputation as a parliamentarian, was selected as the very man who, of all others, was most capable of drawing up a resolution that would meet and cover the emergency. He produced a resolution with a preamble, in which it was stated, substantially, that, whereas the Hon. John Quincy Adams, a Representative from Massachusetts, had presented to the House of Representatives a petition signed by negro slaves, thus "giving *color to an idea*" that bondmen were capable of exercising the right of petition, it was "Resolved, That he be taken to the bar of the House, and be censured by the Speaker thereof."

Mr. Haynes said, the true motion, in his judgment, would be to move that the petition be rejected.

Mr. Lewis hoped that no motion of that kind would come from any gentleman from a slave holding section of the country.

Mr. Haynes said he would cheerfully withdraw his motion.

Mr. Lewis was glad the motion was withdrawn. He believed that the House should punish severely such an infraction of its decorum and its rules; and he called on the members from the slaveholding States to come forward now and demand of the House the punishment of the gentleman from Massachusetts.

Mr. Grantland, of Georgia, would second the motion, and go all lengths in support of it.

Mr. Lewis said, that if the House would inflict no punishment for such flagrant violations of its dignity as this, it would be better for the Representatives from the slaveholding States to go home at once.

Mr. Alford said, if the gentleman from Massachusetts intended to present this petition, the moment it was presented he should move, as an act of justice to the South, which he in part represented, and which he conceived had been treated with indignity, that it be taken from the House and burnt; and he hoped that every man who was a friend to the constitution, would support him. There must be an end to this constant attempt to raise excitement, or the Union could not exist much longer. The moment any man should disgrace the Government under which he lived, by presenting a petition from *slaves,* praying for emancipation, he hoped that petition would, by order of the House, be committed to the flames.

Mr. Waddy Thompson moved the following resolution:—

"Resolved, That the Hon. John Quincy Adams, by the attempt just made by him to introduce a petition purporting on its face to be from slaves, has been guilty of a gross disrespect to this House, and that he be instantly brought to the bar, to receive the severe censure of the Speaker."

The idea of bringing the venerable ex-President to the bar, like a culprit, to receive a reprimand from a comparatively youthful Speaker, would be a spectacle so disgraceful, and withal so absurd, that the proposition met with no favor. An easier way to reprimand was devised. Mr. Haynes introduced the following resolution:—

"Resolved, That John Quincy Adams, a Representative from the State of Massachusetts, has rendered himself justly liable to the severest censure of this House, and is censured accordingly, for having attempted to present to the House the petition of slaves."

Several other resolutions and propositions, from members of slaveholding States, were submitted to the House; but none proved satisfactory even to themselves. Mr. Adams, unmoved by the tempest which raged around him, defended himself, and the integrity of his purpose, with the distinguished ability and eloquence which characterized all his public labors.

"In regard to the resolutions now before the House," said he, "as they all concur in naming me, and in charging me with high crimes and misdemeanors, and in calling me to the bar of the House to answer for my crimes, I have thought it was my duty to remain silent, until it should be the pleasure of the House to act either on one or the other of these resolutions. I suppose that if I shall be brought to the bar of the House, I shall not be struck mute by the previous question, before I have an opportunity to say a word or two in my own defence.

"Now, as to the fact what the petition was for, I simply state to

the gentleman from Alabama, (Mr. D. H. Lewis,) who has sent
to the table a resolution assuming that this petition was for the
abolition of slavery—I state to him that he is mistaken. He must
amend his resolution; for if the House should choose to read this
petition, I can state to them they would find it something very
much the reverse of that which the resolution states it to be. And
if the gentleman from Alabama still chooses to bring me to the
bar of the House, he must amend his resolution in a very important particular; for he may probably have to put into it, that my
crime has been for attempting to introduce the petition of slaves
that slavery should *not* be abolished.

"Sir, it is well known, that from the time I entered this House,
down to the present day, I have felt it a sacred duty to present
any petition, couched in respectful language, from any citizen of
the United States, be its object what it may; be the prayer of it
that in which I could concur, or that to which I was utterly
opposed. It is for the sacred right of petition that I have adopted
this course. Where is your law which says that the mean, and the
low, and the degraded, shall be deprived of the right of petition,
if their moral character is not good? Where, in the land of freemen, was the right of petition ever placed on the exclusive basis
of morality and virtue? Petition is *supplication*—it is *entreaty*—it
is *prayer!* And where is the degree of vice or immorality which
shall deprive the citizen of the right to *supplicate* for a boon, or
to *pray for mercy?* Where is such a law to be found? It does not
belong to the most abject despotism! There is no absolute
monarch on earth, who is not compelled, by the constitution of
his country, to receive the petitions of his people, whosoever they
may be. The Sultan of Constantinople cannot walk the streets
and refuse to receive petitions from the meanest and vilest of the
land. This is the law even of despotism. And what does your law
say? Does it say that, before presenting a petition, you shall look
into it, and see whether it comes from the virtuous, and the great,
and the mighty? No sir; it says no such thing. The right of petition belongs to *all*. And so far from refusing to present a petition

because it might come from those low in the estimation of the world, it would be an additional incentive, if such incentive were wanting.

"But, I must admit," continued Mr. Adams, sarcastically, "that when *color* comes into the question, there may be other considerations. It is possible that this House, which seems to consider it so great a crime to attempt to offer a petition from slaves, may, for aught I know, say that freemen, if not of the *carnation,* shall be deprived of the right of petition, in the sense of the House."

When southern members saw that, in their haste, they had not tarried to ascertain the nature of the petition, and that it prayed for the *perpetuation,* instead of the *abolition* of slavery, their position became so ludicrous, that their exasperation was greatly increased. At the time the petition was announced by Mr. Adams, the House was very thin; but the excitement it produced soon filled it; and, besides, the *sergeant-at-arms* had been instructed to arrest and bring in all absentees. The excitement commenced at about one o'clock, and continued until seven o'clock in the evening, when the House adjourned. Mr. Adams stood at his desk, resolutely refusing to be seated till the matter was disposed of, alleging that if he were guilty, he was not entitled to a seat among high and honorable men. When Mr. Dromgoole's resolution was read to the House for its consideration, Mr. Adams yielded to it one of those sarcastic sneers which he was in the habit of giving, when provoked to satire; and said—"Mr. Speaker, if I understand the resolution of the honorable gentleman from Virginia, it charges me with being guilty of 'giving *color* to *an idea!*'" The whole House broke forth in one common irrepressible peal of laughter. The Dromgoole resolution was actually laughed out of existence. The House now found that it had got itself in a dilemma,—that Mr. Adams was too much for it; and, at last, adjourned, leaving the affair in the position in which they found it.

For several days this subject continued to agitate the House.

Mr. Adams not only warded off the virulent attacks made upon him, but carried the war so effectually into the camp of his enemies, that, becoming heartily tired of the contest, they repeatedly endeavored to get rid of the whole subject by laying it on the table. To this Mr. Adams objected. He insisted that it should be thoroughly canvassed. Immense excitement ensued. Call after call of the House was made. Mr. Henry A. Wise, who was, at the time, engaged on the Reuben Whitney affair, was sent for, with an accompanying message that the stability of the Union was in danger!

Breathless, and impatient, Mr. Wise made his appearance, and inquired what was the matter. He was informed.

"And is that all?" ejaculated Mr. Wise. "The gentleman from Massachusetts has presented a petition signed by slaves! Well, sir, and what of that? Is anybody harmed by it? Sir, in my opinion, slaves are the very persons who should petition. Mine, sir, pray to me, and I listen to them; and shall not the feeble supplicate? Sir, I see no danger,—the country, I believe, is safe."

At length the exciting subject was brought to a termination, by the passage of the following preamble and resolutions; much softened, it will be seen, in comparison with the measures first proposed:—

An inquiry having been made by an honorable gentleman from Massachusetts, whether a paper which he held in his hand, purporting to be a petition from certain slaves, and declaring themselves to be slaves, came within the order of the House of the 18th of January, and the said paper not having been received by the Speaker, he stated that in a case so extraordinary and novel, he would take the advice and counsel of the House.

Resolved, That this House cannot receive said petition without disregarding its own dignity, the rights of a large class of citizens of the South and West, and the Constitution of the United States.

Resolved, That slaves do not possess the right of petition secured to the citizens of the United States by the constitution.

The slave petition is believed to have been a counterfeit,

manufactured by certain members from slaveholding States, and was sent to Mr. Adams by the way of experiment—with the double design of ascertaining if he could be imposed upon; and, if the deception succeeded, those who got it up were curious to know if the venerable statesman would redeem his pledge, and present a petition, no matter who it came from. He was too wily not to detect the plot at the outset; he knew that all was a hoax; but, he resolved to present the paper, and then turn the tables on its authors.

22.

FREDERICK DOUGLASS:
Voice of the Freeman and the Slave

Frederick Douglass's (1817–1895) services touched every aspect of his own people's needs and many of the nation's as a whole. His works of tongue and pen over half a century covered slavery as well as other conditions of Negroes. His works also involved liberty of speech and of press, the country's image at home and abroad, in peace and in war. Douglass began as a Garrisonian. Later events persuaded Douglass that Negroes must engage in politics to reach new friends. As he disturbed idealists by permitting English sympathizers to buy his freedom (his critics argued that property rights in human beings ought not to be respected), so he outraged extremists who held that involvement in politics implicated Douglass in the evils of a slavery-endorsing government. Douglass later fought to gain Negroes the right to bear arms in Federal military units and still later to share in the fruits of victory. His last quarrel was with his own people for marrying a white woman in 1884 following the death of his first wife. Douglass's response was that his first wife "was the color of my mother and the second, the color of my father." (See also page 202.) Charles Lenox Remond, mentioned below, was a free-born Negro whose platform appearances gave him some distinction before Douglass's presence dimmed his light. George Latimer was a fugitive slave seized in Boston in 1842 but rescued by abolitionists who defied Supreme Court interpretations of the Fugitive Slave Act of 1793 to make the issue one of personal liberties.

SOURCE: Liberator, November 18, 1842.

Dear Friend Garrison: Lynn, Mass., Nov. 8, 1842

The date of this letter finds me quite unwell. I have for a week past been laboring, in company with bro. Charles Remond, in New Bedford, with special reference to the case of our outraged brother, George Latimer, and speaking almost day and night, in public and in private; and for the reward of our labor, I have the best evidence that a great good has been done. It is said by many residents, that New Bedford has never been so favorably aroused to her anti-slavery responsibility as at present. Our meetings were characterized by that deep and solemn feeling which the importance of the cause, when properly set forth, is always calculated to awaken. On Sunday, we held three meetings in the new town hall, at the usual meeting hours, morning, afternoon, and evening. In the morning, we had quite a large meeting, at the opening of which, I occupied about an hour, on the question as to whether a man is better than a sheep. Mr. Dean then made a few remarks, and after him, Mr. Clapp of Nantucket arose and gave his testimony to the truth, as it is in anti-slavery. The meeting then adjourned, to meet again in the afternoon. I said that we held our meetings at the regular meeting hours. Truth requires me to make our afternoon meeting an exception to this remark. For long before the drawling, lazy church bells commenced sounding their deathly notes, mighty crowds were making their way to the town hall. . . . After a short space, allotted to secret or public prayer, bro. J. B. Sanderson arose and requested the attention of the audience to the reading of a few passages of scripture, selected by yourself in the editorial of last week. They did give their attention, and as he read the solemn and soul-stirring denunciations of Jehovah, by the mouth of his prophets and apostles, against oppressors, the deep stillness that pervaded that magnificent hall was a brilliant demonstration that the audience felt that what was read was but the reiteration of words which had fallen from the great Judge of the universe. After reading, he proceeded to make some remarks on the general question of human rights. These, too, seemed to sink deep into the hearts of the gathered multitude. Not a word was lost; it was good seed, sown in good ground, by a careful hand; it must, it will bring forth fruit. . . .

The meeting met according to adjournment, at an early hour. The splendid hall was brilliantly lighted, and crowded with an earnest, listening audience, and notwithstanding the efforts of our friends before named to have them seated, a large number had to stand during the meeting, which lasted about three hours; where the standing part of the audience were, at the commencement of the meeting, there they were at the conclusion of it; no moving about with them; any place was good enough, so they could but hear. From the eminence which I occupied, I could see the entire audience; and from its appearance, I should conclude that prejudice against color was not there, at any rate, it was not to be seen by me; we were all on a level, every one took a seat just where they chose; there were neither men's side nor women's side; white pew, nor black pew; but all seats were free, and all sides free. When the meeting was fully gathered, I had something to say, and was followed by bro. Sanderson and Remond. When they had concluded their remarks, I again took the stand, and called the attention of the meeting to the case of bro. George Latimer, which proved the finishing stroke of my present public speaking. On taking my seat, I was seized with a violent pain in my breast, which continued till morning, and with occasional raising of blood; this past off in about two hours, after which, weakness of breast, a cough, and shortness of breath ensued, so that now such is the state of my lungs, that I am unfit for public speaking, for the present. My condition goes harder with me, much harder than it would at ordinary times. These are certainly extraordinary times; times that demand the efforts of the humblest of our most humble advocates of our perishing and dying fellow-countrymen. Those that can but whisper freedom, should be doing even that, though they can only be heard from one side of their short fire place to the other. It is a struggle of life and death with us just now. No sword that can be used, be it never so rusty, should lay idle in its scabbard. Slavery, our enemy, has landed in our very midst, and commenced its bloody work. Just look at it; here is George Latimer a man—a brother—a husband—a father, stamped with the likeness of the eternal God, and redeemed by the blood of Jesus Christ, out-lawed, hunted down like a wild beast, and ferociously dragged through the streets of Boston, and incarcerated within the walls of Leverett-st. jail. And all this is done in Boston—liberty-loving, slavery-hating Boston—intellectual, moral, and religious Boston. And why was this—what crime had George Latimer committed? He had committed the crime of availing himself of his natural rights, in defence of which the founders of this very Boston enveloped her in midnight darkness, with the smoke proceeding from their thundering artillery. What a horrible state of things is here presented. Boston has become the hunting-ground of merciless men-hunters, and man-stealers. Henceforth we need not portray to the imagination of northern people, the flying slave making his way through thick and dark woods of the South, with white fanged blood-hounds yelping on his blood-stained track; but refer to the streets of Boston, made dark and dense by crowds of professed Christians. Take a look at James B. Gray's new pack, turned loose on the track of poor Latimer. I see the blood-thirsty animals, smelling at every corner, part with each other, and meet again; they seem to be consulting as to the best mode of coming upon their victim. Now they look sad, discouraged;—tired, they drag along, as if they were ashamed of their business, and about to give up the chase; but presently they get a sight of their prey, their eyes brighten, they become more courageous, they approach their victim unlike the common hound. They come upon him softly, wagging their tails, pretending friendship, and do not pounce upon him, until they have secured him beyond possible escape. Such is the character of James B. Gray's new pack of two-legged blood-hounds that hunted down George Latimer, and

23.

THOMAS HOOD:
British Reform: I

British reform differed from American in that abolition, relating to far-off slaves, could be separated from the complex questions of domestic "wage slavery." Yet the reform impulse affected abolition as well as the lot of the poor and oppressed. Wrote Gerald Massey, whom Chartists and Christian Socialists claimed as their poet:

And this is merry England,—cradling-place
    Of souls self-deified and glory-crown'd!
Where smiles made splendour in the Peasant's face,
    And Justice reign'd—Her awful eyes close-bound!
Where Toil with open brow went on light-hearted,
    And twain in love Law never thrust apart?
How is the glory of our life departed
    From us, who sit and nurse our bleeding smart;
    And slink, afraid to break the laws that break the heart!

Thomas Hood (1799–1845) was a wit and versifier who concerned himself little with critical social problems. That they should have reached him sufficiently to have inspired "The Song of the Shirt" was a measure of social need more than of social concern. The poem also affected sentiment in the United States.

With fingers weary and worn,
    With eyelids heavy and red,
A woman sat in unwomanly rags,
    Plying her needle and thread—
        Stitch! stitch! stitch!

SOURCE: *The Poetical Works of Thomas Hood* (Boston: Phillips, Sampson and Company, 1853), pp. 123–125.

162   The Antislavery Concert

In poverty, hunger, and dirt,
   And still with a voice of dolorous pitch
She sang the "Song of the Shirt!"

   "Work! work! work!
While the cock is crowing aloof!
   And work—work—work,
Till the stars shine through the roof!
It's O! to be a slave
   Along with the barbarous Turk,
Where woman has never a soul to save,
   If this is Christian work!

   "Work—work—work
Till the brain begins to swim!
   Work—work—work
Till the eyes are heavy and dim!
Seam, and gusset, and band,
   Band, and gusset, and seam,
Till over the buttons I fall asleep,
   And sew them on a dream!

"O, men, with sisters dear!
   O, men, with mothers and wives!
It is not linen you're wearing out,
   But human creatures' lives!
     Stitch—stitch—stitch,
   In poverty, hunger, and dirt,
Sewing at once, with a double thread,
   A shroud as well as a shirt.

"But why do I talk of death?
   That phantom of grisly bone,
I hardly fear his terrible shape,
   It seems so like my own—
It seems so like my own,
   Because of the fasts I keep;
O, God! that bread should be so dear,
   And flesh and blood so cheap!

"Work—work—work!
    My labor never flags;
And what are its wages? A bed of straw,
    A crust of bread—and rags.
That shattered roof—and this naked floor—
    A table—a broken chair—
And a wall so blank, my shadow I thank
    For sometimes falling there!

"Work—work—work!
    From weary chime to chime,
Work—work—work,
    As prisoners work for crime!
Band, and gusset, and seam,
    Seam, and gusset, and band,
Till the heart is sick, and the brain benumbed,
    As well as the weary hand.

    "Work—work—work,
In the dull December light,
    And work—work—work,
When the weather is warm and bright—
While underneath the eaves
    The brooding swallows cling,
As if to show me their sunny backs,
    And twit me with the spring.

    "O! but to breathe the breath
Of the cowslip and primrose sweet—
    With the sky above my head,
And the grass beneath my feet,
For only one short hour
    To feel as I used to feel,
Before I knew the woes of want,
    And the walk that costs a meal!

"O! but for one short hour!
    A respite however brief!
No blessed leisure for love or hope,
    But only time for grief!

A little weeping would ease my heart,
  But in their briny bed
My tears must stop, for every drop
  Hinders needle and thread!"

With fingers weary and worn,
  With eyelids heavy and red,
A woman sat in unwomanly rags,
    Plying her needle and thread—
      Stitch! stitch! stitch!
    In poverty, hunger, and dirt,
And still with a voice of dolorous pitch,—
Would that its tone could reach the rich!—
    She sang this "Song of the Shirt!"

24.

SHAFTESBURY:

British Reform: II

In 1885, the year of Shaftesbury's death, the Duke of Argyll stated in the House of Lords: "[T]he social reforms of the last century [in Great Britain] have not been mainly due to the Liberal Party [but] to the influence, character, and perserverance of one man—Lord Shaftesbury." Lord Shaftesbury's half-century of services affected men, women and children everywhere in industry and the home. Manchester Liberals, operating factories, held they must be free of restrictions and resented Shaftesbury (earlier Lord Ashley). They accused him of diverting attention from the rural poor his landowning class dominated. Liberals demanded, instead, repeal of the Corn [wheat] Laws and free trade, which would prevent competition and therefore war. Shaftesbury did not subscribe to his class's prejudices. He kept a journal from which the following is abstracted. The victory recorded was only a step in Shaftesbury's endless labors which took in factory inspection, lodging houses, schools and missions for boys and girls, sanitary reform in the metropolis, the great suffrage-expanding Reform Bill of 1867 and aid to fugitive slaves in Canada.

February 24th [1842]. . . . All Peel's affinities are towards wealth and capital. His heart is manifestly towards the mill-owners; his lips occasionally for the operatives. *What* has he ever done or proposed for the working classes? His speech of last night was a signal instance of his tendencies. He suppressed all the delin-

SOURCE: Edwin Hodder, *Life and Work of . . . Shaftesbury* (London: Cassell & Co., 1887), pp. 218 ff.

quencies of the manufacturers, bepraised machinery, and treated the distress as severe but temporary. Now, he might have said that no small portion of the suffering was caused by the forced immigration of families in 1836, reducing the already low wages, and aggravating the misery, in the stagnation which followed. He might have said, too, that, while we cannot interdict machinery, we ought not to be blind to its effects: it may cheapen goods for the consumer, but it pauperises irrevocably thousands of work-people, who can never resume their position, whatever be the activity of trade. In short, his speech was a transcript of his mind: cotton is everything, man nothing!

Feb. 25th.—Time creeps on, years fly past, and the city of oppression and vice has not capitulated; the factory system stands erect; millions of infants are consumed in other depart-ments; and, in the course of nature, it seems probable that before long I shall be removed to another scene of action—to the House of Lords. If I regard this event as a man only, I must see in it utter annihilation of all my schemes for the benefit of the working classes, and a total retirement from public life, because in that House, except for one who holds high official station, there is little or no power of originating anything which may conduce to the welfare of the poorer sort. The Peers act as breakwaters, and think as such; this is their office, and they never rise above it. The House of Commons is the depository of Power; any favour ac-quired there is more effective than ten times the amount in the House of Lords; they are won, besides, by different qualities, and the station occupied by different men. I should be quite over-whelmed by such peers as Salisbury, Redesdale, and Wharncliffe. Character of *all kinds* is FAR LESS required and appreciated among the Peers. . . .

March 18th.—Spoke again last night on the Lunacy Bill. I seemed to myself to do it without force or point, and with diffi-culty; half left unsaid and the other half said ill. This is humbling and despairing, because I plough not in hope. How can I look to success in the great measures I propose, if I am so weak in the smaller? The House will despise schemes so brought forward. Am I working *in* the truth and *for* the truth? This doubt often arises now, and yet, what is my guide if I am not?

March 29th—If things are not put down as they arise, they are either lost or are recorded with their point blunted. A reconciliation with Peel. We shook hands, and avoided all explanations. So much the better; an explanation only gets rid, for the moment, of the old quarrel, for the purpose of laying the grounds of a new one. Facts may be set right; but we should have had to deal with opinions and expressions. He was very cordial, and clearly much pleased.

April 9th—This day is, perhaps, the last of leisure I shall have for a long time. Gave it to the reading of the Colliery Report, that I may be thoroughly furnished to the good work. I can never produce, in a speech, one-tenth part of the truth, and yet, unless that be fully told, I shall not accomplish my purpose. Great labour, great difficulty, first to read, and then to select and arrange the matter. . . .

In August 1840, Shaftesbury—then Lord Ashley—had moved in Parliament for a Commission to inquire into the use of children in mines and collieries. In May 1842, the first report was issued. Its accounts of cruelty and depravity caused a sensation. In the United States it was utilized to reinforce the proslavery argument that "free" labor was inferior to slave labor.

May 7th—The Report of the Commission is out—a noble document. The Home Office in vain endeavoured to hold it back; it came by a most providential mistake into the hands of members; and, though the Secretary of State for a long while prevented the sale of it, he could not prevent publicity, or any notice of motion.

Perhaps even "Civilisation" itself never exhibited such a mass of sin and cruelty. The disgust felt is very great, thank God; but will it be reduced to action when I call for a remedy?

May 14th—The Government cannot, if they would, refuse the

Bill of which I have given notice, to exclude females and children from coal-pits—the feeling in my favour has become quite enthusiastic; the Press on all sides is working most vigorously. Wrote pointedly to thank the editor of the *Morning Chronicle* for his support, *which is most effective.* . . .

May 21st—The Government had well-nigh given away Thursday (my day for the Colliery Bill) to C. Buller. It is clear that they desire to get rid of the motion. This day I received a formal proposition from Freemantle to give precedence to the Bridport case. No reason assigned why the Minister demanded precedence; there is quite as good reason why I should precede Buller, as he precede me. I told him that such a request came with a very bad grace from a Government which was hostile, not only to past measures of the kind, but, I really believed, to this one in particular! I, of course, refused; postponement would be total surrender.

May 23rd—Peel, knowing my determination not to give way, advised Wynne this evening (Wynne told me so himself) to take Thursday for a *question of privilege,* thereby destroying me altogether. Never was there such treatment, such abominable trickery.

May 24th—One would have thought that a "paternal" Government would have hastened to originate, certainly to aid, any measures for the removal of this foul and cruel stain! No such thing, no assistance, no sympathy—every obstacle in my way, though I doubt whether they will dare *openly to oppose* me on the Bill itself. Have no time for reflection, no time for an entry. I hear that no such sensation has been caused since the first disclosures of the horrors of the slave trade! . . .

Ashley's crusade called forth criticism not only from John Bright, manufacturer and Corn Law reformer but from Harriet Martineau, a friend of Garrisonians, who claimed his attacks on the factory system was an attack on freedom of contract and that Ashley's own father's estates reduced their laborers "to the lowest

condition then known to Englishmen." Ashley's speech in No-
vember 1843 to the Sturminster Agricultural Society, which in-
cluded "strong truths respecting wages, dwellings, truck, delay of
payments and exclusion from gleaning," in his summary, not only
created a sensation but roused his father's anger. He fought on
though the Peel government sought to divide his supporters by
threatening that the program which would limit hours in industry
would limit hours in agriculture.

March 16th [1844]—Factory Bill last night in Committee. Spoke for two and a quarter hours. What will be the issue? Had we divided last night, we should, I am told, have beaten the Government! The interval will be favourable to them; official whips will produce official votes.

March 18th.—Jocelyn came to me yesterday, after morning service, and said that "he had something important to communicate." Stanley had taken him aside on Saturday evening, and had urged upon him the mischiefs arising from the amendment for "ten hours" that I had proposed. "Ashley," he added, "does not know the condition in which he places the Government. If he carries his point, as it seems probable he will, two courses remain; we must either throw up the Bill, for Graham is pledged to carry it as it is, or throw it into his hands." He then said a great deal more about the effect such success would have in aiding the repeal of the Corn Laws, and remarked: "If Ashley is strong enough to beat the Government, he must take all responsibility: if he thinks himself strong enough to defeat them here, perhaps he thinks himself strong enough to take the Government." Jocelyn said: "What would you have Ashley do? He has given his life, you may say, to the question; what would you have him do? He could not surrender it." Stanley replied in a drawling, uncertain tone: "I don't know; I don't say what he could do." The upshot was that Jocelyn, without delivering a direct message, was to inform me of the Ministerial mind. He did so. I replied that "if my perseverance involved the repeal of ten thousand Corn Laws, and the dissolution of as many Governments, I would go on with all the vigour I could command; that, were I disposed to hold back, I could not do so in the smallest degree; that even in a mere question of politics, a man would be regarded as a sad specimen of faithlessness who retired simply to gratify the convenience of his Parliamentary friends, but that in this case, when I had toiled for so many years, and placed the whole matter on the basis of duty and religion, I should be considered, *and most justly, too,* a hypocrite almost without parallel." We rang the changes on all this, and Jocelyn went away. I saw him again in the street, just before I entered the Chapel Royal. "I have seen Stanley again," he said; "he never thought you could resign the question; you were too deeply pledged." "It would be a sad thing," continued Stanley, "for the Government to appear as alone resisting the wishes and feelings of the people; it would look very ill to the country if the question had a majority in the House, but was rejected solely by the Government." Then Lord Stanley added (*O tempora, O mores!*) "What I meant was that you (Jocelyn) and your friends should not bestir yourselves so much to obtain votes, and Ashley might save his character by maintaining his point, and *yet allow himself to be beaten!*" If ever insult was put on an individual, here it was with a vengeance! I told Jocelyn that "the only difference was whether I should be an open or a secret scoundrel." I added that "I would exhaust all legitimate means to obtain my end, and that if defeated, I would never cease to work on the sympathies of the country." . . .

Finally, despite all opposition, the Factory Bill, limiting hours of labor to ten, passed in the House of Commons and went to the House of Lords.

February 10th [1847]—Factory Bill is under discussion in the House of Commons. I lingered in the lobby; had not spirit to enter the House; should have been nervously excited to reply, and grieved by inability to do so.

March 1st—Intense anxiety about Factory Bill. I dream of it

by day and by night, and work as though I had charge of the Bill.

March 12th—Lady De Grey observed to me, last night, that I was grown silent, and had lost all my spirits. It is quite true. I have, during the last two or three years, been growing more melancholy and even stupid. It is, perhaps, because I have little or no play, and that makes Jack a dull boy.

March 17th—Long labour yesterday in furnishing John Russell, at his request, with notes for a speech. . . .

May 18th—The Bishops behaved gallantly—13 remained to vote; three spoke, and most effectively: London, Oxford, St. David's; Clarendon (!) and Brougham (!!) in opposition. This will do very much to win the hearts of the manufacturing people to Bishops and Lords—it has already converted the hard mind of a Chartist Delegate.

June 1st—Six o'clock. News that the Factory Bill has just passed the third reading. I am humbled that my heart is not bursting with thankfulness to Almighty God—that I can find breath and sense to express my joy. What reward shall we give unto the Lord for all the benefits He hath conferred upon us? . . .

25.

GEORGE THOMPSON:
British Abolitionism

British abolitionists were a force at home and in reform generally. Thompson (1804–1878) was one of the most notable of Englishmen to agitate the question not among parliamentarians —though he later served in Parliament—but among the people. His visit to the United States, 1834–1835, was attended by riot and enthusiasm. Andrew Jackson denounced him in a Presidential Message. Thompson was forced to flee Boston in an open boat to a British vessel which took him to New Brunswick and thence home. He was received back with honor during the Civil War by President Lincoln and the House of Representatives. His career also included distinguished services in behalf of colonial Indians. The following is from his Substance of a Speech . . . Being a Reply to Mr. Borthwick's Statements on the Subject of British Colonial Slavery.

Mr. Borthwick said something very beautiful about the happiness and contentedness of the negro, which would be very elegant, if it were true; but the misfortune is, that most of the things he says are not true, in fact. That he believes them to be true, I must not question. He says the negroes do not care for freedom,—that they set no value upon it,—that if you go round amongst them, and put the question to them, they will say 'No, Massa; me very happy, me want no more, me get all me care for:' that, in fine, they would not have their freedom, if they could get it. Would they not? Then why are the newspapers filled with

SOURCE: Amos A. Phelps, *Lectures on Slavery and Its Remedy* (Boston: New England Anti-Slavery Society, 1834), Appendix B, pp. 251 ff.

advertisements of runaway negroes? Why are the prisons filled with runaway negroes? Why are the mountains peopled with runaway negroes? Why is the bush filled with runaway negroes? Why is a standing army kept to force slavery down the throats of the negroes, if they are in love with it? (Loud applause.) Does the mother hold a rod over the child's head to force it to eat apple tart? (Laughter.) Did Adam and Eve *run* out of Paradise? If the negroes like slavery, then withdraw the troops, and save us the trouble and expense, the loss of life and money needlessly incurred, if the negroes are contented with their condition. (Loud applause.) But they like slavery, and do not wish for liberty; and Mr. Borthwick exclaims they shall not have liberty now, because they do not know its value: but shall man be kept in slavery, because he does not know the value of liberty? See the pitiful dilemma into which Mr. Borthwick has brought himself: the negroes do not like what all men sigh for,—what they would bleed and die to defend,—what they would give house and lands, friends and reputation to obtain; and here is the dilemma,—if it be so, then, planters, proprietors, upholders of slavery, he defends and maintains a vile and brutalizing system, which has extinguished in man the most noble and generous quality that distinguishes him from the brutes. (Loud cheers.) What! because men do not like liberty,—if it be true that they do not like it, are we not to try to make them like it? Mr. Borthwick tells us that the negroes are very happy and contented,—that they want no more; and then he tells us of a man, a most miserable man,—if there ever were so very a wretch,—that bought fifty acres of land, and then said he did not want his own liberty. I should like to see the man who was thus in love with 'going round and round his tub.' Not like liberty for himself—why, then, did he want it for his wife and children? Mr. Borthwick tells us that he might call them 'MY OWN.' (Loud cheers.) Mr. Borthwick tells us that, when asked this question, the man replied, 'I want to call them *mine;*' and I beg Mr. Borthwick to remember that word *mine*. . . .

But I am prepared to show that the slaves *do* value freedom and long to possess it, notwithstanding Mr. Borthwick's declaration to the contrary. I hold in my hand two documents,—the first is a proclamation from Governor Ross, published in the *Antigua Register* of March 29, 1831:

ANTIGUA.

> By his Excellency Sir Patrick Ross, Knight, Commander of the most distinguished Order of St. Michael and St. George, Major-General in the Army, Governor, and Commander-in-Chief in and over his Majesty's Island of Antigua, Montserrat, and Barbuda, Chancellor, Vice-Admiral, and Ordinary of the same, &c. &c. &c.
> Patrick (L. S.) Ross.

WHEREAS by my proclamation bearing date the twenty-first day of this present month, I did, by and with the advice of His Majesty's Privy Council, offer a Reward of One Hundred Pounds to the Person or Persons (except the actual offender) who should give such information as would lead to the conviction of the offender or offenders who set fire to several cane pieces in this Island, and also a free pardon to an accomplice or accomplices on conviction by their means of the actual perpetrator of such diabolical acts. Now, therefore, I do further, in compliance with the joint Address of both Houses of the Legislature, offer

FREEDOM TO ANY SLAVE

who by his or her exertions and evidence may bring to justice any of the incendiaries who have been destroying the canes in various parts of the Island.

> Given under my hand and seal at Government-house, this Twenty-second day of March, One Thousand Eight Hundred and Thirty-one, and in the First Year of His Majesty's Reign.
>> *God save the King.*
> By His Excellency's command,
>> CHARLES TAYLOR, Private Secretary.

Duly published this Twenty-third day of March, One Thousand Eight Hundred and Thirty-one.

> MARTIN NANTON, Deputy Provost Marshal.

—*Weekly Register, Antigua, Tuesday, March 29, 1831.*

Now, Mr. Borthwick, when Governor Ross means to offer the highest reward which it is in his power to confer,—what is it that he does offer? A few more yams, a little more rum, or a little more clothing? No; but he offers the slave the highest boon which the island can grant,—he offers him *freedom*. (Loud cheers.) Another proclamation to the same effect was issued in Jamaica during the late insurrection.

Freedom, Mr. Borthwick, is the highest boon that governors and generals can bestow; and to-day I have been informed, by a gentleman now on this platform, that whilst he was on the island of Nevis, a few years back, the inhabitants were alarmed by a tremendous storm, and found that a vessel had been wrecked, the *crew* of which *were* in danger of perishing. The planters stood on the beach, beholding the desolation on the waters, but they could not induce any person to launch a boat and go to the assistance of the persons in the wreck. At last the planters offered freedom to any slaves who would put off to the assistance of the shipwrecked mariners, and immediately these men, who are said to care nothing for liberty, rushed into the boat, and risked their own existence to save those who were in danger of perishing. (Cheers.) In the year 1794 there was what was termed the Maroon war in Jamaica: and who were the Maroons? Runaway negroes! And where had they run from? From the 'four parlors and a saloon.' What did they run from? From the light work, the beautiful clothing, and abundance of food; from the kind care and culture of the planters. And where did they run to from all this comfort and happiness? To the bleak and desolate mountains, to the fastnesses of Jamaica. Ay, to the desolate mountain, from the four parlors and a saloon. And what did they do there? Why, whilst the negro of Jamaica was enjoying his four parlors and a saloon, drinking his wine, and revelling in all the luxuries of slavery, like another Sardanapalus, the negroes in the mountains were getting strong, increasing and multiplying, and at last down they came upon the whites, and threatened to exterminate them. The whites met together, to consider how they might best resist the aggressions of the Maroons: the standing troops were called out, and found to be insufficient, and with the militia added to them they were still thought insufficient, and the arming of the negroes was talked of: but somebody said, 'How do you know, when you have armed the negroes, that they will fight for you? How do you know that they will not make common cause with the Maroons? You must find some motive sufficiently strong to induce them to fight.' And what was that motive? Was it food, house, a provision ground—No; they promised the slaves *liberty!* (Loud cheers.) And with liberty in their hearts, liberty their watchword, and liberty their expected reward, they went to the battle plain, they fought and bled, and even many of them died, whilst the living returned victorious, not to pull down chapels, not to injure innocent men, but to clasp to their bosoms their wives and their children, to stretch out their *free* hands to Heaven and say, 'Now, indeed, we are men and brethren.' (Hear that, Mr. Borthwick.) I beg my friends will not make any remarks; let them leave that to me, for I am exceedingly jealous of my privileges. (Much laughter.)

And now Mr. Borthwick comes to Hayti; he thinks he has a fine specimen of the dangers of emancipation at Hayti; and he measures the happiness of the inhabitants of that island by the amount of their exports. But this is false philosophy, Mr. Borthwick. Suppose the people of Ireland were to ship less of their produce, less corn, fewer cattle, and fewer potatoes to foreign countries than they now do, and eat it all themselves, would any person assign this as a reason why they should be worse off than they were when they did export a larger quantity. (Cheers.) Mr. Borthwick ought not to measure the comfort and happiness of a people by the amount of their exports. Would he argue because the stage-proprietor did not carry so many passengers, and therefore did not run his horses so frequently, that the *horses* were worse off than they were before? (Loud cheers.) Would he argue that the ox was in a worse condition because he trod out less corn than he did before? How does it happen that the

Haytians have not cultivated so much sugar as they did for-merly? Why did they cultivate so much formerly? Because of the whip, to please their masters, not to please themselves. (Loud cheers.) What is the fact now? A gentleman who is now here is willing to come forward, to state it firmly, fearlessly and openly. (Cheers.) After a twelve years' residence in Hayti, where he kept a regular account of exports and imports, and investigated the manners, motives and desires of the inhabitants, he is ready to testify that the commerce of Hayti is prosperous, and that the peasants of Hayti are as happy and comfortable as any portion of the human family. (Loud cries of 'Name, name.') Mr. Shiel. (Loud and reiterated cheering.)

Mr. Shiel then stood upon the table, and said—Ladies and Gentlemen, called upon as I have been by the gentleman who has already addressed you for upwards of three hours, I do not come forward to make any long oration, I merely come forward to say that the facts stated by that gentleman, with regard to Hayti, are perfectly correct, and that I have witnessed them. I know that the people of Hayti are free, independent, comfort-able, and happy. (Cheers.) There is also another point which I wish to notice, a point which has never yet been laid before the British public;—I allude to the revolution which occurred in Hayti in 1822, when the Spanish part of the colony threw off the yoke of slavery. That revolution was effected by the people, without a single act of violence even of the most trifling charac-ter. (Cheers.) The masters, it is to be observed, were Span-iards—a people who never maltreated their slaves. (Hear, hear.) The slaves declared themselves free, shook off the Spanish yoke, and joined the republican part of Hayti, without a single act of violence or the slightest destruction of property. (Loud cheers.) . . .

26.

PHILLIPS, THOMPSON ET AL.:
World Antislavery

The World Anti-Slavery Convention of 1840 in London was expected to initiate an alliance which would gather strength and erase slavery everywhere. In fact, events in the field continued to be dominated by national considerations of complex and often subtle quality. Thus what could be plainly seen as slavery in Egypt or China or Yucatan by an impertinent stranger could be defended by a native of the derogated country or colony as tradition or religious sanction. In Great Britain and the United States, however, the title of slavery was kept in constant sight, and developments weakened its hold on popular acceptance. The 1840 Convention, sponsored by the British and Foreign Anti-Slavery Society, if it accomplished little, did at least initiate meetings which would in due course be attended by representatives of nations, rather than societies. One of its by-products was to stir a spirit on the part of American men and women in attendance, which in 1848 resulted in the convening of the first Woman's Rights Convention at Seneca Falls, New York.

Mr. [Wendell] Phillips: When the call reached America we found that it was an invitation to the friends of the slave of every nation and of every clime. Massachusetts has for several years acted on the principle of admitting women to an equal seat with men, in the deliberative bodies of anti-slavery societies. When the Massachusetts Anti-Slavery Society received that paper, it interpreted it, as it was its duty, in its broadest and most liberal

SOURCE: Elizabeth Cady Stanton et al., *History of Woman Suffrage* (New York: Fowler & Wells, 1881), vol. I, pp. 55 ff.

sense. If there be any other paper, emanating from the Committee, limiting to one sex the qualification of membership, there is no proof; and, as an individual, I have no knowledge that such a paper ever reached Massachusetts. We stand here in consequence of your invitation, and knowing our custom, as it must be presumed you did, we had a right to interpret "friends of the slave," to include women as well as men. In such circumstances, we do not think it just or equitable to that State, nor to America in general, that, after the trouble, the sacrifice, the self-devotion of a part of those who leave their families and kindred and occupations in their own land, to come three thousand miles to attend this World's Convention, they should be refused a place in its deliberations. . . .

Dr. Bowring: I think the custom of excluding females is more honored in its breach than in its observance. In this country sovereign rule is placed in the hands of a female, and one who has been exercising her great and benignant influence in opposing slavery by sanctioning, no doubt, the presence of her illustrious consort at an anti-slavery meeting. We are associated with a body of Christians (Quakers) who have given to their women a great, honorable, and religious prominence. I look upon this delegation from America as one of the most interesting, the most encouraging, and the most delightful symptoms of the times. I can not believe that we shall refuse to welcome gratefully the cooperation which is offered us. . . .

The Rev. Henry Grew, of Philadelphia: The reception of women as a part of this Convention would, in the view of many, be not only a violation of the customs of England, but of the ordinance of Almighty God, who has a right to appoint our services to His sovereign will.

Rev. Eben Galusha, New York: In support of the other side of this question, reference has been made to your Sovereign. I most cordially approve of her policy and sound wisdom, and commend to the consideration of our American female friends who are so deeply interested in the subject, the example of your noble

Queen, who by sanctioning her consort, His Royal Highness Prince Albert, in taking the chair on an occasion not dissimilar to this, showed her sense of propriety by putting her Head foremost in an assembly of gentlemen. I have no objection to woman's being the neck to turn the head aright, but do not wish to see her assume the place of the head.

George Bradburn, of Mass.: We are told that it would be outraging the customs of England to allow women to sit in this Convention. I have a great respect for the customs of old England. But I ask, gentlemen, if it be right to set up the customs and habits, not to say prejudices of Englishmen, as a standard for the government on this occasion of Americans, and of persons belonging to several other independent nations. I can see neither reason nor policy in so doing. Besides, I deprecate the principle of the objection. In America it would exclude from our conventions all persons of color, for there customs, habits, tastes, prejudices, would be outraged by *their* admission. And I do not wish to be deprived of the aid of those who have done so much for this cause, for the purpose of gratifying any mere custom or prejudice. Women have furnished most essential aid in accomplishing what has been done in the State of Massachusetts. If, in the Legislature of that State, I have been able to do anything in furtherance of that cause, by keeping on my legs eight or ten hours day after day, it was mainly owing to the valuable assistance I derived from the women. And shall such women be denied seats in this Convention? My friend George Thompson, yonder, can testify to the faithful services rendered to this cause by those same women. He can tell you that when "gentlemen of property and standing" in "broad day" and "broadcloth," undertook to drive him from Boston, putting his life in peril, it was our women who made their own persons a bulwark of protection around him. And shall such women be refused seats here in a Convention seeking the emancipation of slaves throughout the world? What a misnomer to call this a World's Convention of Abolitionists, when some of the oldest and most thorough-going

Abolitionists in the world are denied the right to be represented in it by delegates of their own choice. . . .

George Thompson: . . . Let gentlemen, when they come to vote on this question, remember, that in receiving or rejecting these ladies, they acknowledge or despise [loud cries of No, no]. I ask gentlemen, who shout "no," if they know the application I am about to make. I did not mean to say you would despise the ladies, but that you would, by your vote, acknowledge or despise the parties whose cause they espouse. It appears we are prepared to sanction ladies in the employment of all means, so long as they are confessedly unequal with ourselves. It seems that the grand objection to their appearance amongst us is this, that it would be placing them on a footing of equality, and that would be contrary to principle and custom. For years the women of America have carried their banner in the van, while the men have humbly followed in the rear. It is well known that the National Society solicited Angelina Grimké to undertake a mission through New England, to rouse the attention of the women to the wrongs of slavery, and that that distinguished woman displayed her talents not only in the drawing-room, but before the Senate of Massachusetts. Let us contrast our conduct with that of the Senators and Representatives of Massachusetts who did not disdain to hear her. It was in consequence of her exertions, which received the warmest approval of the National Society, that that interest sprung up which has awakened such an intense feeling throughout America. Then with reference to efficient management, the most vigorous anti-slavery societies are those which are managed by ladies. . . .

Mr. Phillips, being urged on all sides to withdraw his motion, said: It has been hinted very respectfully by two or three speakers that the delegates from the State of Massachusetts should withdraw their credentials, or the motion before the meeting. The one appears to me to be equivalent to the other. If this motion be withdrawn we must have another. I would merely ask whether any man can suppose that the delegates from

Massachusetts or Pennsylvania can take upon their shoulders the responsibility of withdrawing that list of delegates from your table, which their constituents told them to place there, and whom they sanctioned as their fit representatives, because this Convention tells us that it is not ready to meet the ridicule of the morning papers, and to stand up against the customs of England. In America we listen to no such arguments. If we had done so we had never been here as Abolitionists. It is the custom there not to admit colored men into respectable society, and we have been told again and again that we are outraging the decencies of humanity when we permit colored men to sit by our side. When we have submitted to brick-bats, and the tar tub and feathers in America, rather than yield to the custom prevalent there of not admitting colored brethren into our friendship, shall we yield to parallel custom or prejudice against women in Old England? We can not yield this question if we would; for it is a matter of conscience. . . .

James Gillespie Birney: It has been stated that the right of women to sit and act in all respects as men in our anti-slavery associations, was decided in the affirmative at the annual meeting of the American Anti-Slavery Society in May, 1839. It is true the claim was so decided on that occasion, but not by a large majority; whilst it is also true that the majority was swelled by the votes of the women themselves. I have just received a letter from a gentleman in New York (Louis Tappan), communicating the fact, that the persistence of the friends of promiscuous female representation in pressing that practice on the American Anti-Slavery Society, at its annual meeting on the twelfth of last month, had caused such disagreement among the members present, that he and others who viewed the subject as he did, were then deliberating on measures for seceding from the old organization.

Rev. C. Stout: My vote is that we confirm the list of delegates, that we take votes on that as an amendment, and that we henceforth entertain this question no more. Are we not met here pledged to sacrifice all but everything, in order that we may do something against slavery, and shall we be divided on this *paltry question* and suffer the whole tide of benevolence to be stopped by *a straw?* No! You talk of being men, then be men! Consider what is worthy of your attention. . . .

Part III: Reform at High Noon

Some of our anti-slavery people . . . are now purblind with the dust of politics. . . . It blinds them to moral truth and renders them insensible to its power and beauty.

Nathaniel P. Rogers

The day for the multitudes has now arrived.

George Bancroft

[Joseph Smith] decides all the great controversies —infant baptism, ordination, the Trinity . . . the general resurrection . . . and even the question of freemasonry, republican government, and the rights of man.

Alexander Campbell

That *screech* of infidelity is a desperate power against us.

Parker Pillsbury

Reformers in the 1840s dominated events in a fashion unknown before in America even during the Revolution. The riots and sensations caused by abolitionists, particularly in the preceding decade, stirred the country mainly because its established habits of thought and action were being disturbed by radical interpretations of the Bill of Rights. In the 1840s reformers became more than a band or fellowship. They became part of the scene itself, challenging the consciences and prestige of the recognized leaders of society.

Before the decade was finished reformers would destroy Henry Clay's hopes for the Presidency and have tarnished the glory of the Mexican War, though it brought with it great land accessions. And they would have changed the vocabulary of public debate on crucial issues, lending it an unprecedentedly moral tone.

The key to these achievements lay in the interrelatedness of reforms and reformers. Thus, Garrison took an increasingly extreme position not only on slavery but on other unrelated matters. His dogmas, if pursued, would have disrupted the lives of most Americans. The unrealistic quality of his views, therefore, should have isolated him from his countrymen and rendered him insignificant. He not only maintained his sweeping testimony favoring abolition, he also demanded that everyone else do so on pain of being held equally responsible for the infamy of slavery. He repelled those who might have agreed with him, but who could not endure his assaults on the clergy and the Constitution or who were disgusted by his encouragement of women's participation in direct abolitionist activities.

Yet Garrison, far from being submerged in the augmented reformist ranks, remained as vivid a figure of scandal or inspiration as before. To an extent this was because he furnished a convenient scapegoat for proslavery debaters who viewed the North as a ferment of madmen and eccentrics. Even so, it was in the power of Northerners to repudiate Garrison and his brilliant and energetic followers.

Why did they not do so? For one thing, reformers were rarely specialized. Dorothea L. Dix was the one major reformer to avoid opinions affecting slavery so as not to inhibit her work for the sick and imprisoned in the South as in the North. Also, the causes of reformers tended to blend with one another. They were all temperance men and women. A majority of them were Whigs, in fact or in sympathy. Though they might deplore aggressive women in principle, they needed their cooperation and direct aid in the unfolding world of industry and western settlement.

Above all, the more "moderate" approach, especially to abolition, by such conservatives as Birney, the Tappans and the Reverend Elizur Wright, Jr., who came east from the Western Reserve, and dreaming of a mass antislavery movement did not avail them with their foes. Even Salmon P. Chase, who protested that he was a Democrat and not an abolitionist and that he was respectful of both law and the Constitution, even Chase could not appease Ohio proslavery conservatives who were outraged by his legal defenses of fugitive slaves and his patent ambition to curb the expansion of the slaveholders' domain.

Garrison's entire program was moral; hence, a silencing of him posed a threat to all reformers, whether sympathetic to him or not. But more important, the destruction of civil liberties could have no other result but to inculpate Northerners at large in the maintenance of the slavery system. Though the majority of them preferred the great simplicities of conventional religion, politics and custom, they had no stomach for law which threatened personal freedoms—first the black then the white—and which aspired to put a firm lid on experimenters and sharp-tongued agitators.

Finally, there was less of a chasm than might have been expected between the adventurers of society and those of more routine habit. John Humphrey Noyes (1811–1886) recruited his "free love" followers not from the dregs of society or from men and women demoralized by economic or personal tragedy but from traditionally-raised elements which sincerely believed that Noyes, in his rejection of sin and belief in "complex" or multiple marriage, had attained a fresh view of religious truth for which they were prepared to suffer. Their faith enabled them to resist the malice, social pressure and personal danger presented by their less tolerant Oneida, New York, neighbors. Their inspiration enabled them to endure until they had put their community on a working basis.

The "free love" aspect of some reforms (notably those proposed by the Mormons) was one of the sensitive areas in the reform wave of the time but created relatively few problems. Reformers tended as a class to be austere and even sanctimonious in their social habits. They gained conviction by believing that their proposals were not only morally just but constituted improvements over traditional processes. Thus Horace Mann condemned rote studies and prison-like deportment in public schools as failing to communicate moral principles and understanding of academic subjects. Anticapital punishment advocates denied that the death penalty reduced crime. Prison reformers, health faddists, women's rights proponents and those who challenged church ordinances all emphasized that society as a whole would gain by their innovations.

The era sought change on every level and in all pursuits, in the process creating new sciences and pseudosciences which, though often false and inaccurate, were influential in human affairs, sometimes with positive results. Phrenology was a pseudoscience, locating qualities in the brain which were not there. Yet Horace

Mann attributed all he had done to the inspiration it had furnished him. Walt Whitman found revelation regarding his self
and destiny in what phrenologists told him.

The food reformers were on somewhat better ground, if only
because they used common sense, and so aided an age which ate
carelessly and without restraint. The great name in the field was
Sylvester Graham (1784–1851) who began with temperance,
studied anatomy and lectured not only on the evils of drink but
on gluttony. For a brief period, Graham was a sensation. His
Journal of Health and Longevity (1837–1839) preached vegetari-
anism and also exercise, good sleeping habits and sexual continence. His advocacy of home-made bread from unbolted wheat,
with which his name was ultimately identified, angered bakers
who in 1847 during a Boston lecture rioted in protest. Graham's
vogue fell partly because his followers divided and went off in
different directions and partly because he turned more and more
to scriptural endorsement of his views.

The question of who among the warring factions of abolition
were the radicals and who were the conservatives was thoroughly
explored during the 1840s. Garrison held that to enter into politics inevitably diluted the abolitionist's testimony against slavery.
His duty lay, rather, in setting antislavery examples. That meant
welcoming Negroes to abolitionist sessions and promoting such
related freedoms as female participation, independence of
churches (especially those condoning slaveholders) and criticism
of government for the same reasons.

To the political-minded this approach seemed without a
future. In 1838 Birney's *Letter on the Political Obligations of
Abolitionists* opened a new perspective for men of his outlook.
Two years later a number of them launched the Liberty party as
an arm of abolition with Birney as their presidential candidate.
The results seemed catastrophic enough to warrant Garrison's
ridicule. Birney received 7,053 votes in an election which gained

William Henry Harrison the Presidency with 1,275,612 votes. Nevertheless the political abolitionists persisted during years which saw new differences separating North and South. With the Republic of Texas, a slave country, being groomed for entrance into the Union, the times seemed to call for a mediator: one who would appease southern dreams of expansion west and also respect the desire of northern settlers not to have to compete with slave labor.

Thus 1844 seemed clearly the year when Henry Clay, author of the Compromise of 1820, would assume the presidency and seek to promote harmony between the anxious sections. In that close election of 1844 the little Liberty party, offering Birney once more, created a sensation. Its 15,814 votes in New York State defeated the Whig Clay and raised to power his Democratic opponent James K. Polk of Tennessee. The Liberty party had elected an aggressive representative of the slave society.

This was a shocking experience for most Liberty party men, though a few professed to prefer a forthright slavery representative to a Janus-faced Clay. It was an even more shocking blow to Northerners whose minds turned westward, and who feared that slavery partisans would extend their power on the frontier.

They therefore learned a new tolerance of abolitionist "fanatics" and sought out antislavery politicians who would distinguish free soil from abolition. They sent to Congress such picturesque spokesmen as Joshua R. Giddings and Benjamin F. Wade, both from the Western Reserve, who did not challenge the Ohio "Black Laws" restricting the privileges of Negroes, but who resisted the demands of their proslavery peers in Congress. They sent Salmon P. Chase to the capitol of Ohio as governor. From New Hampshire they sent to the United States Senate John P. Hale; at home his abolitionist sentiments had caused him to be read out of the Democratic party. Even more significant appeared to be the growing national reputation of Governor William Henry Seward of New York. His career, though marked by firm adherence to the law, was also colored by reform issues. Also he resisted Southern demands for extradition of fugitive slaves in ways promising to broaden the antislavery political front.

Communication was affected by these developments in the stiffening free soil sentiments of Northern newspapers and the proliferation of moral issues in literary writings. Richard Henry Dana, in his well-received *Two Years before the Mast* (1840), responded with pity to the harsh lot of the seaman subject to masters who were wholly despotic and often brutal. Herman Melville, too, in his sea tales, described the miseries of this despised caste and pondered the role of its Negro component. The Navy and merchant marine drew a notable proportion of Negroes, in part because of the onerous conditions of employment which gave them entree unavailable in more humane occupations. Nathaniel Hawthorne's role in reform was curious. He deplored inhumanity as it had been practiced in the past, regretting the harsh treatment his Puritan ancestors had accorded Quakers and other nonconformists. In the present he was a conservative Democrat and a stipendiary of its organization, to whom reform was an illusion and a breeder of hypocrites.

Numerous others helped touch the sensibilities of their generation with essays, verse and fiction. The poetic genius of reform, however, was James Russell Lowell, whose wit contributed zest to the cordial of moral authority and eloquence offered by Whittier, Wendell Phillips and Lydia Maria Child.

The 1840s produced massive reform figures in various fields. A significant phenomenon of the time was Elihu Burritt (1811–1879), a son of Connecticut farmers who became a blacksmith and a self-taught master of numerous languages including Sanskrit. They taught him the brotherhood of man. He was made famous for his learning by accidental publicity and offered a haven at Harvard College by Henry Wadsworth Longfellow. Burritt declined, to embark instead on a crusade for peace, first through his *Christian Citizen* (1844–1851) at home then abroad where he worked to organize international conferences on peace: pioneer assemblies which influenced all later efforts to set up international safeguards against war's carnage.

As significant was the lengthening career of Horace Mann, who in 1837 gave up an established law and legislative career to work for competence and social goals in education. Mann's courage and moral intensity made him a symbol of the struggle for an education which would preserve Democracy's health. In 1848 he succeeded John Quincy Adams in the House of Representatives and added his own eloquence to the gathering antislavery alliance in the Capital.

Still others helped give dimensions to the struggle for human rights. Thus Thomas A. Devyr, born an Englishman, was a leader in the upstate New York battle to break the colonial leases held by Dutch patroons who resisted the will of their tenants to own the farms they tilled. Although such duels progressed on the level of taxes, suffrage limitations, sheriff's warrants and other emblems of material concern, they involved the future as well as the past. Devyr and his associates were land reformers. As one of them put it: "[T]he Anti-Renter who will not set his face like flint against the recurrence of land monopoly in the West, does not deserve success in his own behalf."[1] The war against perpetual leases ultimately resulted in defiance of the law, the tarring of deputies attempting to serve writs and the shedding of blood, as troops strove to uphold a dying system. Although passion and rhetoric concluded in negotiations for sale of property, the struggle earned its place in the history of equity and American opportunity.

Others in and out of politics helped make the 1840s an era of

1. Henry Christman, *Tin Horns and Calico* (New York: Henry Holt and Company, 1945), p. 168. This study recaptures the color and excitement of the upstate farmer's finest hour: one which freed the area for individual enterprise and directly helped define Free Soil as a major slogan. Some Anti-Renters later helped found the Republican party.

unprecedented demand for reform but none better symbolized its ultimate goals than Frederick Douglass, a fugitive slave whose natural abilities, character and strength of mind soon made it difficult for strangers to credit the fact that he had only recently been a chattel in Maryland subject not only to a master but to mean-minded foremen of slaves. Douglass was sponsored by the Garrisonians and as such displayed his awesome gifts in public, though a fugitive slave and subject to the dangers facing a fugitive slave. Douglass's contributions to the abolitionist crusade were many. He aided other fugitive slaves and published his invaluable *North Star:* a beacon light for Negroes. But his most valuable contribution was himself as exemplified in his immortal response to hecklers at a New York meeting who demanded to know who he was. Said Douglass: "I am a man."

Many factors influenced the course of reform. Of great significance were the feelings of Britishers, some of whom honored slavery but perhaps a majority of whom maintained a prejudice favoring liberty. British Quakers gave aid and comfort to American abolitionists abroad. Thomas Carlyle shocked his admirers by writing down Negroes as inferior and suitable for enslavement. But the main battle was necessarily at home. Abolitionists and reformers were now challenged by a powerful combination of patriots and expansionists. War with Mexico promised a union of Americans based on pride of country and faith in her destiny.

Before leaving office President Tyler brought Texas into the Union. Polk, his successor, aspired to be the greatest of American imperialists, at one time considering not only the purchase or seizure of New Mexico, California, and Oregon—the last an obvious propitiation of northern ambitions—but even the total dismemberment of Mexico. All of this was calculated to "solve" the slavery problem by giving southerners and northerners an endless stretch of frontier territory for expansion.

It was a sign of the state of northern opinion that though it was unable to stop Texas accession, elements in the North, especially in New England, could yet be forceful in opposition to imperialism. Ten years of anti-Texas debate had taught northerners that free soil prospects could be jeopardized. Their arguments derogatory of slavery expansion fitted nicely those in praise of free soil.

Polk had his way with Congress, winning a war budget and a vigorous military establishment which employed soldiers who would later be conspicuous on both the Northern and Southern sides of the Civil War.[2] New England, however, picked up the quarrel on war policy it had nourished during the War of 1812 and once again honored its pacifists as true patriots. And though Polk could point to mighty territorial gains, his willingness to concede to the British part of the enormous Oregon claims struck his northern party cohorts as a betrayal of themselves and the work of a southern rather than a national President. Like Tyler before him, Polk was deserted by his party and could not hope for renomination. His political arms in 1848 stretched just far enough to secure the nomination of a "doughface" northerner willing to reassure southern party managers: General Lewis Cass of Michigan.

Sacrificed in this compromise were the ambitions of Martin Van Buren who had served his party faithfully as politician and as President. He led his embittered New York faction out of the Democratic party and joined hands with Liberty men and politicians of the Northwest states and territories to form the Free Soil party of 1848 and receive its presidential nomination.

Garrisonians were appalled; Van Buren had not only been an antiabolition President, he had cooperated freely with proslavery partisans of every description. Many moderate abolitionists were dismayed. But so steadfast a Liberty man as Joshua Leavitt—one of the party's most active editors and organizers—gave himself fully to the enterprise. As he said, while comrades of past cam-

2. Alfred Hoyt Bill, *Rehearsal for Conflict: the War with Mexico, 1846–1848* (New York: A. A. Knopf, 1947).

paigns searched their consciences for reasons enabling them to support Van Buren, "Mr. Chairman, this is the most solemn experience of my life. I feel as if in the immediate presence of the Divine Spirit."

Van Buren's campaign in 1848—a product of spite rather than principle—revealed the growing consciousness of Free Soilers that they would have to fight for their interests. Van Buren split the Democratic vote, permitting the election of the Whig candidate and war hero Zachary Taylor, a Southerner and slaveholder but also a nationalist unwilling to follow in Polk's imperialist footsteps. Taylor's very lack of political experience served him. A nation fearful of sectional dissent hungered for respite and hoped time would teach it how to quell extremists.

A question raised by this election was the future of abolition. Had Garrison and the old Liberty party been made obsolete? Was the United States entering into an era which could only tolerate equivocal personalities? Would they pretend to seek answers but evade the only one actually available: compensated emancipation which recognized the humanity of Negroes and distributed the burden of writing off slavery with taxes on both North and South?

There was another solution at hand; another Compromise of the 1820 variety: divide the booty of the Mexican War; parcel off gains to North and South; maintain the balance of power. But what would such a program do to reform? Were reformers about to become obsolete, juxtaposed with the great goal of preserving the Union and administering the one million square miles which had been added to the nation?

That same year of 1848—famous as bringing with it revolutions throughout Europe—a new weekly paper was founded in New York City: the *Independent*. Among its ministerial editors was Joshua Leavitt. Intended to carry the message of the Congregational Church, it was supported by businessmen to whom religious institutions were no less important than mercantile. One of them was Henry C. Bowen, a son-in-law of Lewis Tappan. In time Bowen would immortalize himself with a public announcement, while under pressure from others of the business community to enforce a conservative policy respecting slavery. Bowen's business card informed them that he and his firm wished it "distinctly understood that our goods, and not our principles, are on the market."[3]

Significant among Bowen's editors and contributors was Henry Ward Beecher, already famous as the worthy son of a distinguished father and with an eloquence of his own. He had recently come east to head the new Plymouth Church of Brooklyn, New York. His imposing figure and rich voice, and especially his flamboyant style, thrilled his parishioners. He drew readers to the *Independent* with essays which as often touched upon contemporary issues as upon the eternal. Beecher came slowly to abolition, and when he did, he rode upon it rather than directed it. The "Beecher Bibles," which Free Soil sympathizers later sent to Kansas—Sharps rifles—were less a tribute to a minister of vision and fortitude than they were an indication of the widening currents of antislavery opinion in the North. The *Independent* was one of many agencies being formed in the North to defend its way of life. Whatever the fate of reform as such, it supplied the people the arguments, the experience and the character which the national campaigns required and from which such personalities as Beecher would profit.

3. Louis Filler, "Liberalism, Anti-Slavery, and the Founders of the *Independent*," *New England Quarterly*, vol. 27 (Brunswick, Me., 1954), p. 297.

27.

RALPH WALDO EMERSON:
The Dial *Speaks for the Mind*

Ralph Waldo Emerson (1803–1882) was the intellectual voice of his generation. No other person sought so persistently to find the essence of personal expression and eternal goals. Others offered more tangible guides to change. Thoreau experimented with living, Bronson Alcott with education and Margaret Fuller with the uses of literature. Many seekers gave of themselves to whole communities, notably Brook Farm. But none so firmly grappled with the mystery of form and freedom. Emerson broke the Puritan cast to assert the rights of the individual. Guided by faith in the human potential, he declared confidence in his intuitions. His essay "Self-Reliance" swept past family, charity, society and religion in pursuit of self. Transcendentalism, the Emerson mystique of God and good, directly affected only a few persons, but it distilled one essence of what inspired numerous workers in more mundane circumstances. Emerson's courage and sincerity caused him to acknowledge Walt Whitman, though the latter's style of living differed drastically from Emerson's. The following statement of intentions appeared in the first issue of the Transcendentalist Dial, *July 1840. Though first drawn up by Margaret Fuller, it was all but rewritten by Emerson and spoke his mind as well as that of his followers.*

We invite the attention of our countrymen to a new design. Probably not quite unexpected or unannounced will our Journal appear, though small pains have been taken to secure its wel-

SOURCE: *The Dial,* July 1840, pp. 1–4.

come. Those, who have immediately acted in editing the present Number, cannot accuse themselves of any unbecoming forwardness in their undertaking, but rather of a backwardness, when they remember how often in many private circles the work was projected, how eagerly desired, and only postponed because no individual volunteered to combine and concentrate the freewill offerings of many coöperators. With some reluctance the present conductors of this work have yielded themselves to the wishes of their friends, finding something sacred and not to be withstood in the importunity which urged the production of a Journal in a new spirit.

As they have not proposed themselves to the work, neither can they lay any the least claim to an option or determination of the spirit in which it is conceived, or to what is peculiar in the design. In that respect, they have obeyed, though with great joy, the strong current of thought and feeling, which, for a few years past, has led many sincere persons in New England to make new demands on literature, and to reprobate that rigor of our conventions of religion and education which is turning us to stone, which renounces hope, which looks only backward, which asks only such a future as the past, which suspects improvement, and holds nothing so much in horror as new views and the dreams of youth.

With these terrors the conductors of the present Journal have nothing to do,—not even so much as a word of reproach to waste. They know that there is a portion of the youth and of the adult population of this country, who have not shared them; who have in secret or in public paid their vows to truth and freedom; who love reality too well to care for names, and who live by a faith too earnest and profound to suffer them to doubt the eternity of its object or to shake themselves free from its authority. Under the fictions and customs which occupied others, these have explored the Necessary, the Plain, the True, the Human,— and so gained a vantage ground, which commands the history of the past and the present.

No one can converse much with different classes of society in New England, without remarking the progress of a revolution. Those who share in it have no external organization, no badge, no creed, no name. They do not vote, or print, or even meet together. They do not know each other's faces or names. They are united only in a common love of truth and love of its work. They are of all conditions and constitutions. Of these acolytes, if some are happily born and well bred, many are no doubt ill dressed, ill placed, ill made—with as many scars of hereditary vice as other men. Without pomp, without trumpet, in lonely and obscure places, in solitude, in servitude, in compunctions and privations, trudging beside the team in the dusty road, or drudging a hireling in other men's cornfields, schoolmasters, who teach a few children rudiments for a pittance, ministers of small parishes of the obscurer sects, lone women in dependent condition, matrons and young maidens, rich and poor, beautiful and hard-favored, without concert or proclamation of any kind, they have silently given in their several adherence to a new hope, and in all companies do signify a greater trust in the nature and resources of man, than the laws or the popular opinions will well allow.

This spirit of the time is felt by every individual with some difference,—to each one casting its light upon the objects nearest to his temper and habits of thought;—to one, coming in the shape of special reforms in the state; to another, in modifications of the various callings of men, and the customs of business; to a third, opening a new scope for literature and art; to a fourth, in philosophical insight; to a fifth, in the vast solitudes of prayer. It is in every form a protest against usage, and a search for principles. In all its movements, it is peaceable, and in the very lowest marked with a triumphant success. Of course, it rouses the opposition of all which it judges and condemns, but it is too confident in its tone to comprehend an objection, and so builds no outworks for possible defence against contingent enemies. It has the step of Fate, and goes on existing like an oak or a river, because it must.

In literature, this influence appears not yet in new books so much as in the higher tone of criticism. The antidote to all narrowness is the comparison of the record with nature, which at once shames the record and stimulates to new attempts. Whilst we look at this, we wonder how any book has been thought worthy to be preserved. There is somewhat in all life untranslatable into language. He who keeps his eye on that will write better than others, and think less of his writing, and of all writing. Every thought has a certain imprisoning as well as uplifting quality, and, in proportion to its energy on the will, refuses to become an object of intellectual contemplation. Thus what is great usually slips through our fingers, and it seems wonderful how a life-like word ever comes to be written. If our Journal share the impulses of the time, it cannot now prescribe its own course. It cannot foretell in orderly propositions what it shall attempt. All criticism should be poetic; unpredictable; superseding, as every new thought does, all foregone thoughts, and making a new light on the whole world. Its brow is not wrinkled with circumspection, but serene, cheerful, adoring. It has all things to say, and no less than all the world for its final audience.

Our plan embraces much more than criticism; were it not so, our criticism would be naught. Everything noble is directed on life, and this is. We do not wish to say pretty or curious things, or to reiterate a few propositions in varied forms, but, if we can, to give expression to that spirit which lifts men to a higher platform, restores to them the religious sentiment, brings them worthy aims and pure pleasures, purges the inward eye, makes life less desultory, and, though raising men to the level of nature, takes away its melancholy from the landscape, and reconciles the practical with the speculative powers.

But perhaps we are telling our little story too gravely. There are always great arguments at hand for a true action, even for the writing of a few pages. There is nothing but seems near it and prompts it,—the sphere in the ecliptic, the sap in the apple tree,—every fact, every appearance seem to persuade to it. . . .

28.

FREDERICK DOUGLASS:
"We . . . bid the women . . . our humble godspeed"

The fight for women's rights resulted in a torrent of eloquence and argument bearing on legal, social, economic and human conditions. Much of it has historical rather than intrinsic appeal. (Thus the argument that women's winning of suffrage would elevate and enrich politics was not borne out by events.) Nevertheless a host of varied and remarkable women came into public view by way of temperance, antislavery and other causes; they achieved their milestone in the Seneca Falls (New York) Convention of 1848. As the women were vital to other crusades of the time, so the support of numerous male reformers was indispensable to advancing the women's fight. Frederick Douglass's expression of sympathy for the Seneca Falls meeting illustrated his keen sense of the indivisibility of reform efforts. It was origially printed in his North Star.

One of the most interesting events of the past week, was the holding of what is technically styled a Woman's Rights Convention at Seneca Falls. The speaking, addresses, and resolutions of this extraordinary meeting was almost wholly conducted by women; and although they evidently felt themselves in a novel position, it is but simple justice to say that their whole proceedings were characterized by marked ability and dignity. No one present, we think, however much he might be disposed to differ from the views advanced by the leading speakers on that occa-

SOURCE: *The North Star* (Rochester, N.Y.), July 28, 1848.

sion, will fail to give them credit for brilliant talents and excellent dispositions. In this meeting, as in other deliberative assemblies, there were frequent differences of opinion and animated discussion; but in no case was there the slightest absence of good feeling and decorum. Several interesting documents setting forth the rights as well as the grievances of women were read. Among these was a Declaration of Sentiments, to be regarded as the basis of a grand movement for attaining the civil, social, political, and religious rights of women. We should not do justice to our own convictions, or to the excellent persons connected with this infant movement, if we did not in this connection offer a few remarks on the general subject which the Convention met to consider and the objects they seek to attain. In doing so, we are not insensible that the bare mention of this truly important subject in any other than terms of contemptuous ridicule and scornful disfavor, is likely to excite against us the fury of bigotry and the folly of prejudice. A discussion of the rights of animals would be regarded with far more complacency by many of what are called the *wise* and the *good* of our land, than would a discussion of the rights of women. It is, in their estimation, to be guilty of evil thoughts, to think that woman is entitled to equal rights with man. Many who have at last made the discovery that the Negroes have some rights as well as other members of the human family, have yet to be convinced that women are entitled to any. Eight years ago a number of persons of this description actually abandoned the anti-slavery cause, lest by giving their influence in that direction they might possibly be giving countenance to the dangerous heresy that woman, in respect to rights, stands on an equal footing with man. In the judgment of such persons the American slave system, with all its concomitant horrors, is less to be deplored than this *wicked* idea. It is perhaps needless to say, that we cherish little sympathy for such sentiments or respect for such prejudices. Standing as we do upon the watch-tower of human freedom, we cannot be deterred from an expression of our approbation of any movement, however

29.

NATHANIEL PEABODY ROGERS:
A *Dissenter of Dissenters*

Nathaniel Peabody Rogers (1794–1846) became a well-respected symbol of the drastic insistence on self which characterized the age. A Dartmouth College graduate and New Hampshire lawyer, he turned from commercial pursuits in 1838 to edit The Herald of Freedom, *a journal dedicated to abolition and universal reform, from which the following selection is taken. Rogers's foe was "Authority," which he found everywhere and finally even among the ardent spirits of Garrisonianism, whom he resisted as he did all threats to his free will and understanding. Thoreau, in* The Dial, *hailed his "genuine Yankee style" and the "unpledged poetry in his prose."*

It is high time this old Incubus [of Authority] were in the sepulchre. It has long enough been the great bug-bear to frighten the spirit of Reform—the giant scare-crow, looming by the road-side of human advancement. And it has long enough flapped its bat-looking wings in the eyes of the anti-slavery movement. It has stood across our path-way in every Protean variety of alarming shape. It has towered before us in the form of "Glorious Constitutions," and "Happy and inviolable Unions;" of "Compromises," and "Guarantees," and "Revolutionary Fathers." The creatures of slavery, all of them, in all that makes them important to the question. The people are getting accustomed to these *sights,* and can almost look these forms of authority steadily in

SOURCE: *A Collection from the Newspaper Writings of Nathaniel Peabody Rogers* (Concord, N.H.: J. R. French, 1847), pp. 280–281.

the face. But Authority has showed itself in the more awful apparition of THE CHURCH, with her dreadful array of Sabbaths and Sanctuaries and Sacraments and Priesthood. With these she has reared herself up across our anti-slavery path, and with hollow admonitions warned us to go back. Her Priesthood have had a Book, now getting into the hands of the people under the requirements of the age—out of which they read the warrant of man to enslave his brother, and God's express command as well as permission for the damnable deed. The Book was handed down from God out of a cloud, on some mountain top half hid in thunder—to some one of "the world's gray fathers"—and so far back in time, that the age itself when it occurred, has become clothed with a kind of prescriptive divinity. Religion pictured the awful tradition—even at this period of the world—respecting the half-seen hand of the Almighty, as the hand of a man, reaching down the terrible trust out of a black cloud, to the implicit and awe-struck receiver, who is honored as the messenger of God to the trembling race. With such pictures as this, does doctorated and learned divinity play upon the apprehensions of the people, and mould their worship. The Book is at length in the hands of the People—but not to be read. They may open it and perform out of it their religious services—but it can be read by the priests alone. For an ordained and learned Priesthood are held necessary to the interpretation of the Book to the people, and to their being instructed in its doctrines. The people can read—and the Bible is amply in their hands. Yet it abates not at all the necessity of an interpreting Priesthood. . . .

The Priest reads out of it that man may enslave and butcher his brother—and the Church receives and inculcates his teachings—and the abolitionist or friend of peace who gainsays the frightful inculcation, is silenced by being branded as an infidel and fanatic. . . .

[of education] has been held. The human mind is so constituted that it cannot embrace any great idea, but, forthwith, all the faculties strive to aggrandize and adorn and dignify it. Let any principle or sentiment be elevated by the public voice,—whether rightfully or wrongfully,—to a station of pre-eminence or grandeur, in the eyes of men, and it is at once personified, and, as it were, consecrated. The arts go, as on a pilgrimage, to do it reverence. Music celebrates it in national songs. Sculpture embodies it in enduring substance, and clothes it in impressive forms. . . .

Without one word from the historian, and only by studying a people's relics, and investigating the figurative expressions in their literature and law, one might see reflected, as from a mirror, the moral scale on which they arranged their idea of good and great. Though history should not record a single line in testimony of the fact, yet who, a thousand years hence, could fail to read, in their symbols, in their forms of speech, and in the technical terms of their law, the money-getting, money-worshipping tendencies of all commercial nations, during the last and the present centuries? The word "sovereign," we know, means a potentate invested with lawful dignity and authority; and it implies subjects who are bound to honor and obey. Hence, in Great Britain, a gold coin, worth twenty shillings, is called a *"sovereign;"* and happy is the political sovereign who enjoys such plenitude of power and majesty, and has so many loyal and devoted subjects as this vicegerent of royalty. An ancient English coin was called an *angel*. Its value was only ten shillings, and yet it was named after a messenger from heaven. In the Scriptures, and in political law, a *crown* is the emblem and personification of might and majesty, of glory and blessedness. The synonym of all these is a piece of silver worth six shillings and seven pence. As the king has his representative in a sovereign, so a duke has his in a ducat,—the inferior value of the latter corresponding with the inferior dignity of its archetype. As Napoleon was considered the mightiest ruler that France ever knew, so, for many years, her highest coin was called a *Napoleon;* though now, in the French mint, they strike double-Napoleons. God grant that the world may never see a double-Napoleon of flesh and blood! Our fore-fathers subjected themselves to every worldly privation for the sake of liberty,—and when they had heroically endured toil and sacrifice for eight long years,—and at last achieved the blessing of independence,—they showed their veneration for the Genius of Liberty by placing its image and superscription—upon a *cent!* . . .

I group together a few of these extraordinary facts, my friends, to illustrate the irresistible tendency of the human mind to dig-nify, honor, elevate, aggrandize, and even sanctify, whatever it truly respects and values. But education,—that synonym of mortal misery and happiness; that abbreviation for earth and heaven and hell,—where are the conscious or unconscious testi-monials to its worth? What honorable, laudatory epithets, what titles of enconium or of dignity, have been bestowed upon its professors? What, save such titles as pedagogue, (which, among the Romans, from whom we derived it, meant a slave,) and pedant, and knight of the birch and ferrule? What sincere or single offering has it received from the hand or voice of genius? Traverse the long galleries of art, and you will discover no tribute to its worth. Listen to all the great masters of music, and you will hear no swelling notes or chorus in its praise. Search all the volumes of all the poets, and you will rarely find a respectful mention of its claims, or even a recognition of its existence. . . .

Both in Europe and in this country, scientific institutions have been founded, and illustrious men, during successive ages, poured the collected light of their effulgent minds upon other departments of science and of art,—upon language, astronomy, light, heat, electricity, tides, meteors, and so forth, and so forth. Such were the Royal Academy of Sciences, in Paris, founded in 1660; the Royal Society of England, founded in 1663; and the American Academy of Arts and Sciences, founded in 1780;—and what ponderous volumes of reports, essays, and transactions, they have published! But when or where have a nation's sages met in council to investigate the principles and to discuss the modes by which that most difficult and delicate work upon earth,—the education of a human soul,—should be conducted? Yet what is there in philology, or the principles of universal grammar; what is there in the ebb and flow of tides, in the shooting of meteors, or in the motions of the planetary bodies;— what is there, in fine, in the corporeal and insensate elements of the earth beneath, or of the firmament above, at all comparable in importance to those laws of growth and that course of training, by which the destiny of mortal and immortal spirits is at least foretokened, if not foredoomed?

So, too, in regard to those ancient and renowned literary institutions, which have been established and upheld by the foremost nations of Christendom,—the Sorbonne in France; the universities of Oxford and Cambridge and Edinburgh, in Great Britain; and the universities and colleges of this country,—the grand object of all these institutions has been, not to educate the general, the common mass of mind, but to rear up men for the three learned professions (as they are called), Physics, Law, and Divinity. For this comparatively narrow and special purpose, vast legislative endowments and munificent private donations have been made, and the highest talents have been called from the community, for presidentships and professorships. . . .

When the law of hereditary distempers shall be as profoundly investigated as the law which regulates the hereditary transmission of property, then may we expect some improvement in the health and robustness and beauty of the race. Compare all the books written on the transmission from parents to children of physical or moral qualities with the law-books and treatises on the descent of estates. When will the current of public opinion, or the stimulus of professional emolument, create a desire to understand the irreversible ordinances and statutes of Nature, on this class of subjects, as strong as that which now carries a student at law through Fearne on Contingent Remainders?—a book which requires the same faculty for divining ideas, that Champollion had for deciphering Egyptian Hieroglyphics.

And how is it with the clerical profession? They enter upon the work of reforming the human character,—not at the earlier stages of its development,—but when it has arrived at, or is approaching to, its maturity;—a period, when, by universal consent, it has become almost unchangeable by secondary causes. They are reformers, I admit, but in regard to any thing that *grows,* one right *former* will accomplish more than a thousand *re*-formers. It is their sacred mission to prepare a vineyard for the Lord, to dress it, and make it fruitful; but I think no one will say that an army of laborers, sent into a vineyard at midsummer, when brambles and thorns have already choked the vines, and the hedges have been broken down, and the unclean beasts of the forest have made their lair therein;—I think no one will say that an army of laborers, entering the vineyard at such a time, will be able to make it yield so abundant a harvest as one faithful, skilful servant would do, who should commence his labors in the spring-time of the year.

The Constitution of the United States makes no provision for the education of the people; and in the Convention that framed it, I believe the subject was not even mentioned. A motion to insert a clause providing for the establishment of a national university was voted down. I believe it is also the fact, that the Constitutions of only *three* of the thirteen original States made the obligation to maintain a system of Free Schools a part of their fundamental law.

On what grounds of reason or of hope, it may well be asked, did the framers of our National and State Constitutions expect that the future citizens of this Republic would be able to sustain the institutions, or to enjoy the blessings, provided for them? And has not all our subsequent history shown the calamitous consequences of their failing to make provision for the educational wants of the nation? Suppose it had been provided, that no person should be a voter who could not read or write, and also that no State should be admitted into the Union which had not established a system of Free Schools for all its people; would not our National history and legislation, our State administrations and policy, have felt the change through all their annals? Great and good men though they were, yet this truth, now so plain and conspicuous, eluded their sagacity. They did not reflect that, in the common course of nature, all the learned and the wise and the virtuous are swept from the stage of action almost as soon as they become learned and wise and virtuous; and that they are succeeded by a generation who come into the world wholly devoid of learning and wisdom and virtue. The parents may have sought out the sublimest truths, but these truths are nothing to the children, until their minds also shall have been raised to the power of grasping and of understanding them. The truths, indeed, are immortal, but the beings who may embrace them are mortal, and pass away, to be followed by new minds, ignorant, weak, erring, tossed hither and thither on the waves of passion. Hence, each new generation must learn all truth anew, and for itself. Each generation must be able to comprehend the principles, and must rise to the practice of the virtues, requisite to sustain the position of their ancestors; and the first generation which fails to do this, loses all, and comes to ruin not only for itself but for its successors.

At what time, then, by virtue of what means, is the new generation to become competent to take upon itself the duties of the old and retiring one? At which of Shakespeare's "Seven Ages" is the new generation expected to possess the ability to stand in the places of the departed? Allow that the vast concerns of our society must be submitted to a democracy,—still, shall they be submitted to the democracy of babyhood,—to those whose country, as yet, is the cradle, and whose universe the nursery? Can you call in children from trundling hoops and catching butterflies, organize them into "Young Men's Conventions," and propound for their decision the great questions of judicature and legislation, of civil, domestic, and foreign policy? Or will you take the youth of the land, from sixteen to twenty-one years of age, in the heyday of their blood, with passions unappeasable in their cry for indulgence, and unquenchable by it; without experience, without sobriety of judgment; whose only notions of the complex structure of our government and of its various and delicate relations have been derived from hearing a Fourth-of-July Oration; with no knowledge of this multiform world into which they have been brought, or of their dangers, duties and destiny, as men,—in one word, with no education,—and is it to such as these that the vast concernments of a nation's well-being can be safely intrusted? . . .

I will never cease to protest that I am not bringing forward these facts for the purpose of criminating the motives, or of invoking retribution upon the conduct of any one. My sole and exclusive object is to show to what menial rank the majesty of this cause has been degraded;—to show that the affections of this community are not clustered around it; that it is not the treasure which their hearts love and their hands guard;—in fine, that the sublime idea of a generous and universal education, as the appointed means, in the hands of Providence, for restoring mankind to a greater similitude to their Divine Original, is but dawning upon the public mind. . . .

31.

ALBERT BRISBANE:
"The Palace of the Collective Man"

Albert Brisbane (1809–1890) was an interpreter of the French utopian Charles Fourier, but in introducing the latter's collectivist ideas to Americans, Brisbane molded them to his own thinking. Half of the volume which Brisbane gave over to his translation of Fourier's The Social Destiny of Man *(1857) was composed of Brisbane's own views on the treatise's plan and implications, of which the following is an example. John Humphrey Noyes, in his* History of American Socialisms, *criticized Brisbane for having spent too much time in the 1840s and 1850s in "drumming and recruiting," rather than in helping to supervise experiments and sharing blame for their failures.*

The Association or Collective Man, composed of its eighteen hundred individual Souls, would require for its field of operations a tract of land about three miles square. This domain would be laid out in fields, gardens, orchards, vineyards, parks, lawns, meadows, woodlands, etc., according to the nature of the soil and the industrial requirements of the Association. In the centre of the domain, a vast Unitary Edifice, a Palace complete in all its appointments, would be erected, serving as the residence of the Associates. This edifice should be planned throughout in conformity with the wants and requirements—material, social, and intellectual—of the Collective Man who is to inhabit it. In conformity with the principle in Nature which coördinates the

SOURCE: Albert Brisbane, *The Social Destiny of Man* . . . (New York: Robert M. DeWitt . . . Calvin Blanchard . . . , 1857), pp. 137–143.

Material and the Spiritual—as illustrated in the co-relation and unity of the body and the soul—the Palace of the Association should be an Architectural Organism perfectly adapted in its distribution and arrangements to the nature and requirements of the Collective Soul that is to inhabit it. We will point out some of the main features of the correspondence which should exist between the Collective Man and his abode.

The Palace of an Association will consist of three great divisions—a Centre and two Wings—forming a Series, and corresponding to the three-fold nature of Man, or to the three classes of Passions—the Material, the Social, and the Intellectual. The Centre of the Palace will correspond to the Social principle or element in Man; it will be devoted to uses, functions, pleasures, etc., of a social character—that is, to the service of the four cardinal Passions. In it will be located the banquet-halls, the halls of reception, the grand saloons, the ball-rooms, and the *Courts of the four Social Passions*. All social relations and pleasures of a collective character will be here concentrated; it will form so to say the Heart of the Edifice.

In one of the Wings will be located some of the workshops or Halls of Industry—those in which branches of manufactures and mechanics of a light and refined character are prosecuted; the heavier branches will be carried on in separate buildings adjoining the palace. In this Wing will be located also the industrial schools, so as not to disturb the other parts of the edifice. This Wing will represent the material or industrial element in Man. The other Wing will be devoted to the intellectual and scientific pursuits and functions of the Association; here will be located the reading-rooms, the library, the scientific collections, the museum, the university, and the studios of the artists: it will represent the intellectual element in human nature.

Thus the Palace of the Collective Man will correspond to the three great divisions of human life and activity, namely, the Industrial, the Social, and the Intellectual.

The private apartments of the members of the Association will be distributed through the upper stories of the entire palace: they will be of various sizes, with proportional rents, so as to suit all degrees of fortune, and all varieties of taste.

Architectural unity requires that all parts of the Edifice should be connected; in consequence, a spacious corridor or gallery, an enclosed piazza, will extend along the whole of one of the fronts of the Palace; by means of this covered communication, which will be spacious and elegant and decorated with works of art, persons will be able to go to all parts of the edifice with ease and facility, and without exposure to the inclemency of the weather or to sudden changes of temperature, which cause an incredible amount of disease under our present defective architectural arrangements. This spacious and elegant Corridor, of the entire height of the building and lighted by wide and lofty windows, will be one of the charms of the Palace of the Association; it will serve at times for exhibitions of works of Art, for horticultural displays, and other collective purposes.

A winter garden, planted with evergreens and exotic plants, and containing the green-houses, will be located in the rear of the central portion of the edifice.

At one end of the Palace will be erected the TEMPLES OF MATERIAL HARMONIES, in which the seven following branches of Material Art, in all the variety and magnificence of which they are susceptible, will be represented:—

1. SINGING, or measured vocal sounds.
2. INSTRUMENTAL MUSIC, or measured artificial sounds.
3. POETRY, or measured language.
4. PANTOMIME, or measured expression.
5. DANCING, or measured movement.
6. GYMNASTICS, or measured action.
7. PAINTING, or measured decoration.

PIVOT.—MEASURED MECHANICAL DISTRIBUTION, AND MEASURED
     COÖPERATION OF BOTH SEXES AND ALL AGES.

The nearest approach in the present Order to the Temple of Material Harmonies, is the Opera. The Opera, however, is merely a place of amusement, or considered in its best aspect, a means of developing one Sense, that of Hearing. The Temple of Material Harmony in the Combined Order will be a school of Universal Art; in it will be presented under the form of material emblems and harmonies the highest conceptions of the intellect; it will be a powerful auxiliary in educating the spiritual Passions through the medium of the Senses.

At the other extreme of the Palace will be located the TEMPLE OF UNITYISM in which Man will celebrate by appropriate rites and symbols, his Unity with the Universe, his association with universal life and harmony.

On the summit of the Edifice will be placed the observatory, telegraph, and signal-tower. From this point, communications with all parts of the domain and with neighboring associations, take place.

In the vicinity of the Palace will be located the granaries, stables, warehouses, manufactories, and other buildings which for various reasons require to be kept separate from the residence of the Association. . . .

UNITARY DOMESTIC ARRANGEMENTS—KITCHENS, NURSERIES, HEATING, LIGHTING, ETC.

The waste, incoherence, and complication of the present System will disappear in the Combined Order. An Association of eighteen hundred persons—equal to say three hundred families—would not have three hundred kitchens, three hundred kitchenfires, three hundred sets of cooking utensils, and prepare three hundred separate meals as three hundred families now do. The Association would have one vast and well-organized kitchen, divided into four or five compartments for the different kinds of culinary preparations, with four or five fires, and the requisite number of skilful cooks, occupied alternately and devoted to a special function. The kitchen of an Association would be fitted up with elegance and with every convenience; machinery and processes of every kind that can abridge or save labor will be introduced, so that culinary occupations will be simplified, and freed from the drudgery now connected with them. Those only who have an Attraction for the function will engage in it, and as their number will be comparatively small, the remuneration will be liberal. By these and other means, culinary labor will, in Association, be rendered honorable and attractive like other industrial occupations; it certainly should be, for the culinary art is one of the most useful and important to man.

The economies and collective arrangements introduced into the cooking department, will be introduced into all other departments of domestic labor, among others, into the Laundry, where a few large vats with proper machinery will take the place of the three hundred little wash-tubs of three hundred isolated households.

In connection with the subject of the Combined Kitchen of Association, we will remark that it is the primary practical condition of the *Emancipation of Woman*—her emancipation from pecuniary dependence on man, from domestic servitude, and from a low sphere of action. Efforts are being made to secure to Woman the rights which belong to her as an independent and rational being, and to elevate her to her true position. This subject may be discussed theoretically, but no important practical reform in this direction is possible so long as the isolated household and the isolated kitchen exist. Woman, or one half of the adult portion of the Human Race, must, under our present domestic arrangements, be absorbed in the petty details of the isolated household—in the kitchen, at the wash-tub, etc.—must spend her life in domestic drudgery and servitude, and be dependant upon Man for her support. If woman were taken out of the kitchen, man would have to take her place, for *the work must be done;* he would, then, sink into the condition in which woman is now placed.

If Woman would emancipate herself from domestic servitude, from dependence on Man, from inferiority of position, and from her present restricted and subordinate sphere of action, the isolated household and kitchen must be abolished, and the combined household and kitchen substituted in their place. In the vast kitchen of an Association, supplied with every variety of labor-saving machinery, thirty women would do the work which now absorbs three hundred; by this means two hundred and seventy would at once be set at liberty and be placed in a position to devote themselves to more useful, productive, elevating, and intellectual pursuits, while the thirty who remained, having an attraction for culinary functions, and working but a few hours a day at some special branch, in a spacious and elegant kitchen, and being well remunerated for their services, would find themselves in an independent and congenial position.

If Woman would free herself from the trammels which now bind her, if she would secure her pecuniary independence and would elevate herself to her true position, she must begin with abolishing the isolated household and the separate kitchen. She must set on foot a Reform which will descend to the pots, kettles, and wash-tubs of the domestic den, which are so many clogs from which she must first free herself as the preliminary condition of her emancipation and improvement. . . .

32.

A. J. MACDONALD:

A Communitarian Failure: Sylvania

The first of the Fourierite-style "Phalanxes" was initiated in 1843 in Pennsylvania with bright promises and the support of Brisbane and Greeley. It was intended to create new avenues of expression and social advancement for New York mechanics, and solicited philanthropic and other support. The reality fell far short of the prospectus. The following is from notes collected by a disappointed Owenite, A. J. Macdonald, who circulated among communitarians to learn the details of their experiences. John Humphrey Noyes consulted these notes while preparing his own History of American Socialisms.

B.—Good morning, Mr. A. I perceive you are busy among your papers. I hope we do not disturb you?

A.—Not in the least, sir. I am much pleased to meet you.

B.—I wish to introduce to you my friend Mr.C. He is anxious to learn something concerning the experiment in which you were engaged in Pike County, Pennsylvania, and I presumed that you would be willing to furnish him with the desired information.

A.—I suppose, Mr. C., like many others, you are doubtful about the correctness of the reports you have heard concerning these Associations.

C.—Yes, sir: but I am endeavoring to discover the truth, and particularly in relation to the causes which produce so many failures. I find thus far in my investigations, that the difficulties

SOURCE: John Humphrey Noyes, *History of American Socialisms* (Philadelphia: J. B. Lippincott & Co., 1870), pp. 239 ff.

which all Associations have to contend with, are very similar in their character. Pray, sir, how and where did the Sylvania Association originate?

A.—It originated partly in New York City and partly in Albany, in the winter of 1842–3. We first held meetings in Albany, and agitated the subject of Socialism till we formed an Association. Our original object was to read and explain the doctrines of Charles Fourier, the French Socialist; to have lectures delivered, and arouse public attention to the consideration of those social questions which appeared to us, in our new-born zeal, to have an important bearing upon the present, and more especially upon the future welfare of the human family. In this we partly succeeded, and had arrived at the point where it appeared necessary for us to think of practically carrying out those splendid views which we had hitherto been dreaming and talking about. Hearing of a similar movement going on in New York City, we communicated with them and ascertained that they thought precisely as we did concerning immediate and practical operations. After several communications the two bodies united, with a determination to vent their enthusiasm upon the land. Our New York friends appointed a committee of three persons to select a desirable location, and report at the next meeting of the Society.

C.—What were the qualifications of the men who were appointed to select the location? I think this very important.

A.—One was a landscape painter, another an industrious cooper, and the third was a homœpathic doctor!

C.—And not a farmer among them! Well, this must have been a great mistake. At what season did they go to examine the country?

A.—I think it was in March; I am sure it was before the snow was off the ground.

C.—How unhappy are the working classes in having so little patience. Every thing they attempt seems to fail because they will not wait the right time. Had you any capitalists among you?

A.—No; they were principally working people, brought up to a city life.

C.—But you encouraged capitalists to join your society?

A.—Our constitution provided for them as well as laborers. We wished to combine capital and labor, according to the theory laid down by Charles Fourier.

C.—Was his theory the society's practice?

A.—No; there was infinite difference between his theory and our practice. This is generally the case in such movements, and invariably produces disappointment and unhappiness.

C.—Does this not result from ignorance of the principles, or a want of faith in them?

A.—To some extent it does. If human beings were passive bodies, and we could place them just where we pleased, we might so arrange them that their actions would be harmonious. But they are not so. We are active beings; and the Sylvanians were not only very active, but were collected from a variety of situations least likely to produce harmonious beings. If we knew mathematically the laws which regulate the actions of human beings, it is possible we might place all men in true relation to each other.

C.—Working people seem to know no patience other than that of enduring the everlasting toil to which they are brought up. But about the committee which you say consisted of an artist, mechanic and a doctor; what report did they make concerning the land?

A.—They reported favorably of a section of land in Pike County, Pennsylvania, consisting of about 2,394 acres, partly wooded with yellow pine and small oak trees, with a soil of yellow loam without lime. It was well watered, had an undulating surface, and was said to be elevated fifteen hundred feet above the Hudson river. To reach it from New York and Albany, we had to take our things first to Rondout on the Hudson, and thence by canal to Lackawanna; then five miles up hill on a bad stony road. There was plenty of stone for building purposes lying all over the land. The soil being covered with snow, the committee did not see it, but from the small size of the trees, they probably judged it would be easily cleared, which would be a great advantage to citychoppers. Nine thousand dollars was the price demanded for this place, and the society concluded to take it.

C.—What improvements were upon it, and what were the conditions of sale?

A.—There were about thirty acres planted with rye, which grain, I understood, had been successively planted upon it for six years without any manure. This was taken as a proof of the strength of the soil; but when we reaped, we were compelled to rake for ten yards on each side of the spot where we intended to make the bundle, before we had sufficient to tie together. There were three old houses on the place; a good barn and cowshed; a grist-mill without machinery, with a good stream for water-power; an old saw-mill, with a very indifferent water-wheel. These, together with several skeletons of what had once been horses, constituted the stock and improvements. We were to pay $1,000 down in cash; the owner was to put in $1,000 as stock, and the balance was to be paid by annual instalments.

C.—How much stock did the members take?

A.—To state the exact amount would be somewhat difficult; for some who subscribed liberally at first, withdrew their subscriptions, while others increased them. On examining my papers, I reckon that in Albany there were about $4,500 subscribed in money and useful articles for mechanical and other purposes. In New York I should estimate that about $6,000 were subscribed in like proportions.

C.—When did the members proceed to the domain, and how did they progress there?

A.—They left New York and Albany for the domain about the beginning of May; and I find from a table I kept of the number of persons, with their ages, sex and occupations, that in the following August there were on the place twenty-eight married men, twenty-seven married women, twenty-four single young men, six single young women, and fifty-one children; making a total of one hundred and thirty-six individuals. These had to be closely packed in three very indifferent two-story frame houses. The upper story of the grist-mill was devoted to as many as could sleep there. These arrangements very soon brought trouble. Children with every variety of temper and habits, were brought in close contact, without any previous training to prepare them for it. . . .

C.—How long did the Association remain on the place?

A.—About a year and a half, and then it was abandoned as rapidly as it was settled. . . .

C.—It appears to me that your society, like many others, lacked a sufficient amount of intelligence, or they never would have sent such a committee to select a domain; and after the domain was selected, sent so many persons to live upon it so soon. Your means were totally inadequate to carry out the undertaking, and you had by far too many children upon the domain. There should have been no children sent there, until ample means had been secured for their care and education under the superintendence of competent persons.

A.—It is difficult to get any but married men and women to endure the hardships consequent on such an experiment. Single young men, unless under some military control, have not the perseverance of married men. . . .

33.

JOHN VAN DER ZEE SEARS:
A Communitarian Success: Brook Farm

Brook Farm symbolized the great effort of community living in the 1840s and 1850s. This was partly because of the varied and famous personalities it attracted, partly because of the unity Brook Farmers achieved and partly because of the writings which memorialized the venture. Hawthorne was of two minds about Brook Farm. It drew him, yet he left it because it infringed upon his solitude. His Blithedale Romance *(1852) derogated reform and Brook Farm. Yet he recalled his stay there as a moving episode in his life. Orestes A. Brownson, Margaret Fuller, Emerson and others visited and contributed to Brook Farm's activities and fame. It was begun in 1841 by the Reverend George Ripley (1802–1880) at West Roxbury, nine miles from Boston. Its major impulse was Transcendental and religious. In 1845 it became a Fourierite Phalanx. March 3, 1846, its major building, The Phalanstery, was destroyed by fire. Whether Brook Farm failed because its emphasis had shifted from empathy to organization or because it had insufficiently linked the two elements is moot. Brook Farmers were outstanding in their education of children as the following memoir by one of them indicates.*

Our slide down the Knoll proved very popular, and, with occasional repairs, lasted all winter, making a welcome addition

SOURCE: John Van Der Zee Sears, *My Friends at Brook Farm* (New York: Desmond FitzGerald, 1912), pp. 80, 81, 102–103, 107–108, 112–113, 117–118.

to our outdoor diversions during the season when these were necessarily limited. . . .

Withal, however, indoor pleasures took the most prominent place, during the winter months. After the reorganization of the Association as a Phalanx, Mr. John Dwight was the Chief of the Festal Series, and as he was, first of all, a musician, it followed that music formed the principal feature of our entertainments. Vocal and instrumental music was thoroughly taught in the school, and, as nearly all the members of the community were music lovers, and many were singers and players, the place was melodious from morning until night. There was always some new song or perhaps some very old one to be tried, some local composition to be heard, or some preparation for future musical events to enlist attention. . . .

With all our love of recreation, there were no sedentary games in our repertoire. Cards were unknown. The General was said to like a quiet game of whist in his own room, but if he had a pack of cards, it was probably the only one on the Farm. There was no prejudice against cards or chess or any other game so far as I know, but no one cared for any form of amusement that separated two or four from all the others. I imagine that even courting, the divine solitude of two, must have been handicapped by this persistent penchant for all being together.

The spell that drew these sympathetic associates like a magnet was in great part that charm of the general conversation, the memory of which still lingers wherever traditions of Brook Farm are cherished. The never failing succession of entertainments especially in summer were enjoyed to the full by the happy Farmers, but it was conversation, the mutual exchange of bright ideas that afforded their chiefest enjoyment. Not literature, not the drama, not the dance, but the fascination of human speech in its best employ attracted and held their enthralled attention. It is impossible to report in writing even the heads of this discourse, pervading as it did the atmosphere of Brook Farm as currents of electricity pervade the air in breaths. . . .

Education at Brook Farm began in the kindergarten—only we did not know it. The word was not in the dictionaries of that period, and Froebel was yet to be heard of in Massachusetts; but the rudiments of the kindergarten system were devised and put in practice by our folk in response to a new demand. The little ones, too old for the nursery and too young for the school, demanded some adequate provision for their care while their mothers were at work. In the community the one person best suited to fill any requirement was directed to the undertaking by natural selection. This was one of the normal though scarcely recognized results of the organization of industry. Among the many workers there was always one who could do whatever was to be done better than any of the others, and to this one, young or old, man or woman, full charge of the work was given.

The one person best qualified to take charge of these toddlers was a charming young lady, Miss Abby Morton, whose sincere interest in children invariably gained their young affections. Miss Morton gathered her group of older babies on the grass or under the elms whenever weather permitted and at other times in the parlor of Pilgrim Hall. Her first object was to make them happy and contented, and to this end she invented and arranged games and songs and stories, contrived little incidents and managed little surprises with never failing ingenuity. Learning as well as teaching, she gradually gave a purposeful bent to her song-and-dance diversions, making them effective lessons as well as pleasant pastimes. . . .

Brook Farm was practically an industrial school, though not so named. It was the first I ever heard of where instruction in the useful arts was regularly given as a part of the educational course. The fine arts were not very extensively taught at the time, and all we had was literature, drawing, music, and dancing.

These four studies were very well supplied with good teachers, everything the school promised to do being well done, but they were not given nearly so much time as the industrial arts. Every pupil old enough to work was expected to give two hours every Monday and Tuesday, and every Thursday and Friday to work under an instructor in the shops on the farm, in the garden or the household. The pupils could select their own work and could make a change of occupation with consent of the instructor. No one was obliged to take the Industrial course, but very few declined, even the aristocratic Spaniards taking hold of work like good fellows as they were. Idling was not in fashion.

I worked, for a while, four hours every day in the week. Cedar was found competent to act as first assistant to the president—in the cow-stable. Care of the cow being regarded as a disagreeable duty, Dr. Ripley took it upon himself, just as Mrs. Ripley took the scrubbing of the kitchen floor. Mrs. Ripley had other little matters to look after, general oversight of the girls, teaching Greek, entertaining distinguished guests, writing clever musical plays for the Festal Series, etc., but she kept the floor clean all the same. . . .

My industrial education was not confined to the cow-stable. At different times I worked in the green-house with John Codman, in the fields and meadows with everybody, and in the orchard and tree-nursery with Mr. Dana. On one occasion teacher and pupil were sitting on the ground, budding peach-seedlings, when a stranger approached and demanded a hearing. Gerrish had brought him out and had directed him to Vice President Dana as the authority he should consult. "Free speech, here," said the vice-president, without looking up from his work.

Speaking freely, the visitor announced that his mission was to save souls, and he had a message of warning to deliver to sinners in danger of eternal punishment. What he wanted was to have the people called together that he might exhort them as to the terror of the wrath to come.

"Our people do not need to be called. They come together every evening without calling."

"Can I have an opportunity to address them this evening?" asked the missionary.

"You can," said Mr. Dana, still busy, "but they have a way of not listening, sometimes. I'll tell you what, if you are able and willing to preach a sound, old-fashioned, blue-blazes, and brimstone sermon, you will get an audience. I would like to hear a real scorcher, once more."

So far from being encouraged the missionary hastily sought Gerrish and departed on that worthy teamster's return trip to Boston. . . .

34.

WILLIAM HENRY SEWARD:
"*I am not the prisoner's lawyer. . . .*
I am the lawyer for society"

William Henry Seward (1801–1872) was one of the great men of his generation, spanning the chasm between law and reform and yet with quirks of character which left him more memorable as the purchaser of Alaska rather than as one of his country's rescuers. Seward sensed the need for bringing the nation forward to new ways of thinking, yet he held to legal processes. His defense of the lunatic murderer William Freeman, a Negro, was his most daring effort. It might have crushed him as too knightly and uncontrollable for high office. (Freeman was convicted, the verdict appealed, and he died in his cell. Accumulated evidence of insanity, however, made his a landmark case and Seward a pioneer in distinguishing insanity from crime.) As governor of New York, Seward augmented his reputation, refusing to surrender fugitive slaves, opposing imprisonment for debt and otherwise shaping a program for the North. He was later victimized by his own prose, his reference to a law "higher than the Constitution" appearing to make him more "radical" than Lincoln, though Seward was as ambitious as Lincoln and anything but an extremist.

[I]f the prisoner *be* guilty of murder, I do not ask remission of punishment. If he be guilty, never was murderer *more* guilty. He has murdered not only John G. Van Nest, but his hands are

SOURCE: George E. Baker, ed., *The Works of William H. Seward* (New York: Redfield, 1853), vol. I, pp. 411 ff.

reeking with the blood of other, and numerous, and even more pitiable victims. The slaying of Van Nest, if a crime at all, was the cowardly crime of assassination. John G. Van Nest was a just, upright, virtuous man, of middle age, of grave and modest demeanor, distinguished by especial marks of the respect and esteem of his fellow-citizens. On his arm leaned a confiding wife, and they supported, on the one side, children to whom they had given being, and, on the other, aged and venerable parents, from whom they had derived existence. The assassination of such a man was an atrocious crime, but the murderer, with more than savage refinement, immolated on the same altar, in the same hour, a venerable and virtuous matron of more than three-score years, and her daughter, the wife of Van Nest, mother of an unborn infant. Nor was this all. Providence, which, for its own mysterious purposes, permitted these dreadful crimes, in mercy suffered the same arm to be raised against the sleeping orphan child of the butchered parents and received it into Heaven. A whole family, just, gentle, and pure, were thus, in their own house, in the night time, without any provocation, without one moment's warning, sent by the murderer to join the assembly of the just; and even the laboring man, sojourning within their gates, received the fatal blade into his breast, and survives through the mercy, not of the murderer, but of God.

For William Freeman, as a murderer, I have no commission to speak. If he had silver and gold accumulated with the frugality of Crœsus, and should pour it all at my feet, I would not stand an hour between him and the avenger. But for the innocent, it is my right, my duty to speak. If this sea of blood was *innocently* shed, then it is my duty to stand beside him until his steps lose their hold upon the scaffold.

"Thou shalt not kill," is a commandment addressed not to him alone, but to me, to you, to the court, and to the whole community. There are no exceptions from that commandment, at least in civil life, save those of self-defence, and capital punishment for crimes in the due and just administration of the law. There is not only a question, then, whether the prisoner has shed the blood of his fellow-man, but the question, whether we shall unlawfully shed his blood. I should be guilty of murder if, in my present relation, I saw the executioner waiting for an insane man, and failed to say, or failed to do in his behalf, all that my ability allowed. I think it has been proved of the prisoner at the bar, that, during all this long and tedious trial, he has had no sleepless nights, and that even in the day time, when he retires from these halls to his lonely cell, he sinks to rest like a wearied child, on the stone floor, and quietly slumbers till roused by the constable with his staff to appear again before the jury. His counsel enjoy no such repose. Their thoughts by day and their dreams by night are filled with oppressive apprehension that, through their inability or neglect, he may be condemned.

I am arraigned before you for undue manifestations of zeal and excitement. My answer to all such charges shall be brief. When this cause shall have been committed to you, I shall be happy indeed if it shall appear that my only error has been, that I have felt too much, thought too intensely, or acted too faithfully.

If error on my part would thus be criminal, how great would yours be if you should render an unjust verdict! Only four months have elapsed since an outraged people, distrustful of judicial redress, doomed the prisoner to immediate death. Some of you have confessed, before you came here, that you approved that lawless sentence. All men now rejoice that the prisoner was saved for this solemn trial. But if this trial, through any wilful fault or prejudice of yours, should prove only a mockery of justice, it would be as criminal as that precipitate sentence. If any prejudice of witnesses, or the imagination of counsel, or any ill-timed jest shall at any time have diverted your attention, or if any pre-judgment which you may have brought into the jury box, or any cowardly fear of popular opinion shall have operated to cause you to deny to the prisoner that dispassionate considera-tion of his case which the laws of God and man exact of you, and if, owing to such an error, this wretched man shall fall from among the living, what will be your crime? You will have violated the commandment, "Thou shalt not kill." . . .

I plead not for a murderer. I have no inducement, no motive to do so. I have addressed my fellow citizens in many various relations, when rewards of wealth and fame awaited me. I have been cheered on other occasions by manifestations of popular approbation and sympathy; and where there was no such encouragement, I have had at least the gratitude of him whose cause I defended. But I speak now in the hearing of a People who have prejudged the prisoner, and condemned me for pleading in his behalf. He is a convict, a pauper, a negro, without intellect, sense, or emotion. My child, with an affectionate smile, disarms my care-worn face of its frown whenever I cross my threshold. The beggar in the street obliges me to give, because he says "God bless you," as I pass. My dog caresses me with fondness if I will but smile on him. My horse recognizes me when I fill his manger. But what reward, what gratitude, what sympathy and affection can I expect here? There the prisoner sits. Look at him. Look at the assemblage around you. Listen to their ill-suppressed censures and their excited fears, and tell me where among my neighbors or my fellow men, where even in his heart, I can expect to find the sentiment, the thought, not to say of reward or of acknowledgment, but even of recognition. I sat here two weeks during the preliminary trial. I stood here between the prisoner and the Jury nine hours, and pleaded for the wretch that he was insane and did not even know he was on trial: and when all was done, the Jury thought, at least eleven of them thought, that I had been deceiving them, or was self-deceived. They read signs of intelligence in his idiotic smile, and of cunning and malice in his stolid insensibility. They rendered a verdict that he was sane enough to be tried, a contemptible compromise verdict in a capital case; and then they looked on, with what emotions God and they only know, upon his arraignment. The District Attorney, speaking in his adder ear, bade him rise, and reading to him one indictment, asked him whether he wanted a trial, and

the poor fool answered, No. Have you Counsel? No. And they
went through the same mockery, the prisoner giving the same
answers, until a third indictment was thundered in his ears, and
he stood before the Court, silent, motionless, and bewildered.
Gentlemen, you may think of this transaction what you please,
bring in what verdict you can, but I asseverate before Heaven
and you, that, to the best of my knowledge and belief, the
prisoner at the bar does not at this moment know why it is that
my shadow falls on you instead of his own.

I speak with all sincerity and earnestness; not because I expect
my opinion to have weight, but I would disarm the injurious
impression that I am speaking, merely as a lawyer speaks for his
client. I am not the prisoner's lawyer. I am indeed a volunteer in
his behalf; but society and mankind have the deepest interests at
stake. I am the lawyer for society, for mankind, shocked beyond
the power of expression, at the scene I have witnessed here of
trying a maniac as a malefactor. In this, almost the first of such
causes I have ever seen, the last I hope that I shall ever see, I
wish that I could perform my duty with more effect. If I suffered
myself to look at the volumes of testimony through which I have
to pass, to remember my entire want of preparation, the pressure
of time, and my wasted strength and energies, I should despair
of acquitting myself as you and all good men will hereafter desire
that I should have performed so sacred a duty. But in the cause
of humanity we are encouraged to hope for Divine assistance
where human powers are weak. As you all know, I provided for
my way through these trials, neither gold nor silver in my purse,
nor scrip; and when I could not think beforehand what I should
say, I remembered that it was said to those who had a beneficent
commission, that they should take no thought what they should
say when brought before the magistrate, for in that same hour it
should be given them what they should say, and it should not be
they who should speak, but the spirit of their Father speaking in
them. . . .

An inferior standard of intelligence has been set up here as a standard of the negro race, and a false one as a standard of the Asiatic race. This prisoner traces a divided lineage. On the paternal side his ancestry is lost among the tiger hunters on the gold coast of Africa, while his mother constitutes a portion of the small remnant of the Narragansett tribe. Hence it is held that the prisoner's intellect is to be compared with the depreciating standard of the African, and his passions with the violent and ferocious character erroneously imputed to the aborigines. Indications of manifest derangement, or at least of imbecility, approaching to idiocy, are therefore set aside, on the ground that they harmonize with the legitimate but degraded characteristics of the races from which he comes. You, gentlemen, have, or ought to have, lifted up your souls above the bondage of prejudices so narrow and so mean as these. The color of the prisoner's skin, and the form of his features, are not impressed upon the spiritual, immortal mind which works beneath. In spite of human pride, he is still your brother, and mine, in form and color accepted and approved by his Father, and yours, and mine, and bears equally with us the proudest inheritance of our race—the image of our Maker. Hold him then to be a MAN. Exact of him all the responsibilities which should be exacted under like circumstances if he belonged to the Anglo-Saxon race, and make for him all the allowances, and deal with him with all the tenderness which, under like circumstances, you would expect for yourselves.

The prisoner was obliged—no, his counsel were obliged, by law, to accept the plea of *Not Guilty,* which the court directed to be entered in his behalf. That plea denies the homicide. If the law had allowed it, we would gladly have admitted all the murders of which the prisoner was accused, and have admitted them to be as unprovoked as they were cruel, and have gone directly before you on the only defence upon which we have insisted, or shall insist, or could insist—that he is irresponsible, because he was and is insane.

We labor, not only under these difficulties, but under the

further embarrassment that the plea of insanity is universally suspected. It is the last subterfuge of the guilty, and so is too often abused. But however obnoxious to suspicion this defence is, there have been cases where it was true; and when true, it is of all pleas the most perfect and complete defence that can be offered in any human tribunal. Our Saviour forgave his judges because "they knew not what they did." The insane man who has committed a crime, knew not what he did. If this being, dyed with human blood, be *insane,* you and I, and even the children of your affections, are not more guiltless than he.

Is there reason to indulge a suspicion of fraud here? Look at this stupid, senseless fool, almost as inanimate as the clay moulded in the brick-yard, and say, if you dare, that you are afraid of being deceived by him. Look at me. You all know me. Am I a man to engage in a conspiracy to deceive you and defraud justice? Look on us all, for although I began the defence of this cause alone, thanks to the generosity, to the magnanimity of an enlightened profession, I come out strong in the assistance of counsel never before attached to me in any relation, but strongly grappled to me now, by these new and endearing ties. Is any one of us a man to be suspected? The testimony is closed. Look through it all. Can suspicion or malice find in it any ground to accuse us of a plot to set up a false and fabricated defence? I will give you, gentlemen, a key to every case where insanity has been wrongfully, and yet successfully maintained. Gold, influence, popular favor, popular sympathy, raised that defence, and made it impregnable. But you have never seen a poor, worthless, spiritless, degraded negro like *this,* acquitted wrongfully. I wish this trial may prove that such an one can be acquitted rightfully. The danger lies here. There is not a WHITE man or WHITE woman who would not have been dismissed long since from the perils of such a prosecution, if it had only been proved that the offender was so ignorant and so brutalized as not to understand that the defence of insanity had been interposed.

If he feign, who has trained the idiot to perform this highest and most difficult of all intellectual achievements? Is it I? Shakespeare and Cervantes only, of all mankind, have conceived and perfected a counterfeit of insanity. Is it I? Why is not the imposition exposed, to my discomfiture and the prisoner's ruin? Where was it done? Was it in public, here? Was it in secret, in the jail? His deafened ears could not hear me there unless I were also overheard by other prisoners, by jailers, constables, the sheriff, and a cloud of witnesses. Who has the keys of the jail? Have I? You have had sheriff, jailer, and the whole police upon the stand. Could none of these witnesses reveal our plot? Were there none to watch and report the abuse? When they tell you, or insinuate, gentlemen, that this man has been taught to feign insanity, they discredit themselves, as did the Roman sentinels, who, appointed to guard the sepulchre of our Saviour, said, in excuse of the broken seal, that while they slept men came and rolled away the stone. . . .

The might that slumbered in this maniac's arm was exhausted in the paroxysm which impelled him to his dreadful deeds. Yet an excited community, whose terror has not yet culminated, declare that, whether sane or insane, he must be executed to give safety to your dwellings and theirs. I must needs then tell you the law, which will disarm such cowardly fear. If you acquit the prisoner, he cannot go at large, but must be committed to jail, to be tried by another jury, for a second murder. Your dwellings therefore will be safe. If such a jury find him sane, he will then be sent to his fearful account, and your dwellings will be safe. If acquitted, he will be remanded to jail, to await a third trial, and your dwellings will be safe. If that jury convict, he will then be executed, and your dwellings will be safe. If they acquit, he will still be detained to answer for a fourth murder, and your dwellings will be safe. Whether the fourth jury acquit or convict, your dwellings will still be safe: for if they convict, he will then be cut off; and if they acquit, he must, according to the law of the land, be sent to the Lunatic Asylum, there to be confined for life. You may not slay him, then, for the public security, because the public security does not demand the sacrifice. No security for home or hearth can be obtained by judicial murder. God will abandon him who, through cowardly fear, becomes such a murderer. *I* also stand for the security of the homes and hearths of my fellow citizens, and have as deep an interest, and as deep a stake as any one of them. *Here* are my home and hearth, exposed to every danger that can threaten theirs; but I know that security cannot exist for any, if feeble man undertakes to correct the decrees of Providence. . . .

The prisoner lived with Nathaniel Lynch, at the age of eight or nine, and labored occasionally for him during the last winter. Lynch visited him in the jail, and asked him if he remembered him, and remembered living with him. The prisoner answered, Yes. Lynch asked the prisoner whether he was whipped while there, and by whom, and why. From his answers, it appeared that he had been whipped by his mistress for playing truant, and that he climbed a rough board fence in his night-clothes and fled to his mother. Upon this evidence, the learned professor from Geneva College, Dr. Spencer, builds an argument that the prisoner has conception, sensation, memory, imagination, and association, and is most competent for the scaffold. Now, here are some verses to which I would invite the doctor's attention:

> Shut up in dreary gloom, like convicts are,
> In company of murderers! Oh, wretched fate!
> If pity e'er extended through the frame,
> Or sympathy's sweet cordial touched the heart,
> Pity the wretched maniac who knows no blame,
> Absorbed in sorrow, where darkness, poverty, and
>   every curse impart.

Here is evidence not merely of memory and other faculties, but of what we call *genius*. Yet these verses are a sad effusion of Thomas Lloyd, a man-slaying maniac in Bedlam.

The first question of fact here, gentlemen, as in every case where insanity is gravely insisted upon, is this:

Is the Prisoner feigning or counterfeiting Insanity?

What kind of man is he? A youth of twenty-three, without learning, education, or experience. Dr. SPENCER raises him just above the brute; Dr. BIGELOW exalts him no higher; and Dr. DIMON thinks that he has intellectual capacity not exceeding that of a child of ten years, with the knowledge of one of two or three. These are the people's witnesses. All the witnesses concur in these estimates of his mind.

Can you conceive of such a creature comprehending such a plot, and standing up in his cell in the jail, hour after hour, day after day, week after week, and month after month, carrying on such a fraud; and all the while pouring freely into the ears of inquisitors curious, inquisitors friendly, and inquisitors hostile, without discrimination or alarm, or apparent hesitation or suspicion, with "child-like simplicity," as our witnesses describe it, and with "entire docility," as it is described by the witnesses for the people, confessions of crime which, if they fail to be received as evidences of insanity, must constitute an insurmountable barrier to his acquittal? . . .

And now, gentlemen, I will give you a proof of the difference between this real science and the empiricism upon which the counsel for the people rely, in this cause. JEAN PIERRE was brought before the Court of Assizes in Paris, in 1824, accused of forgery, swindling, and incendiarism. He feigned insanity. A commission of eminent physicians examined him, and detected his imposture by his pretended forgetfulness, and confusion in answering interrogatories concerning his life and history. The most prominent of these questions are set down in the books. I submitted these questions and answers, with a statement of JEAN PIERRE's case to DR. SPENCER, and he, governed by the rules which have controlled him in the present cause, pronounced the impostor's answers to be evidence of insanity, because they showed a decay of memory. . . .

You have now the fate of this lunatic in your hands. To him as to me, so far as we can judge, it is comparatively indifferent what be the issue. The wisest of modern men has left us a saying, that "the hour of death is more fortunate than the hour of birth," a saying which he signalized by bestowing a gratuity twice as great upon the place where he died as upon the hamlet where he was born. For aught that we can judge, the prisoner is unconscious of danger and would be insensible to suffering, let it come when and in whatever forms it might. A verdict can only hasten, by a few months or years, the time when his bruised, diseased, wandering and benighted spirit shall return to Him who sent it forth on its sad and dreary pilgrimage. . . .

35.

MARGARET FULLER:
The Life of Woman

*Both her life and her death made Margaret Fuller (1810–1850)
a legend of womanhood. She was neither an abolitionist nor a
women's rights crusader, but she contributed to the movement of
reform as certainly as any dedicated activist. Raised by her father
to be a learned woman, she showed strength of character at his
sudden death by assuming command of the household. She translated writings, taught school and made her mark with "conversa-
tions" in which she exhibited her wide reading and thoughtful
views. In the first selection below she writes in 1840 to Mrs.
Maria Weston Chapman, an ardent Garrisonian, repudiating
partisan politics. As a literary critic in New York for Greeley's
Tribune, she won the regard of men and gave inspiration to
women. Her* Woman in the Nineteenth Century, *from which the
second selection is drawn, was a pioneer interpretation of the
female spirit. In Italy she married Giovanni Angelo the Marquis
Ossoli; both worked for the Italian Revolution of the time. They
died together with their child, when their overweighted ship
struck Fire Island beach, just off Long Island and was assaulted
by powerful waves.*

The Abolition course commands my respect, as do all efforts to
relive and raise suffering human nature. The faults of the party
are such as it seems to me must always be incident to the

SOURCE: S. M. Fuller to Maria Weston Chapman, December 26, 1840,
Weston Papers, Boston Public Library; Margaret Fuller Ossoli, *Woman
in the Nineteenth Century* . . . (Boston: John P. Jewett & Company,
1855), pp. 157 ff.

partizan spirit. All that was noble and pure in their zeal has helped us all. For the disinterestedness and constancy of many individuals among you I have a high respect. Yet my own path leads a different course and often leaves me quite ignorant what you are doing as in the present instance of your Fair.

Very probably to one whose heart is so engaged as yours in particular measures this indifference will seem incredible or even culpable. But if indifferent I have not been intolerant: I have wronged none of you by a hasty judgement or careless words, and, when I have not investigated a case so as to be sure of my own opinion, have, at least, never chimed in with the popular hue and cry. I have always wished that efforts originating in a griev-ous sympathy, or a sense of right should have fair play; have had firm faith that they must, in some way, produce eventual good.

The late movements in your party have interested me more than those which had for their object the enfranchisement of the African only. Yet I presume I should still feel sympathy with your aims only not with your measures. Yet I should like to be more fully acquainted with both. The late convention I attended hoping to hear some clear account of your wishes as to religious institutions and the social position of woman. But not only I heard nothing that pleased me, but no clear statement from any one. Have you in print what you consider an able exposition of the views of yourself and friends?—Or if not, should you like yourself to give me an account of how these subjects stand in your mind? As far as I know you seem to me quite wrong as to what is to be done for woman! She needs new helps I think, but not such as you propose. But I should like to know your view and your grounds more clearly than I do. . . .

A crowd of books having been sent me since my friends knew me to be engaged in this way, on Woman's "Sphere," Woman's "Mission," and Woman's "Destiny," I believe that almost all that is extant of formal precept has come under my eye. Among these I read with refreshment a little one called *The Whole Duty of*

Woman, "indited by a noble lady at the request of a noble lord," and which has this much of nobleness that the view it takes is a religious one. It aims to fit Woman for heaven; the main bent of most of the others is to fit her to please, or at least not to disturb, a husband.

Among these I select as a favorable specimen . . . *The Study of the Life of Woman* by Madame Necker de Saussure of Geneva, translated from the French. This book was published at Philadelphia, and has been read with much favor here. Madame Necker is the cousin of Madame de Staël, and has taken from her works the motto prefixed to this:

"Cette vie n'a quelque prix que si elle sert à l'education morale de notre coeur."

Madame Necker is by nature capable of entire consistency in the application of this motto, and therefore the qualifications she makes in the instructions given to her own sex show forcibly the weight which still paralyzes and distorts the energies of that sex.

The book is rich in passages marked by feeling and good suggestions; but taken in the whole, the impression it leaves is this:

Woman is and *shall remain* inferior to Man and subject to his will, and in endeavoring to aid her we must anxiously avoid anything that can be misconstrued into expression of the contrary opinion, else the men will be alarmed and combine to defeat our efforts.

The present is a good time for these efforts, for men are less occupied about women than formerly. Let us then seize upon the occasion, and do what we can to make our lot tolerable. But we must sedulously avoid encroaching on the territory of Man. If we study natural history, our observations may be made useful by some male naturalist; if we draw well, we may make our services acceptable to the artists. But our names must not be known; and to bring these labors to any result, we must take some man for our head and be his hands.

The lot of Woman is sad. She is constituted to expect and need

a happiness that cannot exist on earth. She must stifle such aspirations within her secret heart, and fit herself as well as she can
for a life of resignations and consolations.

She will be very lonely while living with her husband. She
must not expect to open her heart to him fully, or that after
marriage he will be capable of the refined service of love. The
man is not born for the woman, only the woman for the man.
"Men cannot understand the hearts of women." The life of
Woman must be outwardly a well-intentioned, cheerful dissimu-
lation of her real life.

Naturally the feelings of the mother at the birth of a female
child resemble those of the Paraguay woman described by
Southey as lamenting in such heart-breaking tones that her
mother did not kill her the hour she was born—"her mother, who
knew what the life of a woman must be"—or of those women
seen at the north by Sir A. Mackenzie, who performed this pious
duty towards female infants whenever they had an opportunity.

"After the first delight the young mother experiences feelings a
little different, according as the birth of a son or a daughter has
been announced.

"Is it a son? A sort of glory swells at this thought the heart of
the mother; she seems to feel that she is entitled to gratitude. She
has given a citizen, a defender to her country; to her husband an
heir of his name; to herself a protector. And yet the contrast of all
these fine titles with this being so humble soon strikes her. At the
aspect of this frail treasure, opposite feelings agitate her heart;
she seems to recognize in him *a nature superior to her own,* but
subjected to a low condition, and she honors a future greatness in
the object of extreme compassion. Somewhat of that respect and
adoration for a feeble child of which some fine pictures offer the
expression in the features of the happy Mary, seem reproduced
with the young mother who has given birth to a son.

"Is it a daughter? There is usually a slight degree of regret; so
deeply rooted is the idea of the superiority of Man in happiness
and dignity; and yet as she looks upon this child, she is more and

more *softened* towards it. A deep sympathy—a sentiment of identity with this delicate being—takes possession of her; an extreme pity for so much weakness, a more pressing need of prayer stirs her heart. Whatever sorrows she may have felt, she dreads for her daughter; but she will guide her to become much wiser, much better than herself. And then the gaiety, the frivolity of the young woman have their turn. This little creature is a flower to cultivate, a doll to decorate."

Similar sadness at the birth of a daughter I have heard mothers express not unfrequently. . . .

I come now with satisfaction to my own country and to a writer, a female writer, whom I have selected as the clearest, wisest, and kindliest who has as yet used pen here on these subjects. This is Miss Sedgwick.

Miss Sedgwick, though she inclines to the private path and wishes that by the cultivation of character might should vindicate right, sets limits nowhere, and her objects and inducements are pure. They are the free and careful cultivation of the powers that have been given, with an aim at moral and intellectual perfection. Her speech is moderate and sane, but never palsied by fear or skeptical caution.

Herself a fine example of the independent and beneficent existence that intellect and character can give to Woman no less than Man, if she know how to seek and prize it—also that the intellect need not absorb or weaken, but rather will refine and invigorate the affections—the teachings of her practical good sense come with great force, and cannot fail to avail much. Every way her writings please me, both as to the means and the ends. I am pleased at the stress she lays on observance of the physical laws, because the true reason is given. Only in a strong and clean body can the soul do its message fitly.

She shows the meaning of the respect paid to personal neatness, both in the indispensable form of cleanliness and of that love of order and arrangement that must issue from a true harmony of feeling. . . .

Another interesting sign of the time is the influence exercised by two women, Miss Martineau and Miss Barrett, from their sick-rooms. The lamp of life which if it had been fed only by the affections, dependent on precarious human relations, would scarce have been able to maintain a feeble glare in the lonely prison, now shines far and wide over the nations, cheering fellow-sufferers and hallowing the joy of the healthful.

These persons need not health or youth or the charms of personal presence to make their thoughts available. A few more such, and "old woman" shall not be the synonym for imbecility, nor "old maid" a term of contempt, nor Woman be spoken of as a reed shaken by the wind. . . .

36.

LUCY STONE:
Marriage under Protest

Lucy Stone (1818–1893), recalled mainly for having kept her maiden name following marriage, was the greatest of pre-Civil War advocates of woman's rights and later founded and sustained the Woman's Journal, *which, more than any other publication, upheld her major cause. An Oberlin College graduate, she became an antislavery lecturer but soon announced: "I was a woman before I was an abolitionist. I must speak for the women." The two campaigns made her famous. In 1850 she organized the first truly national woman's convention at Worcester, Massachusetts, drawing more representative delegates and (unlike the 1848 convention) having a woman, Paulina Wright Davis, in the chair. Lucy's speech at Worcester converted Susan B. Anthony to the cause and, as reported overseas, influenced the writing of "Enfranchisement of Women" by Harriet Taylor (later Mrs. John Stuart Mill). Lucy's and her husband's "Protest," as printed in 1855 in the Worcester* Spy *and elsewhere, was a landmark. Garrison in the* Liberator *felicitated the couple, expressing regret at losing Lucy Stone and welcoming Lucy Blackwell; but "Lucy Stoners" now succeeded the deceased "Fanny Wright men" as proponents of equal rights.*

MARRIAGE OF LUCY STONE UNDER PROTEST.

It was my privilege to celebrate May day by officiating at a wedding in a farm-house among the hills of West Brookfield. The bridegroom was a man of tried worth, a leader in the Western

SOURCE: Elizabeth Cady Stanton *et al., History of Woman Suffrage,* pp. 260–261.

Anti-Slavery Movement, and the bride was one whose fair name
is known throughout the nation: one whose rare intellectual qualities are excelled by the private beauty of her heart and life.

I never perform the marriage ceremony without a renewed
sense of the iniquity of our present system of laws in respect to
marriage; a system by which "man and wife are one, and that one
is the husband." It was with my hearty concurrence, therefore,
that the following protest was read and signed, as a part of the
nuptial ceremony; and I send it to you, that others may be induced to do likewise.

Rev. THOMAS WENTWORTH HIGGINSON.

PROTEST.

While acknowledging our mutual affection by publicly assuming the relationship of husband and wife, yet in justice to ourselves and a great principle, we deem it a duty to declare that
this act on our part implies no sanction of, nor promise of voluntary obedience to such of the present laws of marriage, as refuse
to recognize the wife as an independent, rational being, while
they confer upon the husband an injurious and unnatural superiority, investing him with legal powers which no honorable man
would exercise, and which no man should possess. We protest
especially against the laws which give to the husband:

1. The custody of the wife's person.

2. The exclusive control and guardianship of their children.

3. The sole ownership of her personal, and use of her real
estate, unless previously settled upon her, or placed in the hands
of trustees, as in the case of minors, lunatics, and idiots.

4. The absolute right to the product of her industry.

5. Also against laws which give to the widower so much larger
and more permanent an interest in the property of his deceased
wife, than they give to the widow in that of the deceased
husband.

6. Finally, against the whole system by which "the legal existence of the wife is suspended during marriage," so that in most

States, she neither has a legal part in the choice of her residence, nor can she make a will, nor sue or be sued in her own name, nor inherit property.

We believe that personal independence and equal human rights can never be forfeited, except for crime; that marriage should be an equal and permanent partnership, and so recognized by law; that until it is so recognized, married partners should provide against the radical injustice of present laws, by every means in their power.

We believe that where domestic difficulties arise, no appeal should be made to legal tribunals under existing laws, but that all difficulties should be submitted to the equitable adjustment of arbitrators mutually chosen.

Thus reverencing law, we enter our protest against rules and customs which are unworthy of the name, since they violate justice, the essence of law.

(Signed), HENRY B. BLACKWELL,
LUCY STONE.

37.

RICHARD HENRY DANA, JR.:

"Don't call on Jesus Christ, he can't help you"

*Humanitarianism was an active force during this era of reform.
Richard Henry Dana's (1815–1882) Two Years before the Mast
drew readers who wished to share his experiences at sea, but it
also moved them with images of man's inhumanity to man. Dana's
book helped to bring on social reform in the United States Navy.
It inspired Herman Melville and others to similar writings. And it
sensitized Dana himself to suffering in ways which made him a
valuable associate of reformers and Free Soilers in Massachusetts.*

For several days the captain seemed very much out of humor.
Nothing went right, or fast enough for him. He quarrelled with
the cook, and threatened to flog him for throwing wood on deck;
and had a dispute with the mate about reeving a Spanish burton;
the mate saying that he was right, and had been taught how to
do it by a man *who was a sailor!* This, the captain took in
dudgeon, and they were at sword's points at once. But his dis-
pleasure was chiefly turned against a large, heavy-moulded fellow from the Middle States, who was called Sam. This man
hesitated in his speech, and was rather slow in his motions, but
was a pretty good sailor, and always seemed to do his best; but
the captain took a dislike to him, thought he was surly, and lazy;
and "if you once give a dog a bad name"—as the sailor-phrase
is—"he may as well jump overboard." The captain found fault

SOURCE: Richard Henry Dana, Jr., *Two Years before the Mast* (New York:
P. F. Collier & Sons, 1909), pp. 104–109.

with everything this man did, and hazed him for dropping a marline-spike from the main-yard, where he was at work. This, of course, was an accident, but it was set down against him. The captain was on board all day Friday, and everything went on hard and disagreeably. "The more you drive a man, the less he will do," was as true with us as with any other people. We worked late Friday night, and were turned-to early Saturday morning. About ten o'clock the captain ordered our new officer, Russell, who by this time had become thoroughly disliked by all the crew, to get the gig ready to take him ashore. John, the Swede, was sitting in the boat alongside, and Russell and myself were standing by the main hatchway, waiting for the captain, who was down in the hold, where the crew were at work, when we heard his voice raised in violent dispute with somebody, whether it was with the mate, or one of the crew, I could not tell; and then came blows and scuffling. I ran to the side and beckoned to John, who came up, and we leaned down the hatchway; and though we could see no one, yet we knew that the captain had the advantage, for his voice was loud and clear—

"You see your condition! You see your condition! Will you ever give me any more of your *jaw?*" No answer; and then came wrestling and heaving, as though the man was trying to turn him. "You may as well keep still, for I have got you," said the captain. Then came the question, "Will you ever give me any more of your jaw?"

"I never gave you any, sir," said Sam; for it was his voice that we heard, though low and half choked.

"That's not what I asked you. Will you ever be impudent to me again?"

"I never have been, sir," said Sam.

"Answer my question, or I'll make a spread eagle of you! I'll flog you, by G—d."

"I'm no negro slave," said Sam.

"Then I'll make you one," said the captain; and he came to the hatchway, and sprang on deck, threw off his coat, and rolling up his sleeves, called out to the mate—"Seize that man up, Mr. A——! Seize him up! Make a spread eagle of him! I'll teach you all who is master aboard!"

The crew and officers followed the captain up the hatchway, and after repeated orders the mate laid hold of Sam, who made no resistance, and carried him to the gangway.

"What are you going to flog that man for, sir?" said John, the Swede, to the captain.

Upon hearing this, the captain turned upon him, but knowing him to be quick and resolute, he ordered the steward to bring the irons, and calling upon Russell to help him, went up to John.

"Let me alone," said John. "I'm willing to be put in irons. You need not use any force;" and putting out his hands, the captain slipped the irons on, and sent him aft to the quarter-deck. Sam by this time was *seized up,* as it is called, that is, placed against the shrouds, with his wrists made fast to the shrouds, his jacket off, and his back exposed. The captain stood on the break of the deck, a few feet from him, and a little raised, so as to have a good swing at him, and held in his hand the bight of a thick, strong rope. The officers stood round, and the crew grouped together in the waist. All these preparations made me feel sick and almost faint, angry and excited as I was. A man—a human being, made in God's likeness—fastened up and flogged like a beast! A man, too, whom I had lived with and eaten with for months, and knew almost as well as a brother. The first and almost uncontrollable impulse was resistance. But what was to be done? The time for it had gone by. The two best men were fast, and there were only two beside myself, and a small boy of ten or twelve years of age. And then there were (beside the captain) three officers, steward, agent and clerk. But beside the numbers, what is there for sailors to do? If they resist, it is mutiny; and if they succeed, and take the vessel, it is piracy. If they ever yield again, their punishment must come; and if they do not yield, they are pirates for life. If a sailor resist his commander, he resists the law, and piracy or submission are his only alternatives. Bad as it was, it must be borne. It is what a sailor ships for. Swinging the rope over his head, and bending his body so as to give it full force, the captain brought it down upon the poor fellow's back. Once, twice,—six times. "Will you ever give me any more of your jaw?" The man writhed with pain, but said not a word. Three times more. This was too much, and he muttered something which I could not hear; this brought as many more as the man could stand; when the captain ordered him to be cut down, and to go forward.

"Now for you," said the captain, making up to John and taking his irons off. As soon as he was lose, he ran forward to the forecastle. "Bring that man aft," shouted the captain. The second mate, who had been a shipmate of John's, stood still in the waist, and the mate walked slowly forward; but our third officer, anxious to show his zeal, sprang forward over the windlass, and laid hold of John; but he soon threw him from him. At this moment I would have given worlds for the power to help the poor fellow; but it was all in vain. The captain stood on the quarterdeck, bareheaded, his eyes flashing with rage, and his face as red as blood, swinging the rope, and calling out to his officers, "Drag him aft!—Lay hold of him! I'll *sweeten* him!" etc., etc. The mate now went forward and told John quietly to go aft; and he, seeing resistance in vain, threw the blackguard third mate from him; said he would go aft of himself; that they should not drag him; and went up to the gangway and held out his hands; but as soon as the captain began to make him fast, the indignity was too much, and he began to resist; but the mate and Russell holding him, he was soon seized up. When he was made fast, he turned to the captain, who stood turning up his sleeves and getting ready for the blow, and asked him what he was to be flogged for. "Have I ever refused my duty, sir? Have you ever known me to hang back, or to be insolent, or not to know my work?"

"No," said the captain, "it is not that that I flog you for; I flog you for your interference—for asking questions."

"Can't a man ask a question here without being flogged?"

"No," shouted the captain; "nobody shall open his mouth aboard this vessel, but myself;" and began laying the blows upon his back, swinging half round between each blow, to give it full effect. As he went on, his passion increased, and he danced about the deck, calling out as he swung the rope,—"If you want to know what I flog you for, I'll tell you. It's because I like to do it!—because I like to do it!—It suits me! That's what I do it for!"

The man writhed under the pain, until he could endure it no longer, when he called out, with an exclamation more common among foreigners than with us—"Oh, Jesus Christ! Oh, Jesus Christ!"

"Don't call on Jesus Christ," shouted the captain; *"he can't help you. Call on Captain T——*, he's the man! He can help you! Jesus Christ can't help you now!"

At these words, which I never shall forget, my blood ran cold. I could look on no longer. Disgusted, sick, and horror-struck, I turned away and leaned over the rail, and looked down into the water. A few rapid thoughts of my own situation, and of the prospect of future revenge, crossed my mind; but the falling of the blows and the cries of the man called me back at once. At length they ceased, and turning round, I found that the mate, at a signal from the captain had cut him down. Almost doubled up with pain, the man walked slowly forward, and went down into the forecastle. Every one else stood still at his post, while the captain, swelling with rage and with the importance of his achievement, walked the quarter-deck, and at each turn, as he came forward, calling out to us,—"You see your condition! You see where I've got you all, and you know what to expect!"—"You've been mistaken in me—you didn't know what I was! Now you know what I am!"—"I'll make you toe the mark, every soul of you, or I'll flog you all, fore and aft, from the boy, up!"—"You've got a driver over you! Yes, a *slave-driver—a negro-driver!* I'll see who'll tell me he isn't a negro slave!" . . .

After the day's work was done, we went down into the forecastle, and ate our plain supper; but not a word was spoken. It was Saturday night; but there was no song—no "sweethearts and wives." A gloom was over everything. The two men lay in their berths, groaning with pain, and we all turned in, but for myself, not to sleep. A sound coming now and then from the berths of the two men showed that they were awake, as awake they must have been, for they could hardly lie in one posture a moment; the dim, swinging lamp of the forecastle shed its light over the dark hole in which we lived; and many and various reflections and purposes coursed through my mind. I thought of our situation, living under a tyranny; of the character of the country we were in; of the length of the voyage, and of the uncertainty attending our return to America; and then, if we should return, of the prospect of obtaining justice and satisfaction for these poor men; and vowed that if God should ever give me the means, I would do something to redress the grievances and relieve the sufferings of that poor class of beings, of whom I then was one. . . .

38.

DOROTHEA L. DIX:
"I tell what I have seen"

Dorothea L. Dix (1802–1887), one of the greatest women of the nineteenth century, was mainly inspired by William Ellery Channing to serve society. Her dedication to institutional reform became the great motif of her life. Before her work was done she had transformed attitudes toward the helpless and confined throughout the United States and abroad. Her Memorial to the Legislature of Massachusetts *inaugurated her career.*

GENTLEMEN: . . . About two years since, leisure afforded opportunity, and duty prompted me, to visit several prisons and almshouses in the vicinity of this metropolis. . . . Evey investigation has given depth to the conviction that it is only by decided, prompt, and vigorous legislation that the evils to which I refer, and which I shall proceed more fully to illustrate, can be remedied. I shall be obliged to speak with great plainness, and to reveal many things revolting to the taste, and from which my woman's nature shrinks with peculiar sensitiveness. But truth is the highest consideration. *I tell what I have seen,* painful and shocking as the details often are, that from them you may feel more deeply the imperative obligation which lies upon you to prevent the possibility of a repetition or continuance of such outrages upon humanity. . . . If my pictures are displeasing, coarse, and severe, my subjects, it must be recollected, offer no tranquil, refining, or composing features. The condition of human

SOURCE: Francis Tiffany, *Life of Dorothea Lynde Dix* (Boston: Houghton, Mifflin and Company, 1891), pp. 76 ff.

beings reduced to the extremest state of degradation and misery cannot be exhibited in softened language, or adorn a polished page.

I proceed, gentlemen, briefly to call your attention to the *present* state of insane persons confined within this Commonwealth, in *cages, closets, cellars, stalls, pens; chained, naked, beaten with rods,* and *lashed* into obedience! . . .

I give a few illustrations but description fades before reality.

DANVERS. November. Visited the almshouse; a large building, much out of repair; understand a new one is in contemplation. Here are from fifty-six to sixty inmates: one idiotic; three insane; one of the latter in close confinement at all times.

Long before reaching the house, wild shouts, snatches of rude songs, imprecations, and obscene language, fell upon the ear, proceeding from the occupant of a low building, rather remote from the principal building, to which my course was directed. Found the mistress, and was conducted to the place, which was called "*the home*" of the *forlorn* maniac, a young woman, exhibiting a condition of neglect and misery blotting out the faintest idea of comfort, and outraging every sentiment of decency. She had been, I learnt, a respectable person, industrious and worthy; disappointments and trials shook her mind, and finally laid prostrate reason and self-control; she became a maniac for life! She had been at Worcester Hospital for a considerable time, and had been returned as incurable. The mistress told me she understood that, while there, she was comfortable and decent. Alas! what a change was here exhibited! She had passed from one degree of violence and degradation to another, in swift progress; there she stood, clinging to, or beating upon, the bars of her caged apartment, the contracted size of which afforded space only for increasing accumulations of filth,—a *foul* spectacle; there she stood, with naked arms and disheveled hair; the unwashed frame invested with fragments of unclean garments; the air so extremely offensive, though ventilation was afforded on all sides save one, that it was not possible to remain beyond a few moments without retreating for recovery to the outward air. Irritation of body, produced by utter filth and exposure, incited her to the horrid process of tearing off her skin by inches; her face, neck, and person were thus disfigured to hideousness.

Is the whole story told? What was seen is; what is reported is not. These gross exposures are not for the pained sight of one alone; all, all, coarse, brutal men, wondering, neglected children, old and young, each and all, witness this lowest, foulest state of miserable humanity. And who protects her, that worse than Pariah outcast, from other wrongs and blacker outrages?

Some may say these things cannot be remedied; these furious maniacs are not to be raised from these base conditions. I *know* they are; could give *many* examples; let *one* suffice. A young woman, a pauper in a distant town, Sandisfield, was for years a raging maniac. A cage, chains, and the whip were the agents for controlling her, united with harsh tones and profane language. Annually, with others (the town's poor) she was put up at auction, and bid off at the lowest price which was declared for her. One year not long past, an old man came forward in the number of applicants for the poor wretch; he was taunted and ridiculed. What would he and his old wife do with such a mere beast? "My wife says yes," replied he, "and I shall take her." She was given to his charge; he conveyed her home; she was washed, neatly dressed, and placed in a decent bedroom, furnished for comfort and opening into the kitchen. How altered her condition! As yet the *chains* were not off. The first week she was somewhat restless, at times violent, but the quiet ways of the old people wrought a change: she received her food decently; forsook acts of violence, and no longer uttered blasphemous or indecent language. After a week the chain was lengthened, and she was received as a companion into the kitchen. Soon she engaged in trivial employments. "After a fortnight," said the old man, "I knocked off the chains and made her a free woman." She is at times excited, but not violently; they are careful of her diet, they keep her very clean; she calls them father and mother. Go there now, and you will find her "clothed," and though not perfectly in her "right mind," so far restored as to be a safe and comfortable inmate. . . .

SHELBURNE. I had heard, before visiting this place, of the bad condition of a lunatic pauper. . . . I desired to see him, and, after some difficulties raised and set aside, was conducted into the yard, where was a small building of rough boards imperfectly joined. All was still, save now and then a low groan. The person who conducted me tried, with a stick, to rouse the inmate; I entreated her to desist; the twilight of the place making it difficult to discern anything within the cage; there at last I saw a human being, partially extended, cast upon his back amidst a mass of filth, the sole furnishing, whether for comfort or necessity, which the place afforded; there he lay, ghastly, with upturned, glazed eyes and fixed gaze, heavy breathings, interrupted only by faint groans, which seemed symptomatic of an approaching termination of his sufferings. Not so thought the mistress. "He has all sorts of ways; he'll soon rouse up and be noisy enough; he'll scream and beat about the place like any wild beast, half the time." "And cannot you make him more comfortable? Can he not have some clean, dry place and a fire?" "As for clean, it will do no good; he's cleaned out now and then; but what's the use for such a creature? His own brother tried him once, but got sick enough of the bargain." "But a fire; there is space even here for a small box stove." "If he had a fire he'd only pull off his clothes, so it's no use." I made no impression; it was plain that to keep him securely confined from escape was the chief object. "How do you give him his food? I see no means of introducing anything here." "Oh!" pointing to the floor, "one of the bars is cut shorter there; we push it through there." "There? Impossible! you cannot do that; you would not treat your lowest dumb animals with that disregard to *decency!*" "As for what he eats or where he eats, it makes no difference to him; he'd as soon swallow one thing as another." . . .

Of the dangers and mischiefs sometimes following the location of insane persons in our almshouses I will record but one more example. In Worcester has for several years resided a young woman, a lunatic pauper, of decent life and respectable family. I have seen her as she usually appeared, listless and silent, almost or quite sunk into a state of dementia, sitting one amidst the family, "but not of them." A few weeks since, revisiting that almshouse, judge my horror and amazement to see her negligently bearing in her arms a young infant, of which I was told she was the unconscious parent! Who was the father none could or would declare. Disqualified for the performance of maternal cares and duties, regarding the helpless little creature with a perplexed or indifferent gaze, she sat a silent, but oh, how eloquent, a pleader for the protection of others of her neglected and outraged sex! Details of that black story would not strengthen the cause; needs it a weightier plea than the sight of that forlorn creature and her wailing infant? Poor little child, more than orphan from birth, in this unfriendly world,—a demented mother, a father on whom the sun might blush or refuse to shine! . . .

Men of Massachusetts, I beg, I implore, I demand, pity and protection for these of my suffering, outraged sex. Fathers, husbands, brothers, I would supplicate you for this boon—but what do I say? I dishonor you, divest you at once of Christianity and humanity, does this appeal imply distrust. . . . Here you will put away the cold, calculating spirit of selfishness and self-seeking, lay off the armor of local strife and political opposition; here and now, for once, forgetful of the earthly and perishable, come up to these halls and consecrate them with one heart and one mind to works of righteousness and just judgment. . . . . Gentlemen, I commit to you this sacred cause. Your action upon this subject will affect the present and future condition of hundreds and thousands. In this legislation, as in all things, may you exercise that wisdom which is the breath of the power of God.

look for with high hope, mingled with no fear. I cannot fear that the Spirit which led you to take the first great step at Huntsville—which inspired your letters on Colonization, which sustained you through the mobs of Cincinnati, which dwelt on your lips through our Anti Slavery campaign, which fortified you to accept the nomination of our little "forlorn hope" convention at Albany to cope with the legions of slavery in 1840, will desert you now. The Almighty God wants a man to stand up for Him and be shown to the people as a sample of *the* manhood which He requires and loves; and *you* are the man. Hear the voices of the Vermont and Maine elections. But enough. You will not fail to hear. Now for the object of this letter. We want to see you here. We must see you. Your expenses you must permit us to bear, and to remunerate you for your labor and loss from leaving your business at Saginaw [Michigan]. This, if you signify your willingness, your friends here will gladly do—and we promise you moreover, in case you consent, that the electoral vote of Massachusetts shall be given to you, if to any one. Your friends in Maine, too, will do as much and promise as much for their state, I am persuaded. Perhaps the same may be said of Vermont. New York will speak for herself. Now, as a Southern man, you ought not to be afraid of the "Stump." With all good conscience and heavenly enthusiasm you ought to take it. What! if a worn out gambler can take it to replenish his pockets and eke out his fame, cannot you save humanity, honor God and make the history of this glorious country which He has given us fit to be written? Your presence here will strengthen the hands of all those who are laboring in the good cause—such men as Whittier, Pierpont, Stanton, Sewall etc. etc. and you will call out men whom they cannot. Your presence will give double or triple activity to every canvasser, and tract distributor and vote distributor. It will be all that is wanting to bring our present improved system of anti-slavery action—combining moral and political power, to full perfection, this ability to see and hear the chosen representative and impersonation of our principles. It will also do much to cicatrize the healing wounds of our anti-slavery dissensions. Now, steam and wheels will bring you to us in three or four days—and the great work is upon us—pressing most urgently. Our Bay State must not fall behind Maine and Vermont or her sisters west. We have abundance of gatherings before us. One at the Lexington Battle Ground on the 28th inst. If we do not see you there shall we not at least have a line from you to be read there, in as free and bold a spirit as that which showed itself in that valley sixty eight years ago? I do not speak by any special authority, but nevertheless I know that I speak the voice of our State Central Committee and of all voting abolitionists to a man. And I will take the responsibility, if you come right on. If more convenient, let us know what we can do to aid you to meet us on this New England soil. I do hope in God that there is no obstacle in the way of your visiting us shortly which we cannot remove. Therefore leave the City of Saginaw to grow as it may for a season. We are on the road to victory, and our leader must not be browsing on the solitary and humid plains of Saginaw, among the reeds and alders and *weeping* willows. We want him to water the cedars which are sticking their roots down among the *granite* foundations of this continent. . . .

40.

JAMES G. BIRNEY:
II: Liberty Party Candidate

Others besides James G. Birney expected that his peculiar credentials—distinguished Southerner, former slaveholder and principled abolitionist—entitled him to preside as chief executive over the liquidation of the slavery system. His letter which follows, addressed to Leicester King, an Ohio antislavery leader who had chaired the Liberty party convention in Buffalo, New York, in September 1843, implicitly projected Birney's political program; one destined never to be realized. The details of slavery were too tightly meshed with the nation's traditions and laws and its ethnic relations to be as cleanly settled as Birney imagined. Like Adams, like Garrison, like Douglass, Birney could no more than contribute to its solution. This he did with great effect in 1844 but not beyond.

Your letter of September 13, communicating to me the result of the deliberations of the National Convention, recently assembled in Buffalo, was received at my home, after I had left it on a visit to New England, whence I have not very long since returned.

To learn that my constancy as an Abolitionist and my steadfastness in the principles of the Liberty party from the time of its being organized, have drawn toward me the confidence of that party, is too gratifying not to be acknowledged. To be selected as the representative of that party in its eventful struggle for the liberties of our country against their worst enemies, and with the single view to practically setting up among us the political truths

SOURCE: Signal of Liberty (Ann Arbor, Mich.), January 29, 1844.

of the Declaration of Independence, would under the commonest circumstances of selection, be gratifying even to the most unambitious. How much more so ought it to be, when it is made unanimously, by an unusually large Convention, coming from all parts of the free States, and distinguished for its weight of moral and intellectual character, as the Buffalo Convention was, by the concession of all persons, not excepting those who are the most opposed to its objects? . . .

Most sincerely do I lament that Mr. Adams's course in relation to the Anti-Slavery movement does not permit me, as a friend of Emancipation, to unite with you in the eulogy, which you have thought proper to bestow on his public conduct. The prominent part taken by Mr. Adams in the early stages of the Anti-Slavery agitation in Congress, and the essential aid he might have given to the cause, had he chosen to do so, led me, from the first, to pay particular attention to what he said and did concerning it. His course, in my judgment, has been eccentric, whimsical, inconsistent, defended, in part, by weak and inconclusive, not to say, frivolous arguments; and taken as a whole thus far is unworthy of a statesman of large views and right temper in a great national conjuncture. From this remark I except his defense of the Right of Petition, and his opposition to the schemes for annexing Texas to the Union:—two matters that have been *accidentally* connected with Immediate Emancipation, but with which they have, in reality, no closer or more natural connexion, than with any other of the great interests of the country. For these instances of Mr. A.'s political firmness and ability I cheerfully accord to him as large a measure of honor as his most devoted friends and admirers can claim for them.

The abolitionists, carried away by their admiration of Mr. Adams's spirited defense of the Right of Petition, and his not less spirited opposition to the bold attempt to annex Texas to the Union, as well as by his often eloquent, though splenetic effusions against Southern Slavery and Southern *duelling*, have been well inclined to make his case an exception to their rule of dealing with public men, found substantially siding with the Slavocracy in any important particular. In 1838, when "questioning" candidates was in use, Mr. A. was not subjected, if I remember right, to that test, ineffectual as it generally turned out to be, and as it could be always made, by the ingenuity of the persons to whom it was applied.

But aside from the kind feelings which, for these causes, abolitionists cherished for Mr. Adams, not a few of them—especially such as were personally and politically friendly to Mr. A. were led to believe from his unqualified expressions of regard for the *object* of abolitionists, as well as detestation of slavery, that maturer consideration had determined him quietly to abandon the grounds on which he had heretofore differed with them about abolition in the District of Columbia and in Florida, and as to the admission of the latter into the Union as a Slave State. . . .

Mr. Adams was elected. The next spring (1839) he published, of his own mere notion, so far as any thing to the contrary appears, two letters filling fourteen columns of the National Intelligencer, addressed to the persons who had forwarded Petitions to him to be presented in the House. Neither the length nor the character of the address—for it dwelt on an exuberant variety of topics—would seem to have been called for, by the avowed object of it, which was to inform the petitioners in gross, instead of individually, as a matter of convenience, what disposition had been made of their respective petitions. In this address Mr. *Adams* laments the temper mutually rankling between the slaveholders and the abolitionists; and is convinced, that so long as it shall exist, the abolition of slavery in the Union, or even in the District of Columbia, is as far beyond the regions of possibility as any project of the philosophers of Laputa.

He expresses the opinion, that the multiplication in Anti-Slavery Societies rather weakens than promotes the prospect of immediate or early success.

He finds fault with the encouragement given to slaves to escape from their masters—with the exaggerated representations of the miseries of their condition—with the annoyance of candidates for popular elections by putting searching questions, etc.

He re-affirms the right of Florida to admission into the Union as a slave-State; also, his opposition to the abolition of Slavery in that Territory and in the District of Columbia. Respecting the latter, he says, he should in a special manner be opposed to the enactment of a law to operate exclusively on the people of the District against the will of that people, and in compliance with petitions from persons not to be affected themselves by the law. True, Mr. A. holds the opinion, that one human being cannot be made the property of another—that persons and things are, by the laws of Nature and of Nature's God so distinct, that no human laws can transform either into the other—but that the people of the District do not think so, and that in this case he must be guided by their opinion and not his own.

He assures the abolitionists that he desires not to interfere with the institutions of slavery where they are established—that he would not abolish slavery without a due regard to indemnify the slaveholder for his loss—that he can lend his hand to no project for the abolition of slavery in the United States without the consent of the master, and that Immediate Emancipation is a moral and physical impossibility!

Notwithstanding the creed of Mr. Adams differed so widely from that of the abolitionists, it turned out, that, at the election of 1840, his was the only Congressional district in Massachusetts where a candidate of the Liberty party was not presented to the people. The abolitionists seemed willing again to receive anti-slavery declamation in lieu of anti-slavery action, on the part of Mr. Adams, or, what is perhaps more probable, they expected that Mr. A.'s personal difficulties with the slaveholders in Congress, and the ill suppressed disgust with which his own party looked on his course, would, in the end, lead him to abandon his equivocal position, and take ground with *them.*

So it was again at the election of 1842—no Liberty party candidate was offered in Mr. A.'s district. It is but reasonable to

suppose, that, under such circumstances, the abolitionists generally supported Mr. Adams; and as his majority was small over
his Democratic opponent, that his election was owing to the
abolitionists having cast their votes in his favor.

This departure from rule in Mr. Adams's case has been followed by the consequences that usually attend, either directly or
indirectly departures from rules that have been deliberately
adjusted, for the management of large affairs. The abolitionists,
in electing Mr. Adams, made him *their own* witness—hoping like
an eager but inexperienced litigant, that his testimony would be
favorable to them, because he was heard to speak freely of the
general bad character of their adversary.—But the upshot of the
matter is, that every thing that is *substantial* in his testimony is
favorable to their adversary. To *them* he gives "words—words—
words!" The effect has been as it always is in such cases. . . .

The abolitionists insist on Immediate Emancipation as the
most practicable, and safest mode of emancipation, for all
parties: Mr. Adams despatches it as "a moral and physical impossibility!" . . .

For the logic by which Mr. Adams, after asseverating in almost
every variety of form our language can supply, that no laws can
confer or sanction property in human beings, has arrived at the
conclusion, that this barbarian, brutal usurpation ought to be
endured at the heart of the government till the wrong-doers
voluntarily relinquish their hold on their victims; that Florida
ought to be admitted into the Union, with a slave-holding constitution—as if an immunity to annihilate the inalienable rights of
the weaker portion of society were an essential element in our
republican forms of State Government; that Immediate Emancipation in this country is a moral and physical impossibility—in
view of the instances of its success on this continent, with which
Mr. Adams must be familiar—that Slavery must first be abolished among the Moham[me]dan and Pagan chiefs of Africa,
before it can be possible to put an end to it in Christian America
—for such logic, I say, I can entertain but little respect. . . .

41.

JAMES RUSSELL LOWELL:
"*Ez fer war, I call it murder*"

James Russell Lowell (1819–1891) was far from a radical in temper or deportment. In youth his idealism helped establish him with sentimental readers. Yet the era of reform also unlocked wit, satire and social radicalism in his mind which compare startlingly with his stiff, formal verse and essays of later years. Lowell suffered a general let-down in post-Civil War decades as a result of doubts raised by the Darwinian hypothesis and rude industrialism. But his earlier respect for the language of the folk, his merry puns and his keen ear and eye for people, as illustrated by his "Fable for Critics" (1848), added color and insight to abolitionism. The following was the first of his Biglow Papers *and furnished propaganda against the Mexican War.*

THRASH away, you'll *hev* to rattle
   On them kittle-drums o'yourn,—
'Taint a knowin' kind o' cattle
   Thet is ketched with mouldy corn;
Put in stiff, you fifer feller,
   Let folks see how spry you be,—
Guess you'll toot till you are yeller
   'Fore you git ahold o' me!

Thet air flag's a leetle rotten,
   Hope it aint your Sunday's best;—
Fact! it takes a sight o' cotton
   To stuff out a soger's chest:
Sence we farmers hev to pay fer 't,
   Ef you must wear humps like these,

SOURCE: James Russell Lowell, *The Biglow Papers* (Boston: Ticknor, Reed, and Fields, 1853), pp. 3–11.

S'posin' you should try salt hay fer 't,
   It would du ez slick ez grease.

'T would n't suit them Southun fellers,
   They 're a dreffle graspin' set,
We must ollers blow the bellers
   Wen they want their irons het;
May be it 's all right ez preachin',
   But *my* narves it kind o' grates,
Wen I see the overreachin'
   O' them nigger-drivin' States.

Them thet rule us, them slave-traders,
   Haint they cut a thunderin' swarth
(Helped by Yankee renegaders),
   Thru the vartu o' the North!
We begin to think it 's nater
   To take sarse an' not be riled;—
Who'd expect to see a tater
   All on eend at bein' biled?

Ez fer war, I call it murder,—
   There you hev it plain an' flat;
I don't want to go no furder
   Than my Testyment fer that;
God hez sed so plump an' fairly,
   It 's ez long ez it is broad,
An' you 've gut to git up airly
   Ef you want to take in God.

'Taint your eppyletts an' feathers
   Make the thing a grain more right;
'Taint afollerin' your bell-wethers
   Will excuse ye in His sight;
Ef you take a sword an' dror it,
   An' go stick a feller thru,
Guv'ment aint to answer for it,
   God 'll send the bill to you.

Wut's the use o' meetin'-goin'
   Every Sabbath, wet or dry,

Ef it 's right to go amowin'
   Feller-men like oats an' rye?
I dunno but wut it 's pooty
   Trainin' round in bobtail coats,—
But it 's curus Christian dooty
   This 'ere cuttin' folks's throats.

They may talk o' Freedom's airy
   Tell they 're pupple in the face,—
It's a grand gret cemetary
   Fer the barthrights of our race;
They jest want this Californy
   So 's to lug new slave-states in
To abuse ye, an' to scorn ye,
   An' to plunder ye like sin.

Aint it cute to see a Yankee
   Take sech everlastin' pains,
All to get the Devil's thankee
   Helpin' on 'em weld their chains?
Wy, it 's jest ez clear ez figgers,
   Clear ez one an' one make two,
Chaps thet make black slaves o' niggers
   Want to make wite slaves o' you.

Tell ye jest the eend I've come to
   Arter cipherin' plaguy smart,
An' it makes a handy sum, tu,
   Any gump could larn by heart;
Laborin' man an' laborin' woman
   Hev one glory an' one shame.
Ev'y thin' thet 's done inhuman
   Injers all on 'em the same.

'Taint by turnin' out to hack folks
   You 're agoin' to git your right,
Nor by lookin' down on black folks
   Coz you 're put upon by wite;
Slavery aint o' nary color,
   'Taint the hide thet makes it wus,
All it keers fer in a feller

'S jest to make him fill its pus.

Want to tackle *me* in, du ye?
 I expect you 'll hev to wait;
Wen cold lead puts daylight thru ye
 You'll begin to kal'late;
S'pose the crows wun't fall to pickin'
 All the carkiss from your bones,
Coz you helped to give a lickin'
  To them poor half-Spanish drones?

Jest go home an' ask our Nancy
 Wether I'd be sech a goose
Ez to jine ye,—guess you 'd fancy
 The etarnal bung wuz loose!
She wants me fer home consumption,
 Let alone the hay 's to mow,—
Ef you 're arter folks o' gumption,
 You 've a darned long row to hoe.

Take them editors thet 's crowin'
 Like a cockerel three months old,—
Don't ketch any on 'em goin',
 Though they *be* so blasted bold;
Aint they a prime lot o' fellers?
 'Fore they think on 't guess they 'll
  sprout
(Like a peach thet 's got the yellers),
 With the meanness bustin' out.

Wal, go 'long to help 'em stealin'
 Bigger pens to cram with slaves,
Help the men thet 's ollers dealin'
 Insults on your fathers' graves;
Help the strong to grind the feeble,
 Help the many agin the few,
Help the men thet call your people
 Witewashed slaves an' peddlin' crew!

Massachusetts, God forgive her,
 She 's akneelin' with the rest,

She, thet ough' to ha' clung ferever
   In her grand old eagle-nest;
She thet ough' to stand so fearless
   W'ile the wracks are round her hurled,
Holdin' up a beacon peerless
   To the oppressed of all the world!

Ha'n't they sold your colored seamen?
   Ha'nt they made your env'ys w'iz?
Wut 'll make ye act like freemen?
   Wut 'll git your dander riz?
Come, I'll tell ye wut I'm thinkin'
   Is our dooty in this fix,
They 'd ha' done 't ez quick ez winkin'
   In the days o' seventy-six.

Clang the bells in every steeple,
   Call all true men to disown
The tradoocers of our people,
   The enslavers o' their own;
Let our dear old Bay State proudly
   Put the trumpet to her mouth,
Let her ring this messidge loudly
   In the ears of all the South:—

"I'll return ye good fer evil
   Much as we frail mortils can,
But I wun't go help the Devil
   Makin' man the cus o' man;
Call me coward, call me traiter,
   Jest as suits your mean idees,—
Here I stand a tyrant-hater,
   An' the friend o' God an' Peace!"

Ef I'd *my* way I hed ruther
   We should go to work an' part,
They take one way, we take t' other,
   Guess it would n't break my heart;
Man hed ough' to put asunder
   Them thet God has noways jined;
An' I should n't gretly wonder
   Ef there's thousands o' my mind.

42.

THOMAS CORWIN:
"*Let us call home our armies*"

Thomas Corwin (1794–1865), governor of Ohio, United States Senator and later Secretary of the Treasury, delivered one of the greatest speeches in the nation's history: his protest against the Mexican War. Corwin was representative of tendencies in American life which gave essentially conservatives, of whom he was one, rapport on specific issues with the most unqualified radicals. Such tendencies ensured a flexible politics not readily controlled by the most adroit party managers. Under Lincoln, Corwin served as ambassador to Mexico.

If war is made [in England] by the Crown, and the Commons do not approve of it, refusal to grant supplies is the easy remedy—one, too, which renders it impossible for a king of England to carry forward any war which may be displeasing to the English people. Yes, sir, in England, since 1688, it has not been in the power of a British sovereign to do that, which in your boasted Republic, an American president, under the auspices of what you call Democracy, has done—make war, without consent of the legislative power. In England, supplies are at once refused, if Parliament does not approve the objects of the war. *Here,* we are told, we must not look to the objects of the war, being *in the war*—made by the President—we must help him to fight it out, should it even please him to carry it to the utter extermination of the Mexican race. Sir, I believe it must proceed to this shocking extreme, if you are, by war, to "conquer a peace." Here, then, is your condition. The President involves you in war without your

SOURCE: Josiah Morrow, ed., *Life and Speeches of Thomas Corwin* (Cincinnati, O.: W. H. Anderson & Co., 1896), pp. 300 ff.

consent. Being *in* such a war, it is demanded as a duty, that we grant men and money to carry it on. The President tells us he shall prosecute this war, till Mexico pays us, or agrees to pay us, all its expenses. I am not willing to scourge Mexico thus; and the only means left me is to say to the commander-in-chief, "Call home your army, I will feed and clothe it no longer; you have whipped Mexico into three pitched battles, this is revenge enough; this is punishment enough."

The President has said he does not expect to hold Mexican territory by conquest. Why then conquer it? Why waste thousands of lives and millions of money fortifying towns and creating governments, if, at the end of the war, you retire from the graves of your soldiers and the desolated country of your foes, only to get money from Mexico for the expense of all your toil and sacrifice? Who ever heard, since Christianity was propagated among men, of a nation taxing its people, enlisting its young men and marching off two thousand miles to fight a people merely to be paid for it in money? What is this but hunting a market for blood, selling the lives of your young men, marching them in regiments to be slaughtered and paid for, like oxen and brute beasts? Sir, this is, when stripped naked, that atrocious idea first promulgated in the President's message, and now advocated here, of fighting on till we can get our indemnity for the past as well as the present slaughter. We have chastised Mexico, and if it were worth while to do so, we have, I dare say, satisfied the world that we can fight. What now? Why the mothers of America are asked to send another of their sons to blow out the brains of Mexicans because they refuse to pay the price of the first who fell there, fighting for glory! And what if the second fall, too? The Executive, the parental reply is, "we shall have him paid for, we shall get full indemnity!" Sir, I have no patience with this flagitious notion of fighting for indemnity, and this under the equally absurd and hypocritical pretense of securing an honorable peace. An honorable peace! If you have accomplished the objects of the war (if indeed you had an object which you dare to avow), cease to fight, and you will have peace. Conquer your insane love of false glory, and you will "conquer a peace." Sir, if your commander-in-chief will not do this, I will endeavor to compel him, and as I find no other means, I shall refuse supplies—without the money of the people, he cannot go further. He asks me for that money; I wish him to bring your armies home, to cease shedding blood *for* money; if he refuses, I will refuse supplies, and then I know he *must,* he will cease his further sale of the lives of my countrymen. May we not, *ought* we not now to do this? I can hear no reason why we should not, except this: It is said that we are *in* war, wrongfully it may be, but, being in, the President is responsible, and we must give *him* the means *he* requires! He responsible! Sir, we, we are responsible, if having the power to stay this plague, we refuse to do so. . . .

Mr. President, I dismiss this branch of the subject, and beg the indulgence of the Senate to some reflections on the particular bill now under consideration. I voted for a bill somewhat like the present at the last session—our army was then in the neighborhood of our line. I then hoped that the President did sincerely desire a peace. Our army had not then penetrated far into Mexico and I did hope that with the two millions then proposed, we might get peace, and avoid the slaughter, the shame, the crime, of an aggressive, unprovoked war. But now you have overrun half of Mexico, you have exasperated and irritated her people, you claim indemnity for all expenses incurred in doing this mischief, and boldly ask her to give up New Mexico and California; and, as a bribe to her patriotism, seizing on her property, you offer three millions to pay the soldiers she has called out to repel your invasion, on condition that she will give up to you at least one-third of her whole territory. This is the modest—I should say, the monstrous—proposition now before us, as explained by the Chairman of the Committee on Foreign Relations [Mr. SEVIER], who reported the bill. I cannot now give my assent to this. . . .

You may wrest provinces from Mexico by war—you may hold

them by the right of the strongest—you may rob her, but a treaty of peace to that effect with the people of Mexico, legitimately and freely made, you never will have! I thank God that it is so, as well for the sake of the Mexican people as ourselves, for, unlike the Senator from Alabama [Mr. BAGBY], I do not value the life of a citizen of the United States above the lives of a hundred thousand Mexican women and children—a rather cold sort of philanthropy, in my judgment. For the sake of Mexico then, as well as our own country, I rejoice that it is an impossibility, that you can obtain by treaty from her those territories, under the existing state of things.

I am somewhat at a loss to know, on what plan of operations gentlemen having charge of this war intend to proceed. We hear much said of the terror of your arms. The affrighted Mexican, it is said, when you shall have drenched his country in blood, will sue for peace, and thus you will indeed "conquer peace." This is the heroic and savage tone in which we have heretofore been lectured by our friends on the other side of the chamber, especially by the Senator from Michigan [GENERAL CASS]. But suddenly the Chairman of the Committee on Foreign Relations comes to us with a smooth phrase of diplomacy, made potent by the gentle suasion of gold. The Chairman of the Committee on Military Affairs calls for thirty millions of money and ten thousand regular troops; these, we are assured, shall "conquer peace," if the obstinate Celt refuses to treat till we shall whip him in another field of blood. What a delightful scene in the nineteenth century of the Christian era? What an interesting sight to see these two representatives of war and peace moving in grand procession through the halls of the Montezumas! The Senator from Michigan [GENERAL CASS], red with the blood of recent slaughter, the gory spear of Achilles in his hand and the hoarse clarion of war in his mouth, blowing a blast "so loud and deep" that the sleeping echoes of the lofty Cordilleras start from their caverns and return the sound, till every ear from Panama to Santa Fe is deafened with the roar. By his side, with "modest mien and downcast look," comes the Senator from Arkansas [Mr. SEVIER], covered from head to foot with a gorgeous robe, glittering and embossed with three millions of shining gold, putting to shame "the wealth of Ormus or of Ind." The olive of Minerva graces his brow; in his right hand is the delicate rebec, from which are breathed, in Lydian measure, notes "that tell of naught but love and peace." I fear very much you will scarcely be able to explain to the simple, savage mind of the half-civilized Mexicans, the puzzling dualism of this scene, at once gorgeous and grotesque. . . .

What is the territory, Mr. President, which you propose to wrest from Mexico? It is consecrated to the heart of the Mexican by many a well-fought battle, with his old Castilian master. His Bunker Hills, and Saratogas, and Yorktowns are there. The Mexican can say, "There I bled for liberty! and shall I surrender that consecrated home of my affections to the Anglo-Saxon invaders? What do they want with it? They have Texas already. They have possessed themselves of the territory between the Nueces and the Rio Grande. What else do they want? To what shall I point my children as memorials of that independence which I bequeath to them, when those battle-fields shall have passed from my possession?"

Sir, had one come and demanded Bunker Hill of the people of Massachusetts, had England's lion ever showed himself there, is there a man over thirteen, and under ninety who would not have been ready to meet him—is there a river on this continent that would not have run red with blood—is there a field but would have been piled high with the unburied bones of slaughtered Americans before these consecrated battle-fields of liberty should have been wrested from us? But this same American goes into a sister republic, and says to poor, weak Mexico, "Give up your territory—you are unworthy to possess it—I have got one-half already—all I ask of you is to give up the other!" England might as well, in the circumstances I have described, have come and demanded of us, "Give up the Atlantic slope—give up this trifling territory from the Alleghany mountains to the sea; it is only from Maine to St. Mary's—only about one-third of your Republic, and the least interesting portion of it." What would be the response? They would say, we must give this up to John Bull. Why? "He wants room." The Senator from Michigan says he must have this. Why, my worthy Christian brother, on what principle of justice? "I want room!"

Sir, look at this pretense of want of room. With twenty millions of people, you have about one thousand millions of acres of land, inviting settlement by every conceivable argument—bringing them down to a quarter of a dollar an acre, and allowing every man to squat where he pleases. But the Senator from Michigan says we will be two hundred millions in a few years, and we want room. If I were a Mexican I would tell you, "Have you not room in your own country to bury your dead men? If you come into mine we will greet you with bloody hands, and welcome you to hospitable graves."

Why, says the Chairman of this Committee of Foreign Relations, it is the most reasonable thing in the world! We ought to have the Bay of San Francisco. Why? Because it is the best harbor on the Pacific! It has been my fortune, Mr. President, to have practiced a good deal in criminal courts in the course of my life, but I never yet heard a thief, arraigned for stealing a horse, plead that it was the best horse that he could find in the country! We want California. What for? Why, says the Senator from Michigan, we will have it; and the Senator from South Carolina, with a very mistaken view, I think, of policy, says, you can't keep our people from going there. I don't desire to prevent them. Let them go and seek their happiness in whatever country or clime it pleases them. . . .

Sir, I have read, in some account of your battle of Monterey, of a lovely Mexican girl, who, with the benevolence of an angel in her bosom, and the robust courage of a hero in her heart, was busily engaged, during the bloody conflict, amid the crash of falling houses, the groans of the dying, and the wild shriek of battle, in carrying water to slake the burning thirst of the wounded of either host. While bending over a wounded American soldier, a cannon-ball struck her and blew her to atoms! Sir, I do not charge my brave, generous-hearted countrymen who fought that fight with this. No, no! We who send them—we who know that scenes like this, which might send tears of sorrow "down Pluto's iron cheek," are the invariable, inevitable attendants on war—*we* are accountable for this. And this—this is the way we are to be made known to Europe. This—*this* is to be the undying renown of free, republican America! "She has stormed a city—killed many of its inhabitants of both sexes—she has room!" *So* it will read. Sir, if this were our only history, then may God of His mercy grant that its volume may speedily come to a close. . . .

Let us abandon all idea of acquiring further territory, and by consequence cease at once to prosecute this war. Let us call home our armies, and bring them at once within our own acknowledged limits. Show Mexico that you are sincere when you say you desire nothing by conquest. She has learned that she cannot encounter you in war, and if she had not, she is too weak to disturb you here. Tender her peace, and my life on it, she will then accept it. But whether she shall or not, you will have peace without her consent. It is your invasion that has made war, your retreat will restore peace. Let us then close forever the approaches of internal feud, and so return to the ancient concord and the old way of national prosperity and permanent glory. Let us here, in this temple consecrated to the Union, perform a solemn lustration; let us wash Mexican blood from our hands, and on these altars, in the presence of that image of the Father of his country that looks down upon us, swear to preserve honorable peace with all the world, and eternal brotherhood with each other.

43.

MONCURE DANIEL CONWAY:
I: Reform in the South: A Tortuous Path

Moncure Daniel Conway (1832–1907), like many Southerners troubled by problems related to slavery, spent most of his life in the North. He became a minister, an abolitionist and a literary figure. His efforts at growth and understanding were constricted in ways little known farther North to many young persons of his social status.

My pamphlet on Free Schools excited no discussion in Virginia. My only important sympathizers were Law Professor Minor of the University of Virginia and Samuel M. Janney, Quaker preacher in Loudoun. My father was pleased, though he did not express agreement.

I looked eagerly into my New York "Tribune" to see what Greeley would say about it. His paragraph (editorial) was friendly, but I only remember the closing words: "Virginia's white children will never be educated till its coloured children are free." This shaft went very deep into me, for I found that proslavery "philosophers" considered the Free School system a dangerous Northern "ism."

My mere Virginianism had received a number of blows during my residence in Warrenton,—notably by the mob murder of a free negro named Grayson, at Culpeper Court House. The man had been sentenced for murdering a Mr. Miller, but the evidence against him was weak, while the local demand for a victim was

SOURCE: Moncure Daniel Conway, *Autobiography* (Boston: Houghton, Mifflin and Company, 1904), vol. II, pp. 88 ff.

furious. The Court of Appeals had ordered a new trial, to take place at Warrenton. Grayson was taken from gaol by a mob of several hundred who, as their victim was nobody's property, met but feeble resistance, and hanged,—protesting his innocence to the last. On this I wrote in the Warrenton paper, July 20, 1850: "The whole affair would read better among the records of the Spanish Inquisition, or of the feudal age of Britain, than by the light of the full noon of the nineteenth century."

The innocence of Grayson was afterwards established, as no doubt the innocence of many of the victims of the bloodhounds euphemistically called lynchers would be by fair trial.

This was the only case of the negro murder called "lynching" that I ever heard of before the Union war, and the indignation throughout the South prevented its being made a count against slavery.

I never up to that time had heard any person say a word against the rectitude of slavery. The nearest to it was what my father had said, "It is a doomed institution." It was too close to my eyes to be seen. That it would ever end was not even prophesied by its Northern antagonists. Now, however, when a moral cause—universal education—had taken possession of me, slavery barred my way in every direction. Before my radical Jeffersonianism the negro stood demanding recognition as a man and a brother; else he must be treated as an inferior animal.

At this moment the new theory of Agassiz appeared—that the races of mankind are not from a single pair. I had conversed with Professor Baird of the Smithsonian Institution on the subject, and found that he agreed with Agassiz. In June, 1850, Agassiz delivered a lecture on the subject in Cambridge, Mass., which was expanded into a long article in the "Christian Examiner" for July. In this manifesto the professor argued only by implication against the unity of human species; but where he feared to tread my crudity rushed in. It was not the vanity of a youth under nineteen, but a spirit struggling for existence amid fatal conditions, which led me to announce in the Franklin Lyceum (Warrenton), of which I was secretary, a theory that the negro was not a man within the meaning of the Declaration of Independence. All of the other members, though not antislavery, exclaimed against the "infidelity" of the theory, though none answered my argument that negroes, if human, were entitled to liberty. My eccentric views were talked about, and I found myself the centre of a religious tempest in little Warrenton. If the negro was not descended from Adam he had not like us whites inherited depravity. And wherefore our missions to the many non-Caucasian races?

I sat down as wrangler of the new theory, surrounded myself with books on races, mental philosophy, and Biblical criticism, and achieved fifteen closely written letter pages to prove that mankind are not derived from one pair; that the "Caucasian" race is the highest species; and that this supreme race has the same right of dominion over the lower species of his genus that he has over quadrupeds,—the same right in kind but not in degree.

This elaborate essay was not printed, and I had forgotten that wrappings of my dead self. It is dated "Warrenton, Va., Dec., 1850." It vaguely recalls to me the moral crisis in my life. Whether it was the dumb answers of the coloured servants moving about the house, cheerfully yielding me unrequited services, or whether my eyes recognized in the completed essay a fallacy in the assumption of a standard of humanity not warranted by the facts, the paper was thrown aside. The so-called "conversion" of my college days had been a boyish delusion; the real conversion came now at the end of 1850. I had caught a vision of my superficiality, casuistry, perhaps also of the ease with which I could consign a whole race to degradation. I do not remember whether or not my theory of negro inferiority was consciously altered, but an overwhelming sense of my own inferiority came upon me. The last words of my Warrenton diary are, "Had a violent fever that night." The fever was mental and spiritual more than physical; when it passed away it left me with a determination to devote my life to the elevation and welfare of my fellow-beings, white and black. The man of Nazareth had drawn near and said, "What thou doest to the least of these my brothers, thou art doing to me." . . .

On my homeward way I passed a week in Washington. "Senator Hunter smuggled me into the Senate lobby so that I heard the great debate on the Boston riot." This was on February 18, 1851. Three days before, when the fugitive slave Shadrach was on trial in Boston, the case was postponed till next day, and at that moment about forty coloured men swarmed into the court-room, Shadrach became undistinguishable among them, and was spirited away to Canada. Not a blow was struck. "Nobody injured, nobody wronged, but simply a chattel transformed into a man," wrote Garrison in the "Liberator," but the incident caused excitement in Congress and was described as a "riot." The new Fugitive Slave Law was beginning to bear its fatal fruits. Only a few months before I had been assisting at the banquet given at Warrenton to its author, Senator Mason, but now for the first time discovered that the new law was of serious importance. I shall never forget the wrath that shrivelled up the already wrinkled face of Henry Clay, nor his sharp voice, as he leaped forward and cried, "This outrage is the greater because it was by people not of our race, by persons who possess no part in our political system, and the question arises whether we shall have a government of white men or of blacks."[1] I was not antislavery, and did not doubt at the time that it was a murderous attack on the court, but Clay's speech and manner grated on me, and I was more pleased with the speech of Jefferson Davis. The Massachusetts Senator Davis had tried to soothe the wrath of the compro-

1. In the *Life of Garrison*, Vol. 3, p. 326, Clay is said to have used the phrase "a band who are not of our people." The *Congressional Globe* rightly reports the word "race," but for the rest I have an impression that the speech is considerably manipulated in the official report. On May 23 at Albany Daniel Webster declared the rescue of Shadrach "an act of clear treason," but being, according to Clay, by persons with "no part in our political system," there was no treason in the case. [Conway's note.]

misers who had predicted the reign of peace to follow their "Omnibus Bill;" but when he alluded to the "common sentiment" in Massachusetts against the rendition of fugitives, a voice (that of Hale, I think) cried, "Universal sentiment." Whereupon Jefferson Davis said calmly, "If that be so the law is dead in that State. Wherever mobs can rule, and law is silenced beneath tumult, this is a wholly impracticable government. It was not organized as one of force, its strength is moral, and moral only. I for one will never give my vote to extend a single arm of the Federal power for the coercion of Massachusetts." This was in reply to Foote, who said he had private knowledge that the President, Fillmore, had ordered Commodore Read at Philadelphia to use all of his marine force if necessary to sustain this law, and cited the action of President Washington in marching into Pennsylvania to crush the "Whiskey Rebellion." The debate gave me much to think of. . . .

The Baltimore Conference, February, 1852, gave me Frederick Circuit, now "Liberty Circuit," in Frederick County, Md. Heavy-hearted for the loss of my brother, I started from home, March 26, for my new field.

On the Potomac boat I met Rev. Dr. William Smith (Methodist), president of Randolph-Macon College, Virginia, distinguished by his propaganda of a new proslavery sociology. We had some conversation, and he asked me, "What is the principle of slavery?" I answered, "It has no principle." He said, "The principle of slavery clearly is the submission of one will to another, and government is inconceivable without it." "Then," said I, "government is inconceivably wrong." He said, "You ought to marry Fanny Wright. The best government is where the two elements of slavery and freedom balance. I only wish I had you in my senior class, to which I lecture on this subject every week."

Thus were the winds sown from which whirlwinds were presently reaped!

44.

JAMES McCUNE SMITH:
II: *The South as Reaction: A Negro Response*

Southern apologists did not hesitate to distort reality in the interests of their point of view. A notorious case was their influence upon the first United States census of the insane (1840) which offered invidious and frequently false data calculated to prove Negro inferiority. In 1844 John C. Calhoun, then Secretary of State, during official correspondence bearing on the case of the Creole, *a slave ship on which Negroes mutinied, made gratuitous remarks impugning the character and intelligence of Negroes. A New York meeting of Negroes resulted in a statesmanlike reply by one of them: Dr. James McCune Smith (1813–1867), born free in New York, a graduate of the University of Glasgow and one of the most effective writers on themes concerning his people. His detail and precision made him formidable on this and other occasions. His reply, endorsed by another convocation of Negroes, was presented to the United States Senate, printed in the* New York Tribune *and reprinted in the* Liberator.

The memorial of the undersigned, free colored citizens of the city and county of New York, respectfully showeth, that

Whereas, in a letter, addressed to the Right Hon. Richard Pakenham, &c (bearing date April 18th, 1844,) the Hon. John C. Calhoun, Secretary of State for these United States, saith,

First, "That in the States which have changed their former relations, (the States which have emancipated their slaves, meaning,) the African race has sunk into vice and pauperism";

SOURCE: Liberator, May 31, 1844.

Secondly, That this "vice and pauperism" is "accompanied by the bodily and mental afflictions incident thereto—deafness, blindness, insanity and idiocy"; and that "the number of deaf, dumb, blind, idiots and insane of the Negroes in the States which have changed the ancient relation between the races is one out of every ninety-six"; and, that, "in the State of Maine, the number of Negroes returned as deaf, dumb, blind, insane and idiots, by the census of 1840, is one out of every twelve";

Thirdly, "And the number of Negroes, who are deaf and dumb, blind, idiots, insane, paupers and in prison, in the States that have changed, (the free States, meaning,) is one out of every six";

Fourthly, While in all other States that have retained the ancient relations (the slave States, meaning,) between them (the races, meaning,) "they (the slaves, meaning,) have improved greatly in every respect, in number, comfort, intelligence and morals";

And whereas, in regard to these allegations,

First, Your memorialists have great reason to doubt the accuracy of the first; because,

Secondly, It appears in regard to the second allegation, which is the particular proof of the first, that in an examination of the census of 1840, it is found to be self-contradictory: to wit, in asserting the existence of the free colored persons insane, blind, deaf, dumb, in certain towns in free States, in which towns, it appears by the same census of 1840, there are no free colored persons whatever of any condition:

For example, in

	Insane	Blind	Deaf & Dumb
MAINE			
In 8 towns containing no colored— there are reported,	27	1	2

NEW HAMPSHIRE

11 towns containing no colored— there are reported,	12	0	3

VERMONT

2 towns containing no colored— there are reported,	2	2	1

MASSACHUSETTS

5 towns containing no colored— there are reported,	10	1	0
1 town Worcester, the white insane at the Asylum are returned as colored	133	0	0

NEW YORK

19 towns containing no colored— there are reported,	29	8	5

PENNSYLVANIA

11 towns containing no colored— there are reported,	20	6	6

OHIO

33 towns containing no colored— there are reported,	48	9	5

INDIANA

4 towns containing no colored— there are reported,	6	9	7

ILLINOIS

9 towns containing no colored— there are reported,	18	0	3

MICHIGAN

12 towns containing no colored— there are reported,	12	2	5

IOWA

1 town containing no colored—there are reported,	2	0	4

Showing

	Colored Insane	Blind	Deaf & Dumb
Total colored inhabitants—000	186	38	36

By the same census, it appears that in the above, and other towns in the free States, there is—

An excess of colored insane over colored residents,	213
Error in the return of colored for white insane at Worcester, Mass.	133
Total,	346

The whole number of colored insane in the free States being stated to be 1,199 by the census of 1840; if from this number we deduct the 346 shown to be not colored persons, there remains 853 colored insane in the free States, or one in about 200, which your memorialists are satisfied is greatly beyond the actual proportion; because, so far as your memorialists have been able to ascertain, the proportion of the insane among the free colored is not greater than among the white population of the free States. It is stated, for example, by Dr. J. Ray, the physician of the Lunatic Asylum of the State of Maine, that there are not five colored lunatics or insane in that State. In the Lunatic Asylum at Blackwell's Island, in the county of New York, there are but 17 colored insane, or about 1 to 1000 colored inhabitants of this county. In 1837, the same proportion existed in the free colored population of Philadelphia.

In regard to the deaf, dumb and blind, it will be seen that the census is likewise self contradictory, asserting that there are 74 free colored afflicted with these dispensations, in towns which contain no colored inhabitants.

Thirdly, In regard to the third allegation, which asserts that one in every six of the free colored in the free States are either "deaf, dumb, blind, insane, or in prison," or, in other words, that there are 30,000 free colored supported at the public charge in the free States, your memorialists humbly think that they have furnished, in answer to the second allegation, sufficient facts to disprove the entire accuracy of this astounding assertion. And your memorialists further believe, that the same errors have crept into the census and other documents based thereon, in regard to the pauperism of the free colored, as they have shown to have crept into the census in regard to the insane, &c. Especially when your memorialists know, from the books of the alms-houses of New York and Philadelphia, there are in these places one colored pauper to about 100 of the colored population, a proportion which is about the same as the pauperism of the free white citizens of these cities; and as these cities contain 37,000, more than one sixth part of the entire colored population of the free States; and as it is known that the proportion of paupers in this as well as in other classes is greatest in large cities, it is a fair inference that the third allegation, at least so much of it as relates to pauperism, cannot be accurate.

Fourthly, In relation to the fourth allegation, which is in substance, that the slaves have improved in morals, intelligence, comfort and number—reversing the order of the items; your memorialists would observe, that the natural increase of the slaves (which is greater than the natural increase of the whites or of the free colored) is a measure of their relative fecundity, not of their relative condition. Whilst the percentage of longevity, and the ratio of mortality, which are tests of relative condition, are greatly in favor of the free colored, the more remotely they may be removed in time from slavery. For the slaves who live beyond 36 years are only 15.49 per cent, while free colored in the free States who live beyond 36 years are 22.68, showing a balance of 7.19 per cent in favor of the condition of the free colored.

In the cities of New York and Philadelphia (by the city Inspector's reports), it appears that a joint population of 37,000 free colored have diminished their ratio of mortality from 1 in 17 in Philadelphia, and 1 in 21 in New York in 1820; to 1 in 40, in both places in 1843, being a distinct improvement in *condition* of at least 100 per cent in 23 years! There are no records of the mortality among slaves!

In regard to *intelligence* there are in the free States, to a total population of 170,000 free colored persons, 40,000 children of an age to go to school, one school to every 543 children, in addition to a large number of children attending white schools, and a number of colored students who are pursuing their studies at Oberlin Western Theological Seminary, and Dartmouth College whilst the children of slaves are forbidden to be taught to read, under heavy penalties, in the States which have not changed the *ancient relations—death* being the penalty for the second offence. Your memorialists do not deem it irrelevant to state, in this connexion, that the proportion of adults above 20 years of age, who cannot read or write, is 1 in 1081, in the States which have changed the *ancient relations* (the free States) whilst the number of adults who cannot read and write is 1 in 144, in the States that have not changed the ancient relations (the slave States).

In regard to morals, believing that religion is the only basis of sound morals, your memorialists would state that there are to the 170,000 free colored people of the free States—

Denominations	Churches
Independent Methodists	2
Baptist Association	2
Methodist	284
Baptist	15
Presbyterian & Congregational	3
Episcopal	6
Lutheran	1
Total	318

Making about one church to every 543 of the free colored of the free States.

At the same time, granting that all the churches in the South are promiscuously attended by the slaves and whites, it appears, taking the eleven cities of Baltimore, Richmond, Petersburgh, Virginia, Norfolk, Charleston, Savannah, Mobile, New Orleans, Louisville, St. Louis and Washington, with a total population, of all classes, of 360,905; these cities contain only 167 churches; or one church to every 2,161 inhabitants; from which it follows that the free colored people of the North have a greater number of churches by nearly four fold, than have the entire population of these slave-holding cities. They have, also, 340 Benevolent societies; and 7 newspapers are printed by the free colored people of the free States.

For all of which reasons, your memorialists would humbly pray—

1st. That your honorable body would cause the Census of 1840 to be reexamined, and so far as possible, corrected anew, in the Department of State, in order that the head of that Department may have facts upon which to found his arguments.

2d. That your honorable body would establish at Washington, a general office of Registration, with a proper officer at its head, who shall cause to be returned from each county in the United States, a yearly report of the sanitary condition of each class of inhabitants, as well as the births, deaths, and marriages.

3d. That your honorable body will cause to be taken, in the Census of 1850, the number of adults who cannot read and write among the whites, the slaves, and the free people of color, in every county of the United States.

And your Memorialists will ever pray.

45.

ESTEBAN MONTEJO:

Cuban Slavery

Slavery outside the United States was treated politically, rather than in terms of nations and traditions. Abolitionists praised the Haitian revolutionaries and revered Toussaint L'Ouverture as a Moses of his people. They praised British emancipation in the Caribbean and defended its social and material results in Jamaica and elsewhere. Southern partisans, on the other side, scorned Haiti as a land of chaos and barbarism. They denounced the British as fools and hypocrites. Cuba was viewed as being naturally an American island, and in the notorious Ostend Manifesto of 1854 American ministers to Spain, France and Great Britain, including James Buchanan, who became President in 1856, recommended the acquisition of Cuba by purchase or seizure. In such politicalized circumstances it was difficult to humanize the people involved. The following is by Esteban Montejo, a Negro born in slavery who lived more than a hundred years through emancipation, revolution, American relations and into the regime of Fidel Castro. His memoirs, carefully collected by a talented poet and litterateur Miguel Barnet and published as The Autobiography of a Runaway Slave, *are unique in their precise sense of people and relationships. Though wholly illiterate and superstitious, Montejo, in all his gusto and dignity, compels respect.*

Because of being a runaway I never knew my parents. I never even saw them. But this is not sad, because it is true.

SOURCE: From *Autobiography of a Runaway Slave,* by Esteban Montejo, translated by Jocasta Innes, edited by Miguel Barnet. Copyright © 1968 by The Bodley Head, Ltd. Reprinted by permission of Pantheon Books, a division of Random House, Inc.

Like all children born into slavery, *criollitos*[1] as they called them, I was born in an infirmary where they took the pregnant Negresses to give birth. I think it was the Santa Teresa plantation, but I am not sure. I do remember my godparents talking a lot about this plantation and its owners, people called La Ronda. My godparents were called by this name for a long time, till slavery left Cuba.

Negroes were sold like pigs, and they sold me at once, which is why I remember nothing about the place. I know it was somewhere in the region where I was born, in the upper part of Las Villas, Zulueta, Remedios, Caibarién, all the villages before you come to the sea. Then the picture of another plantation comes to mind: the Flor de Sagua. I don't know if that was the place where I worked for the first time, but I do remember running away from there once; I decided I'd had enough of that bloody place, and I was off! But they caught me without a struggle, clapped a pair of shackles on me (I can still feel them when I think back), screwed them up tight and sent me back to work wearing them. You talk about this sort of thing today and people don't believe you, but it happened to me and I have to say so.

The owner of that plantation has a funny name, one of those long ones with lots of parts. He was everything bad: stupid, evil-tempered, swollen-headed. . . . He used to ride past in the fly with his wife and smart friends through the cane-fields, waving a handkerchief, but that was as near as he ever got to us. The owners never went to the fields. One odd thing about this man: I remember he had a smart Negro, a first-rate driver, with gold rings in his ears and everything. All those drivers were scabs and tale-bearers. You might say they were the dandies of the coloured people.

At the Flor de Sagua I started work on the *bagasse*[2] wagons. I sat on the box and drove the mule. If the wagon was very full I

1. Little Creole. Creole was a first-generation Cuban, black or white. [Barnet's note, here and elsewhere.]
2. The fibres left after the juice has been extracted from sugar-cane.

stopped the mule, got down and led it by the rein. The mules were hardmouthed and you had to bear down on the reins like the devil. Your back began to grow hunched. A lot of people are walking around now almost hunchbacked because of those mules. The wagons went out piled to the top. They were always unloaded in the sugar-mill town, and the *bagasse* had to be spread out to dry. It was scattered with a hook, then it was taken, dried, to the furnaces. This was done to make steam. I suppose that was the first work I did. At least, that's what my memory tells me.

All the indoor parts of the plantation were primitive; not like today with their lights and fast machinery. They were called *cachimbos,* because that is the word for a small sugar-mill. In them the sugar was evaporated and drained. There were some which did not make sugar, but syrup and pan sugar. Almost all of them belonged to a single owner; these were called *trapiches*. There were three sugar-boilers in the *cachimbos*—big copper ones with wide mouths. The first cooked the cane-juice, in the next the froth was taken off, and in the third the treacle was boiled tiil ready. *Cachaza* was what we called the froth which was left over from the cane-juice. It came off in a hard crust and was very good for pigs. When the treacle was ready, you took a ladle with a long wooden handle and poured it into a trough and from there into the sugarlocker, which stood a short distance from the boilers. That was where they drained the *muscovado*, or unrefined sugar, which had most of the syrup left in it. In those days the centrifuge, as they call it, did not exist.

Once the sugar in the locker had cooled, you had to go in barefoot with spade and shovel and a hand barrow. One Negro always went in front and another behind. The barrow was to take the hogsheads to the *tinglado,* a long shed with two beams where the hogsheads were stacked to drain the sugar. The syrup which drained off the hogsheads was given to the mill-town people and was given to the pigs and sheep. They got very fat on it.

To make refined sugar there were some big funnels into which the raw sugar was poured to be refined. That sugar looked like the sort we have today, white sugar. The funnels were known as "moulds."

I know that part of sugar-making better than most people who only know the cane as it is outside, in the fields. And to tell the truth I preferred the inside part, it was easier. At Flor de Sagua I worked in the sugarlocker, but this was after I had got experience working with *bagasse*. That was spade-and-shovel work. To my mind even cane-cutting was preferable. I must have been ten years old then, and that was why they had not sent me to work in the fields. But ten then was like thirty now, because boys worked like oxen.

If a boy was pretty and lively he was sent inside, to the master's house. And there they started softening him up and . . . well, I don't know! They used to give the boy a long palm-leaf and make him stand at one end of the table while they ate. And they said, 'Now see that no flies get in the food!' If a fly did, they scolded him severely and even whipped him. I never did this work because I never wanted to be on closer terms with the masters. I was a runaway from birth.

Sunday was the liveliest day in the plantations. I don't know where the slaves found the energy for it. Their biggest fiestas were held on that day. On some plantations the drumming started at midday or one o'clock. At Flor de Sagua it began very early. The excitement, the games, and children rushing about started at sunrise. The barracoon came to life in a flash; it was like the end of the world. And in spite of work and everything the people woke up cheerful. The overseer and deputy overseer came into the barracoon and started chatting up the black women. I noticed that the Chinese kept apart; those buggers had no ear for drums and they stayed in their little corners. But they thought a lot; to my mind they spent more time thinking than the blacks. No one took any notice of them, and people went on with their dances.

The one I remember best is the *yuka*. Three drums were played for the *yuka*: the *caja*, the *mula*, and the *cachimbo*, which was the smallest one. In the background they drummed with two sticks on hollowed-out cedar trunks. The slaves made those themselves and I think they were called *catá*. The *yuka* was danced in couples, with wild movements. Sometimes they swooped about like birds, and it almost looked as if they were going to fly, they moved so fast. They gave little hops with their hands on their waists. Everyone sang to excite the dancers. . . .

As soon as the drums started on Sunday the Negroes went down to the stream to bathe—there was always a little stream near every plantation. It sometimes happened that a woman lingered behind and met a man just as he was about to go into the water. Then they would go off together and get down to business. If not, they would go to the reservoirs, which were the pools they dug to store water. They also used to play hide-and-seek there, chasing the women and trying to catch them.

The women who were not involved in this little game stayed in the barracoons and washed themselves in a tub. These tubs were very big and there were one or two for the whole settlement.

Shaving and cutting hair was done by the slaves themselves. They took a long knife and, like someone grooming a horse, they sliced off the woolly hair. There was always someone who liked to clip, and he became the expert. They cut hair the way they do now. And it never hurt, because hair is the most peculiar stuff; although you can see it growing and everything, it's dead. The women arranged their hair with curls and little partings. Their heads used to look like melon skins. They liked the excitement of fixing their hair one way one day and another way the next. One day it would have little partings, the next day ringlets, another day it would be combed flat. They cleaned their teeth with strips of soap-tree bark, and this made them very white. All this excitement was reserved for Sundays.

Everyone had a special outfit that day. The Negroes bought

themselves rawhide boots, in a style I haven't seen since, from nearby shops where they went with the master's permission. They wore red and green *vayajá* scarves around their necks, and round their heads and waists too, like in the *maní* dance. And they decked themselves with rings in their ears and rings on all their fingers, real gold. Some of them wore not gold but fine silver bracelets which came as high as their elbows, and patent leather shoes.

The slaves of French descent danced in pairs, not touching, circling slowly around. If one of them danced outstandingly well they tied silk scarves of all colours to his knees as a prize. They sang in patois and played two big drums with their hands. This was called the French dance.

I remember one instrument called a *marímbula,* which was very small. It was made of wickerwork and sounded as loud as a drum and had a little hole for the voice to come out of. They used this to accompany the Congo drums, and possibly the French too, but I can't be sure. The *marímbulas* made a very strange noise, and lots of people, particularly the *guajíros,*[3] didn't like them because they said they sounded like voices from another world.

As I recall, their own music at that time was made with the guitar only. Later, in the Nineties, they played *danzónes*[4] on pianolas, with accordions and gourds. But the white man has always had a very different music from the black man. White man's music is without the drumming and is more insipid.

More or less the same goes for religion. The African gods are different, though they resemble the others, the priests' gods. They are more powerful and less adorned. Right now if you were to go to a Catholic church you would not see apples, stones or cock's feathers. But this is the first thing you see in an African house. The African is cruder.

3. Peasants, originally white settlers, but by this time black and Mulatto also.
4. *Danzón:* a slow, stately Cuban dance popular in the last century.

I knew of two African religions in the barracoons: the Lucumí and the Congolese. The Congolese was the more important. It was well known at the Flor de Sagua because their magic-men used to put spells on people and get possession of them, and their practice of soothsaying won them the confidence of all the slaves. I got to know the elders of both religions after Abolition.

I remember the *Chicherekú*⁵ at Flor de Sagua. The *Chicherekú* was a Congolese by birth who did not speak Spanish. He was a little man with a big head who used to run about the barracoons and jump upon you from behind. I often saw him and heard him squealing like a rat. This is true. Until recently in Porfuerza there was a man who ran about in the same way. People used to run away from him because they said he was the Devil himself and he was bound up with *mayombe* and death. . . .

The other religion was the Catholic one. This was introduced by the priests, but nothing in the world would induce them to enter the slaves' quarters. They were fastidious people, with a solemn air which did not fit the barracoons—so solemn that there were Negroes who took everything they said literally. This had a bad effect on them. They read the catechism and read it to the others with all the words and prayers. Those Negroes who were household slaves came as messengers of the priests and got together with the others, the field slaves, in the sugarmill towns. The fact is I never learned that doctrine because I did not understand a thing about it. I don't think the household slaves did either, although, being so refined and well-treated, they all made out they were Christian. The household slaves were given rewards by the masters, and I never saw one of them badly punished. When they were ordered to go to the fields to cut cane or tend the pigs, they would pretend to be ill so they needn't work. For this reason the field slaves could not stand the sight of them. The household slaves sometimes came to the barracoons to visit relations and used to take back fruit and vegetables for the

5. African word for bogey-man.

master's house; I don't know whether the slaves made them presents from their plots of land or whether they just took them. They caused a lot of trouble in the barracoons. The men came and tried to take liberties with the women. That was the source of the worst tensions. I was about twelve then, and I saw the whole rumpus.

There were other tensions. For instance, there was no love lost between the Congolese magic-men and the Congolese Christians, each of whom thought they were good and the others wicked. This still goes on in Cuba. The Lucumi and Congolese did not get on either; it went back to the difference between saints and witchcraft. The only ones who had no problems were the old men born in Africa. They were special people and had to be treated differently because they knew all religious matters.

Many brawls were avoided because the masters changed the slaves around. They kept them divided among themselves to prevent a rash of escapes. That was why the slaves of different plantations never got together with each other. . . .

In the plantations there were Negroes from different countries, all different physically. The Congolese were black-skinned, though there were many of mixed blood with yellowish skins and light hair. They were usually small. The Mandingas were reddish-skinned, tall and very strong. I swear by my mother they were a bunch of crooks, too! They kept apart from the rest. The Gangas were nice people, rather short and freckled. Many of them became runaways. The Carabalís were like the Musungo Congolese, uncivilised brutes. They only killed pigs on Sundays and at Easter and, being good businessmen, they killed them to sell, not to eat themselves. From this comes a saying, "Clever Carabalí, kills pig on Sunday," I got to know all these people better after slavery was abolished.

nations manacled hand and foot, by tyrants; their rights, liberties, hopes, and aspirations, trodden out of existence by the iron heel of oppression." The imputation of cowardice, unmanly imbecility, a crouching, abject spirit, is involved in this charge. "What! would you have us lie down in the dust, and be trampled upon by these despotic powers and governments! Would you have us permit them to enslave us, and hold out our arms and feet to the fettering without a struggle or a murmur?" And then, having filled their bosoms to bursting with patriotic indignation at the course and disposition described interrogatively by these triumphant questions, they exclaim, "No! we would spill the last drop of our blood;—we would see our cities burned with fire;—we would perish with arms in our hands on the battlefield, or pine in exile in Siberia or Botany Bay, before we would tamely submit to be slaves! Liberty or death!" These are the most striking and usual terms of comparison in the vocabulary of martial patriotism. Frequently the sentiments they express take a figurative form more fearful still. We recollect one employed by the editor of an American journal, pending the Oregon controversy, to this effect: "Sooner than relinquish our just rights to the disputed territory, we would shed every drop of blood in the heart of the nation!" Mr. Barrow, agent of the Bible Society, records "a broken prayer for my native land, which, after my usual thanksgiving, I breathed forth to the Almighty, ere retiring to rest that Sunday night at Gibraltar"; a prayer *for* his native country which contains this passage—"May'st thou sink, if thou dost sink, amidst blood and flame, with a mighty noise, causing more than one nation to participate in thy downfall!" And these are regarded as the outbursts of a patriotic feeling—of a love of country so intense that they would see it engulfed in fire and blood, and even the last vein of the nation's heart pierced, and its existence extinguished, rather than endure insult, injury, or oppression! They measure their attachment and devotion to their country and its institutions by the awful calamities which they would bring upon it, in defending its honour and rights. What a fearful antithesis of alternatives! How many peoples and nations have "sunk, amidst blood and flame, and with a mighty noise," in the abyss which yawns between these alternative conditions! How many patriots of this order have seen their country a smoking sea of ruin, without finding a bulrush ark in which to float "the immediate jewel of its soul"—the charter of its existence as a nation!

We wish no one to accept or share the responsibility of our convictions, or of the views we wish to express in reference to this aspect of the subject. If peace has its victories no less than war, it has its heroism and its patriotism. The men of peace can find no attribute, in the great Gospel principles of their faith, that can side with despotism, or wink with indifference at oppression. They are not cowards. They counsel no tame, unmanly submission to wrong; but to oppose to wrong a courage of the human will that shall never faint or waver at any extremity of endurance;—aye, to "resist unto blood," if it be unavoidable,—to give their own necks to the axe or to the halter, on the block or the scaffold, but never to shed themselves a single drop, or perpetrate a single act of malevolent injury on any human being, under the severest pressure of despotic rule. Peace has its heroism, serene and dauntless, that neither trembles nor pales before the guillotine, the halter, or the knout. Peace has its patriotism; deep, earnest, unselfish, self-sacrificing, and sensitive,—a love of country that would bleed to the last vein, but never wound, for its rights, honour, and prosperity. Peace has its battlefields; bloodless, but brave to a degree of heroic endurance of wrong and outrage to which martial courage could never attain. The patriotism of peace, like the first grace of Christianity, "is first pure, then peaceable;" pure from those intense emotions of selfishness which are generally the heart and soul of the patriotism of the warrior. The history of nations, from its first to its last chapter, is full of the examples of those who have gloried in dying for their country. These last years have produced multitudes of the like. This patriotic sentiment is popularised among the millions, and set to the music of the songs of labour; and the hardy, humble men of the sewers often cheer the hours of their toil by singing, *sotto voce,* the joy and the glory *"Mourir pour sa patrie."* The leaders of the depressed peoples of Europe, who have struggled, again and again, to recover their freedom and independence by the sword, are loud in the profession of their readiness to die for their country, and thousands of their countrymen echo the same sentiment. But under what circumstances would you die for your nation's freedom? Would you mount the scaffold, and die for your country, as Jesus Christ died on the cross for the world, amid the scoffs and scorn, and cutting taunts of your own countrymen? How would your patriotism stand the test of such an ordeal? How would the military heroes of the world, who have acquired fame for dying on the battlefield for their country's good, have trembled and recoiled like cowards from such a scaffold! Tried by such a test, how often would the patriotism of the warrior be seen to be nothing more or better than an intense love of self, the eager ambition for a name that shall outlive the memory of the good!

47.

JOHN HUMPHREY NOYES:
The Dream of Community:
A Summary of Results

John Humphrey Noyes (1811–1886) could take satisfaction that his "free love" Oneida Community, though denounced as immoral and degrading, had survived numerous experiments in community living and proved the integrity of "complex" marriage. Noyes was a thinker as well as an organizer. His Male Continence *(1848) and pioneer work in eugenics,* Scientific Propagation *(1873), testified to his consistency of ideas. His analyses of reasons why other communities had failed, in his* History of American Socialisms *(1870), helped explain the impulses which had dominated the cooperative movement. When Noyes prepared his critique, he could not know that dissatisfaction within his own community, as well as without, would force him to adopt monogamy in 1879 and the next year abandon communism for a joint stock ownership arrangement.*

Looking back now over the entire course of this history, we discover a remarkable similarity in the symptoms that manifested themselves in the transitory Communities, and almost entire unanimity in the witnesses who testify as to the causes of their failure. GENERAL DEPRAVITY, all say, is the villain of the whole story.

In the first place Macdonald himself, after "seeing stern reality," confesses that in his previous hopes of Socialism he "had imagined mankind better than they are."

SOURCE: John Humphrey Noyes, *History of American Socialisms* (Philadelphia: J. B. Lippincott & Co., 1870), pp. 646 ff.

Then Owen, accounting for the failure at New Harmony, says, "he wanted honesty, and he got dishonesty; he wanted temperance, and instead he was continually troubled with the intemperate; he wanted cleanliness, and he found dirt," and so on.

The Yellow Spring Community, though composed of "a very superior class," found in the short space of three months, that "self-love was a spirit that would not be exorcised. Individual happiness was the law of nature, and it could not be obliterated; and before a single year had passed, this law had scattered the members of that society which had come together so earnestly and under such favorable circumstances, back into the selfish world from which they came."

The trustees of the Nashoba Community, in abandoning Frances Wright's original plan of common property, acknowledge their conviction that such a system can not succeed "without the members composing it are superior beings. That which produces in the world only common-place jealousies and every-day squabbles, is sufficient to destroy a Community." . . .

Brook Farm alone is reported as harmonious to the end.

It should be observed that the foregoing disclosures of disintegrating infirmities were generally made reluctantly, and are necessarily very imperfect. Large departments of dangerous passion are entirely ignored. For instance, in all the memoirs of the Owen and Fourier Associations, not a word is said on the "Woman Question!" Among all the disagreements and complaints, not a hint occurs of any jealousies and quarrels about love matters. In fact women are rarely mentioned; and the terrible passions connected with distinction of sex, which the Shakers, Rappites, Oneidians, and all the rest of the religious Communities have had so much trouble with, and have taken so much pains to provide for or against, are absolutely left out of sight. . . . The only conclusion we can come to is, that some of the most important experiences of the transitory Communities have not been surrendered to history.

Nevertheless the troubles that do come to the surface show, as we have said, that human depravity is the dread "Dweller of the Threshold," that lies in wait at every entrance to the mysteries of Socialism.

Shall we then turn back in despair, and give it up that Association on the large scale is impossible? This seems to have been the reaction of all the leading Fourierists. . . .

And yet, to contradict these disheartening persuasions and forbid our settling into despair, we have a respectable series of successes that can not be ignored. Mr. Greeley recognizes them, though he hardly knows how to dispose of them. "The fact," he says, "stares us in the face that, while hundreds of banks and factories, and thousands of mercantile concerns managed by shrewd, strong men, have gone into bankruptcy and perished, Shaker Communities, established more than sixty years ago, upon a basis of little property and less worldly wisdom, are living and prosperous to-day. And their experience has been imitated by the German Communities at Economy, Zoar, the Society of Ebenezer, etc. Theory, however plausible, must respect the facts."

Let us look again at these exceptional Associations that have not succumbed to the disorganizing power of general depravity. Jacobi's record of their duration and fortunes is worth recapitulating. Assuming that they are all still in existence, their stories may be epitomized as follows:

Beizel's Community has lasted one hundred and fifty-six years; was at one time very rich; has money at interest yet; some of its grand old buildings are still standing.

The Shaker Community, as a whole, is ninety-five years old; consists of eighteen large societies; many of them very wealthy.

Rapp's Community is sixty-five years old, and very wealthy.

The Zoar Community is fifty-three years old, and wealthy.

The Snowberger Community is forty-nine years old and "well off."

The Ebenezer Community is twenty-three years old; and said to be the largest and richest Community in the United States.

The Janson Community is twenty-three years old and wealthy.

The Oneida Community (frequently quoted as belonging to this class) is twenty-one years old, and prosperous. . . .

The logic of our facts may be summed up thus: The non-religious party has tried Association under the lead of Owen, and failed; the semi-religious party has tried it under the lead of Fourier, and failed; the thoroughly religious party has not yet tried it; but sporadic experiments have been made by various religious sects, and so far as they have gone, they have indicated by their success, that earnest religion may be relied upon to carry Association through to the attainment of all its hopes. The world then must wait for this final trial; and the hope of the triumph of Association can not rationally be given up, till this trial has been made.

The question for the future is, Will the Revivalists go forward into Socialism; or will the Socialists go forward into Revivalism? We do not expect any further advance, till one or the other of these things shall come to pass; and we do not expect overwhelming victory and peace till both shall come to pass. . . .

There's a good time coming, boys,
    A good time coming;
There's a good time coming, boys;
    Wait a little longer.
We may not live to see the day,
But earth shall glisten in the ray,
    Of the good time coming.
Cannon-balls may aid the truth,
    But thought's a weapon stronger;
We'll win our battle by its aid,
    Wait a little longer.

                                        The Hutchinsons

We have nothing to say to the South. The real
holder of the slave is not there. He is in the
North—the *free* North, the *anti-slavery* North! The
South have not the *power* to hold the slave.

                              Nathaniel Peabody Rogers

The movement which made reform popular and multiplied the ranks of reformers, in some measure spelled the decline of reform. It had been born of an individual need for a new and vital sense of society's conditions. The crisis which now intensified, so that it engaged all elements of the American people, forced its majority to develop attitudes on matters which they had previously evaded: toward Negroes, toward fugitive slaves, toward the sanctity of law and toward political parties.

Such figures as Garrison, Mann and Douglass could no longer carry the burden of their causes. They were too deeply involved in them. They saw them in too pertinacious detail to blend them effectively with the great binding events dominating the public mind. The reformers had created the language of debate. They had provided the entire tissue of a reform program, and they would continue to be the moral force behind the new men and women who spoke the minds of the masses.

The times made Charles Sumner the symbol of abolitionism, rather than any of its original sponsors. Congregations thrilled to the forensics of the Reverend Henry Ward Beecher in Brooklyn's Plymouth Church more than they did to any of the inspired ministers who had struggled to make their churches instruments of social change.

At no time prior to the Civil War did compromisers and political wheel-horses cease their efforts to put out the fires of sectional differences while using them for their own purposes. To the end they exuded confidence that new means would be found to appease the conservative majority and curb the radicals. Yet each successive plan for minimizing slavery as a national issue no more than aggravated feelings respecting its numerous by-products and raised new belligerents to defy solutions.

Reformers played a role to the very last. But whereas Garrison, the Tappans and others had dramatized the battle for an abolitionist program in the 1830s, and such figures as Birney and Joshua Leavitt had shown its organizing potential in the decade following, a new multifaceted vanguard of leaders, intermixed with seasoned performers of previous years, spoke for an aroused North in fresh accents and slogans. They precipitated Free Soil partisans of varied qualities and interests, organizers of a new Republican party and critics of Federal law and order, especially as they concerned fugitives from slavery, Although they would strive to disassociate themselves from "extremists," they would find themselves sometimes on paper, as in the *National Era,* sometimes on common platforms, voicing similar sentiments and goals.

The crisis was exposed by a massive effort to settle it once and for all. Behind the events of the 1850s stood the fugitive slave: silent, anonymous, under rigorous controls, yet somehow responsive to the atmosphere of freedom and natural rights which had been created by the clamor of libertarians and appeals to the American revolutionary tradition. Between the fugitive slave and their own free Negroes Northerners were forced to choose phrases and spokesmen that would define for them the limits of freedom. The Compromise of 1850 was intended to reassure proslavery and antislavery forces that their best interests were being respected by government. It failed to satisfy either.

The national leaders for forty years—Clay, Calhoun and Webster—all speaking at the edge of the grave, stood on the Senate floor and pleaded for the nation as it had been and as they hoped to see it continue. Webster's rhetoric was in no wise inferior to that which he had displayed in his Union speech twenty years before. He spoke, he said, not as a Massachusetts man or as a Virginian but as an American: "Hear me for my cause." He argued that the great accessions of the Mexican War could nourish both slaveholder and freeman, harming neither. Climate and soil would keep slavery from flourishing in New Mexico. California and the Oregon Territory amply compensated the Northern land hungry for any gains accruing to the South.

Webster endorsed the Fugitive Slave Law, intended to end completely the troublesome quarrels over state and federal authority. It was designed to end the slave rescues which impugned law, the agitation which accompanied every movement of slave catchers. Once and for all, runaways would be stopped and returned to their owners. Federal marshals would supervise the action. Peace and quiet would abide along the Mason-Dixon line. The nation would get on with its work of expansion and enjoyment of the largesse afforded by nature and armed might to this most prosperous of peoples.

Although there were great Northern meetings convened to express endorsement of the Fugitive Slave Act and Webster's appeal, there was also a shock of Northern dismay that Webster should have lent his approval to slave-hunting. The North made famous Whittier's awed vision of Webster as "Ichabod," the inglorious, to be memorialized as was the loss by biblical Jews of their holy Ark (see page 325). But it was William Henry Seward, then a Senator from New York and a power in Zachary Taylor's ill-fated Administration, who inadvertently gave the North a momentous slogan. Ambitious and intelligent, Seward denounced the Compromise and the Fugitive Slave Law as he knew his constituents would expect. He invoked in his rhetoric a concept which had passed among orators and clergy for years as proper to a religious nation with a sense of destiny. In repudiating the expansion of slavery and its prerogatives, he made reverential note of the responsibility American authority involved:

The Constitution regulates our stewardship; the Constitution de-votes the domain to union, to justice, to defence, to welfare, and to liberty.

But there is a higher law than the Constitution, which regulates our authority over the domain, and devotes it to the same noble purposes. The territory is a part, no inconsiderable part, of the common heritage of mankind, bestowed upon them by the Creator of the universe. We are his stewards, and must so discharge our trust as to secure in the highest attainable degree their happiness.[1]

Seward's almost casual mention of a law "higher" than the Constitution, however, caused a reaction staggering to one, like himself, who expected to become President of the United States. It was denounced in the South as an invitation to violence. It was turned by abolitionists and Free Soil ministers into a wholesale repudiation of the legal machinery set up to expunge the fugitive slave from contemporary life.

Yet a nation so deeply divided concluded in 1852 to elect as President not General Winfield Scott, the greatest living war hero and a Virginian loyal to national purposes. (Scott would end his half century of services to the government during the Civil War helping to build breastworks to defend the Capi-tal.) The nation chose, instead, Franklin Pierce of New Hamp-shire: a Democratic regular and "doughface," eager to propitiate the South.

The electorate craved peace; yet it could not control its sym-pathies. That same year it responded with passion to Harriet Beecher Stowe's tale of Uncle Tom, who was resolute in defense of his Bible. It was horrified and excited by the licentious and uncontrollable brutalities of Simon Legree, a New Englander. The North and then the South and then the civilized world pondered Mrs. Stowe's message that there were kind and well-

1. George E. Baker, ed., *The Works of William Henry Seward* (New York: Redfield, 1853), vol. 1, pp. 74–75.

intentioned slaveholders in the South who were, however, unable to make slavery a humane and civilized institution.

Abolitionists were critical of Mrs. Stowe's pages in *Uncle Tom's Cabin* which depicted such humanity. They observed that she was not so much an abolitionist as she was a colonizationist. They found it necessary, in any case, to join the multiplying throngs of readers who learned intense antislavery sympathies from her book. Her key achievement was that she had made individuals of her fictional Negroes, rather than stereotyped pawns in a sectional argument. The historic triumph of her book—which counterfiction by southern writers could not approach—was to give northern readers of various persuasions a common bond in the conviction that slavery was wrong.

A rash of Personal Liberty laws appeared in the North in order to aid the safety of fugitives or others threatened by irresponsible slave catchers or harsh constructionists of the Fugitive Slave Law. Various legal actions kept the issue heated, but in 1854 the Anthony Burns case further divided the nation. A young runaway had been seized in Boston. The abolitionists determined to free him by legal or illegal means. Prominent in these proceedings were such Free Soilers as the dedicated Reverend Thomas Wentworth Higginson and Richard Henry Dana, Jr., who worked frantically to interpose law to prevent Burns's return to slavery. Dr. Samuel G. Howe labored for the cause, as did, for the more impassioned advocates, Wendell Phillips and the independent and somewhat heretical Boston minister Theodore Parker. They gave to Free Soil a moral dimension it had not previously achieved or, as in Van Buren's 1848 campaign, tried to achieve.

Burns was returned to slavery. Federal authorities lined the Boston streets with troops and militia from the courthouse to the harbored ship. It was an expensive rendition not only in terms of money but in governmental prestige. For though the Fugitive Slave Law continued in force and claimed some victims,[2] it was

2. Stanley W. Campbell, *The Slave Catchers: Enforcement of the Fugitive Slave Law, 1850–1860* (Chapel Hill: University of North Carolina Press, 1970).

accorded an open contempt and defiance which augured ill for
law and order in general and became more flagrant still as the
crisis intensified. At Framingham, Massachusetts, on July 4, 1854,
at an abolitionist meeting, Garrison burned a copy of the Constitution of the United States and the Fugitive Slave Law, crying:
"So perish all compromises with tyranny. And let all the people
say, Amen!" The answering shout of the spectators was evidence
that some Northerners had made their peace with Higher Law
doctrine. Henry David Thoreau, who had already (1849) committed himself to civil disobedience as valid social deportment,
was on hand as a speaker, though he was only intermittently an
activist of any sort.

In 1854 occurred an experiment in popular democracy which
once again revealed its true nature. Stephen A. Douglas of Illinois, another aspirant to the presidency, hoped that "squatter
sovereignty" would open the Kansas Territory and permit its
settlers to vote slavery up or down as they pleased. Instead, they
elected to quarrel and to turn the border into a scene of agitation
and political strife. It is perhaps true that "Bleeding Kansas" was
actually no more bloody than any other frontier area and involved material goals more than ideal.[3] But, as in other crises,
the manner in which it was viewed nationally affected the Territory's development.

Northern and southern editors urged their countrymen to send
arms and emigrants to Kansas to win it for their section. It was a
momentous fact that, although the proslave faction had every
advantage, it was unable to gain control of the Territory. Neither
the material aid the faction received from proslavery associates in
adjacent Missouri and nearby Kentucky, nor the political aid
granted by the Pierce and then the Buchanan Administrations
availed it. Free Soil advocates as far away as Massachusetts were
manifestly more active in support of their own in Kansas than
were their southern counterparts, though the bulk of northern

3. James C. Malin, *John Brown and the Legend of Fifty-Six* (Philadelphia: American Philosophical Society, 1942), pp. 498 ff. and 509 ff.

settlers were from Ohio, Indiana and other more neighboring areas. Free Soil engaged efficient participants from the conservative businessman Amos Lawrence to the restless and contriving John Brown.

Such events should not have contributed to shattering the Union. The Kansas-Nebraska Act did for all practical purposes destroy the Missouri Compromise line of 36°30', which was to have permitted slave partisans and free to expand west side by side. But it also resulted, by the exercise of popular force, in the gaining of another free state. Kansas Free Soilers finally shook off their proslavery antagonists and came into the Union—and with a constitution which discriminated against its Negro community as other free states did. Such struggles for political control and more or less humanistic legislation might have been expected to continue indefinitely.

Indeed, the national Whig alliance fell apart, and Free Soilers appeared in its stead to create the Republican party. But the latter was as heavy with compromises as the former. The Republicans' first national convention in January of 1856 was chaired by an old follower of Andrew Jackson, Francis P. Blair, who was himself a slaveholder. The Republican presidential candidate of that year was the explorer, John C. Frémont, chosen not for his political record which was no more Republican than Democratic but for his popular appeal. It was a sign of the hectic, experimental nature of the times that the Republican standard-bearer of 1856 was of no political consequence in 1860.

Once again the nation concluded to elect a slavery-oriented candidate: Democrat James Buchanan of Pennsylvania. Birney, retired in Michigan, had already despaired of seeing Americans soften on the race question and returned to his earliest solution, urging Negroes to leave the country and colonize in Africa.

Yet Northerners were unwilling to give up the moral precepts they had learned from him, from Jay, from Garrison and from others—precepts which were being repeated in louder and more

blatant tones by such new leaders as Sumner and Thaddeus
Stevens in Washington and by others who would soon stand
before the nation as Radical Republicans. Such willingness as the
public had to accept peaceable compromise was frustrated by the
Supreme Court ruling of 1857 on the slave Dred Scott, who had
been taken into free territory and thereby, under terms of the
Missouri Compromise, been rendered free. In his immortal decision, Justice Roger B. Taney held the Missouri Compromise officially void and Scott a slave whether on free soil or not. Taney
thus sought to nationalize slavery: an old dream of southern leaders uncomfortable with their sectional disabilities. Horace Greeley's voice was now that of a united North, making cause not only
with the once-despised abolitionists, but even, in sentimental
fashion, with the Negroes threatened by a more powerful and
implemented South.

48.

WILLIAM JAY:
War and Peace

One of William Jay's most important books was A Review of the Causes and Consequences of the Mexican War, *which offered not only devastating analyses of the Polk Administration's policies and deeds but a survey of peaceful alternatives which affected the thinking of pacifists and peace negotiators into the twentieth century.*

Of all the false and hoary maxims by which mankind have been deluded, perhaps none has ever exerted such baneful influence on human happiness as that scrap of counterfeit wisdom, "IN PEACE, PREPARE FOR WAR." The proposed object of the counsel, is to *preserve peace* by being prepared to repel, and thereby to prevent aggression. The reasoning is contradicted by the testimony of history and by the character of human nature. No nation was ever better prepared for war than France under Napoleon, and no nation was ever more fiercely and violently attacked; and seldom has any nation been more humbled, compelled not only to receive a sovereign from the hands of her enemies, but to pay the expenses of a foreign army to whose custody she was consigned. Great military strength has no tendency to foster pacific dispositions in its possessor. While the character of man remains unchanged, his cupidity, oppression, and injustice will ordinarily be proportioned to his means of indulging them. Hence, in all ages those nations which have been the best prepared for war, have drank most deeply of its bloody

SOURCE: William Jay, *A Review of the Causes and Consequences of the Mexican War* (Boston: Benjamin B. Mussey & Co., 1849).

cup. If we examine the history of Europe from 1700, to the general peace in 1815, we shall find that during the 115 years,

Great Britain was engaged in war	69	years.
Russia,	68	"
France,	63	"
Holland,	43	"
Portugal,	40	"
Denmark,	28	"

Pride, arrogance, and the lust of conquest, are the natural and bitter fruits of military preparation—fruits fatal to national peace and happiness.

Strange as may seem the assertion, it is, we believe, nevertheless true, that both Europe and America have expended more money in preparing for war, than in actual hostilities.

In the old world, every important city was anciently walled and fortified, and even in our own days, we have seen the French people already burthened with debt, lavishing millions in erecting a wall thirty miles in circumference around their Capital.[1] . . .

We are fond of comparing our own republican frugality with monarchical prodigality. National vanity, like charity, covers not only a multitude of sins, but also a multitude of follies. The average expenditure of the Federal Government, for the six years, ending with 1840, *exclusive of payments on account of debt,* was $26,474,892. During the same years, the average payments for military and naval purposes, were $21,328,903. Being EIGHTY PER CENT of the whole amount! A greater ratio than is expended by any monarchy in Europe, in preparing for war.[2] . . .

1. This work of prodigal folly has been falsely ascribed to the late King; it was demanded by the liberal or popular party, under the leadership of Mr. Thiers. The *Republic,* instead of lessening the burdens of the people, have actually, although unmenaced by a single State in Europe, *increased* their military preparations. On the 1st December, 1848, the effective force of the French army amounted to 502,196 men, and 100,432 horses; and to this was added a large navy, with between twenty and thirty thousand seamen. [Jay's note]

2. It is true, that during a portion of these six years, we were fighting a few Seminole Indians in Florida. If, then, we take the six years, ending with 1836, a time of profound peace, the ratio is *seventy-seven per cent,* still greater than that of Great Britain. See *American Almanac for 1845,* p. 143.

Happily there is a mode of "international jurisdiction," more simple, speedy, and practicable, and of which any two nations may at any time avail themselves, without waiting for the co-operation of others. This mode is faintly shadowed forth in our late treaty with Mexico, but in terms—

> "Which keep the word of promise to the ear,
> And break it to the hope."

The 21st Article is as follows: "If unhappily any disagreement should hereafter arise between the Governments of the two Republics, whether with respect to the interpretation of any stipulation in this treaty, or with respect to any other particular concerning the political or commercial relations of the two nations, the said Governments, in the name of those nations, *do promise* to each other, that they will *endeavor* in the most sincere and earnest manner, to settle the differences so arising, and to preserve the state of peace and friendship, in which the two countries are now placing themselves, using for this end mutual representations and pacific negotiations; and if by these means they should not be enabled to come to an agreement, a resort shall not on this account be had to reprisals, aggressions, or hostilities of any kind, by the one Republic against the other, until the Government of that which deems itself aggrieved, shall have *maturely considered*, in the spirit of peace and good neighborship, whether it would not be better that such difference should be settled by the arbitration of commissioners appointed on each side, or by that of a friendly nation; and should such course be proposed by either party, *it shall be acceded* to by the other, *unless* deemed by it altogether incompatible with the nature of the difference, or the circumstances of the case."

This stipulation, it is obvious, amounts to nothing more than an acknowledgment that there is an equitable mode of preventing future hostilities, and a promise to adopt it, unless either party shall think it more *advantageous* to trust to the arbitrament of the sword.

Had the reference to arbitration been made imperative instead of discretionary, the treaty of peace would have done much to atone for the iniquity of the war. It would have secured Mexico from future spoliation, and by guaranteeing our own rights, would have removed all pretext for military preparation on our Mexican frontier; and it would, moreover, have set a glorious example of a victorious people debarring themselves from future conquests, and have taught the world how its swords might be beaten into ploughshares, and its spears into pruninghooks.

Let us suppose that instead of this quibbling, shuffling, non-committal Article, the following had been substituted for it.

"It is agreed between the contracting parties, that, if unhappily any controversy shall arise between them, in respect to the true intent of any stipulation in this treaty, or in respect to any other matter, which controversy cannot be satisfactorily adjusted by negotiation neither party shall resort to hostilities against the other, but the matter in dispute shall, by a special convention, be submitted to the arbitrament of some friendly power; and the parties do hereby agree to abide by the award which may be given in pursuance of such submission."

To such an Article, what valid objection can be offered? The reference would be made only after negotiation had failed, of course it would be the alternative of WAR. Now whatever might be the award, each party would be the gainer, for each would be saved the expenditure of blood and treasure. The successful party would establish his claims without cost; and to the losing party, the remark of Franklin would be strictly applicable: "Whatever advantage one nation would obtain of another, it would be cheaper to purchase such advantage with ready money, than to pay the expense of acquiring it by war."

But it may be doubted by some, whether the award would be in accordance with justice. Why such a doubt? Would an impartial disinterested umpire, selected or agreed to by ourselves, and with the gaze of the world fixed upon him, be less able, or less inclined, to understand and determine the merits of the question submitted to him, than the Government of Mexico, or of our own country smarting under the irritation of real or imaginary wrong, seeking popularity by a show of patriotism and sensibility to national honor, and goaded on by politicians seeking for office, and by needy adventurers eager for the commissions, contracts, and spoils of war? The people at large have no interest in war; on the contrary, it is upon them its burdens press and its calamities fall.

We have seen how crushing is the weight of war-taxes upon the multitude; and yet they seem, for the most part, utterly ignorant of the true cause of their poverty and wretchedness. Deluded by demagogues, they ascribe their sufferings to kings, and nobles, and priests, but render a willing homage to SOLDIERS, who are in fact their real oppressors. The French people restless under the burthen of taxation, drove their monarch into exile, and seizing in their own hands the reins of Government, immediately enlarged their army, and have thus swelled their taxes beyond what they were under the monarchy. The suffering masses of England cry aloud against the political institutions of their country, and seek relief in annual parliaments, vote by ballot, &c., apparently unconscious that they are pressed to the earth by *war and military preparation*. Let them rid themselves of these plagues, and their taxes for the support of the Government, including all the appropriations for the maintenance of royalty in all its splendor, would be so trivial as to be scarcely perceptible. Does this statement excite the smile of incredulity? We appeal to facts.

The average expenditure of the British Government for the six years ending with 1836, including interest on the National-Debt, was	£ 45,676,357
Now of this immense sum, there was paid for the *civil* expenses of the Government, only	4,387,214
Leaving, for military preparation and interest on the war-debt	£ 41,289,143

Here we have disclosed the secret agent of those mighty upheavings which are causing the political world to reel to and fro like a drunken man. Men are wasting their lives and energies in toil, yet eat not the fruit of their labor, for it is wrested from them and offered on the altar of Moloch. Yet they perceive not the hand that robs them; and vainly attribute their poverty to defective political institutions. Hence, revolution follows revolution in rapid succession, like the waves of a troubled sea, but no relief is found. . . .

Let, then, the friends of human progress and of public peace, of happiness, and virtue, the patriot and the Christian, all unite in one loud and unceasing demand, for treaties of arbitration. In this blessed reform any nation may take the lead; would that our own had seized the opportunity offered by the recent negotiation! Let Congress by a joint resolution, express its desire that an arbitration clause shall be inserted in all our future treaties, and the great work will be commenced. Such a resolution, would be like the first beams of light breaking upon the darkness of night, and shining more and more unto the perfect day, gradually dispelling the baneful mists of military glory and ambition, and diffusing life, and joy, and abundance, among the suffering millions of our distracted world.

49.

JOHN GREENLEAF WHITTIER:
"Ichabod!"

It was a token of the love northerners bore their country that, although events were carrying them on dangerous waters, they continued to honor Daniel Webster. Since his great speeches on the Union of January 19–27, 1830, other issues had grown big and received northern sympathies: issues involving free speech and Negro rights. Nonetheless, in January of 1850, Henry Clay sought to curb secessionists and abolitionists with his compromise measures, including a Fugitive Slave Law. On March 7, Webster, speaking to a packed Senate chamber, pleaded for the Compromise as the one solution short of war which could ensure national harmony. Northern response shook the country. Conservatives rallied to Webster's support, but their rhetoric faded before John Greenleaf Whittier's. His indictment subtly bridged the gap between old admiration for Webster and new, poignant chagrin over his "fall." It enabled nonabolitionists to join abolitionists in repudiation of their master spokesman. "Ichabod" became one of Whittier's best-remembered antislavery verses.

So fallen! so lost! the light withdrawn
    Which once he wore!
The glory from his gray hairs gone
    Forevermore!

Revile him not, the Tempter hath
    A snare for all;

SOURCE: *The Poetical Works of John Greenleaf Whittier* (Boston: Houghton, Mifflin and Co., 1888), pp. 146–147.

And pitying tears, not scorn and wrath,
  Befit his fall!

Oh, dumb be passion's stormy rage,
    When he who might
Have lighted up and led his age,
    Falls back in night.

Scorn! would the angels laugh, to mark
    A bright soul driven,
Fiend-goaded, down the endless dark,
    From hope and heaven!

Let not the land once proud of him
    Insult him now,
Nor brand with deeper shame his dim,
    Dishonored brow.

But let its humbled sons, instead,
    From sea to lake,
A long lament, as for the dead,
    In sadness make.

Of all we loved and honored, naught
    Save power remains:
A fallen angel's pride of thought,
    Still strong in chains.

All else is gone; from those great eyes
    The soul has fled:
When faith is lost, when honor dies,
    The man is dead!

Then, pay the reverence of old days
    To his dead fame;
Walk backward, with averted gaze,
    And hide the shame!

50.

SOLOMON NORTHUP:
The Shadow of Bondage on Free Men

Abolitionists worked to persuade their Northern neighbors of their own stake in emancipation. They repeated many times and in many ways that a system which could betray a Negro could betray a white man. Many northerners were uneasily aware that not a few "blacks" were whiter than certified whites. Slave narratives brought out aspects of this fact but were of uneven quality. Solomon Northup's (1808–?) Twelve Years a Slave. Narrative of . . . a Citizen of New-York, Kidnapped in Washington City in 1841 . . . was one of the best. Its judicious tone and vivid details brought home to readers how readily slavery, whether conducted with civility or not, could diminish American freedom. Northup was later rescued in 1853 by a series of efforts on his part which permitted his long-lost wife to determine his whereabouts and bring the State of New York into the case in aid of one of its citizens.

On leaving the New-Orleans slave pen, Harry and I followed our new master through the streets, while Eliza, crying and turning back, was forced along by Freeman and his minions, until we found ourselves on board the steamboat Rodolph, then lying at the levee. In the course of half an hour we were moving briskly up the Mississippi, bound for some point on Red River. There were quite a number of slaves on board beside ourselves, just purchased in the New-Orleans market. I remember a Mr.

SOURCE: Solomon Northup, *Twelve Years a Slave. Narrative of . . . a Citizen of New-York, Kidnapped in Washington City in 1841* . . . (New York: Millar, Orton & Co., 1857), pp. 89–90, 106 ff.

Kelsow, who was said to be a well known and extensive planter, had in charge a gang of women.

Our master's name was William Ford. He resided then in the "Great Pine Woods," in the parish of Avoyelles, situated on the right bank of Red River, in the heart of Louisiana. He is now a Baptist preacher. Throughout the whole parish of Avoyelles, and especially along both shores of Bayou Bœuf, where he is more intimately known, he is accounted by his fellow-citizens as a worthy minister of God. In many northern minds, perhaps, the idea of a man holding his brother man in servitude, and the traffic in human flesh, may seem altogether incompatible with their conceptions of a moral or religious life. From descriptions of such men as Burch and Freeman, and others hereinafter mentioned, they are led to despise and execrate the whole class of slaveholders, indiscriminately. But I was sometime his slave, and had an opportunity of learning well his character and disposition, and it is but simple justice to him when I say, in my opinion, there never was a more kind, noble, candid, Christian man than William Ford. . . . Were all men such as he, Slavery would be deprived of more than half its bitterness.

William Ford unfortunately became embarrassed in his pecuniary affairs. A heavy judgment was rendered against him in consequence of his having become security for his brother, Franklin Ford, residing on Red River, above Alexandria, and who had failed to meet his liabilities. He was also indebted to John M. Tibeats to a considerable amount in consideration of his services in building the mills on Indian Creek, and also a weaving-house, corn-mill and other erections on the plantation at Bayou Bœuf, not yet completed. It was therefore necessary, in order to meet these demands, to dispose of eighteen slaves, myself among the number. Seventeen of them, including Sam and Harry, were purchased by Peter Compton, a planter also residing on Red River.

I was sold to Tibeats, in consequence, undoubtedly, of my

slight skill as a carpenter. This was in the winter of 1842. The deed of myself from Freeman to Ford, as I ascertained from the public records in New-Orleans on my return, was dated June 23d, 1841. At the time of my sale to Tibeats, the price agreed to be given for me being more than the debt, Ford took a chattel mortgage of four hundred dollars. I am indebted for my life, as will hereafter be seen, to that mortgage. . . .

Ford's overseer on this plantation, and who had the exclusive charge of it, was a Mr. Chapin, a kindly-disposed man, and a native of Pennsylvania. In common with others, he held Tibeats in light estimation, which fact, in connection with the four hundred dollar mortgage, was fortunate for me.

I was now compelled to labor very hard. From earliest dawn until late at night, I was not allowed to be a moment idle. Notwithstanding which, Tibeats was never satisfied. He was continually cursing and complaining. He never spoke to me a kind word. I was his faithful slave, and earned him large wages every day, and yet I went to my cabin nightly, loaded with abuse and stinging epithets.

We had completed the corn mill, the kitchen, and so forth, and were at work upon the weaving-house, when I was guilty of an act, in that State punishable with death. It was my first fight with Tibeats. The weaving-house we were erecting stood in the orchard a few rods from the residence of Chapin, or the "great house," as it was called. One night, having worked until it was too dark to see, I was ordered by Tibeat to rise very early in the morning, procure a keg of nails from Chapin, and commence putting on the clapboards. I retired to the cabin extremely tired, and having cooked a supper of bacon and corn cake, and conversed a while with Eliza, who occupied the same cabin, as also did Lawson and his wife Mary, and a slave named Bristol, laid down upon the ground floor, little dreaming of the sufferings that awaited me on the morrow. Before daylight I was on the piazza of the "great house," awaiting the appearance of overseer Chapin. To have aroused him from his slumbers and stated my errand, would have been an unpardonale boldness. At length he came out. Taking off my hat, I informed him Master Tibeats had directed me to call upon him for a keg of nails. Going into the storeroom, he rolled it out, at the same time saying, if Tibeats preferred a different size, he would endeavor to furnish them, but that I might use those until further directed. Then mounting his horse, which stood saddled and bridled at the door, he rode away into the field, whither the slaves had preceded him, while I took the keg on my shoulder, and proceeding to the weaving-house, broke in the head, and commenced nailing on the clapboards.

As the day began to open, Tibeats came out of the house to where I was, hard at work. He seemed to be that morning even more morose and disagreeable than usual. He was my master, entitled by law to my flesh and blood, and to exercise over me such tyrannical control as his mean nature prompted; but there was no law that could prevent my looking upon him with intense contempt. I despised both his disposition and his intellect. I had just come round to the keg for a further supply of nails, as he reached the weaving-house.

"I thought I told you to commence putting on weather-boards this morning," he remarked.

"Yes, master, and I am about it," I replied.

"Where?" he demanded.

"On the other side," was my answer.

He walked round to the other side, examined my work for a while, muttering to himself in a fault-finding tone.

"Didn't I tell you last night to get a keg of nails of Chapin?" he broke forth again.

"Yes, master, and so I did; and overseer said he would get another size for you, if you wanted them, when he came back from the field."

Tibeats walked to the keg, looked a moment at the contents, then kicked it violently. Coming towards me in a great passion, he exclaimed,

"G—d d—n you! I thought you *knowed* something."

I made answer: "I tried to do as you told me, master. I didn't mean anything wrong. Overseer said—" But he interrupted me with such a flood of curses that I was unable to finish the sentence. At length he ran towards the house, and going to the piazza, took down one of the overseer's whips. The whip had a short wooden stock, braided over with leather, and was loaded at the butt. The lash was three feet long, or thereabouts, and made of raw-hide strands.

At first I was somewhat frightened, and my impulse was to run. There was no one about except Rachel, the cook, and Chapin's wife, and neither of them were to be seen. The rest were in the field. I knew he intended to whip me, and it was the first time any one had attempted it since my arrival at Avoyelles. I felt, moreover, that I had been faithful—that I was guilty of no wrong whatever, and deserved commendation rather than punishment. My fear changed to anger, and before he reached me I had made up my mind fully not to be whipped, let the result be life or death.

Winding the lash around his hand, and taking hold of the small end of the stock, he walked up to me, and with a malignant look, ordered me to strip.

"Master Tibeats," said I, looking him boldly in the face, "I will *not*." I was about to say something further in justification, but with concentrated vengeance, he sprang upon me, seizing me by the throat with one hand, raising the whip with the other, in the act of striking. Before the blow descended, however, I had caught him by the collar of the coat, and drawn him closely to me. Reaching down, I seized him by the ankle, and pushing him back with the other hand, he fell over on the ground. Putting one arm around his leg, and holding it to my breast, so that his head and shoulders only touched the ground, I placed my foot upon his neck. He was completely in my power. My blood was up. It seemed to course through my veins like fire. In the frenzy of my madness I snatched the whip from his hand. He struggled with all his power; swore that I should not live to see another day; and that he would tear out my heart. But his struggles and his threats were alike in vain. I cannot tell how many times I struck him. Blow after blow fell fast and heavy upon his wriggling form. At length he screamed—cried murder—and at last the blasphemous tyrant called on God for mercy. But he who had never shown mercy did not receive it. The stiff stock of the whip warped round his cringing body until my right arm ached.

Until this time I had been too busy to look about me. Desisting for a moment, I saw Mrs. Chapin looking from the window, and Rachel standing in the kitchen door. Their attitudes expressed the utmost excitement and alarm. His screams had been heard in the field. Chapin was coming as fast as he could ride. I struck him a blow or two more, then pushed him from me with such a well-directed kick that he went rolling over on the ground.

Rising to his feet, and brushing the dirt from his hair, he stood looking at me, pale with rage. We gazed at each other in silence. Not a word was uttered until Chapin galloped up to us.

"What is the matter?" he cried out.

"Master Tibeats wants to whip me for using the nails you gave me," I replied.

"What is the matter with the nails?" he inquired, turning to Tibeats.

Tibeats answered to the effect that they were too large, paying little heed, however, to Chapin's question, but still keeping his snakish eyes fastened maliciously on me.

"I am overseer here," Chapin began. "I told Platt[1] to take them and use them, and if they were not of the proper size I would get others on returning from the field. It is not his fault. Besides, I shall furnish such nails as I please. I hope you will understand *that*, Mr. Tibeats."

Tibeats made no reply, but, grinding his teeth and shaking his fist, swore he would have satisfaction, and that it was not half over

1. Northrup's name as a slave. [Ed.]

yet. Thereupon he walked away, followed by the overseer, and entered the house, the latter talking to him all the while in a suppressed tone, and with earnest gestures.

I remained where I was, doubting whether it was better to fly or abide the result, whatever it might be. Presently Tibeats came out of the house, and, saddling his horse, the only property he possessed besides myself, departed on the road to Chenyville.

When he was gone, Chapin came out, visibly excited, telling me not to stir, not to attempt to leave the plantation on any account whatever. He then went to the kitchen, and calling Rachel out, conversed with her some time. Coming back, he again charged me with great earnestness not to run, saying my master was a rascal; that he had left on no good errand, and that there might be trouble before night. But at all events, he insisted upon it, I must not stir.

As I stood there, feelings of unutterable agony overwhelmed me. . . . I could only bow my head upon my hands and weep. For at least an hour I remained in this situation, finding relief only in tears, when, looking up, I beheld Tibeats, accompanied by two horsemen, coming down the bayou. They rode into the yard, jumped from their horses, and approached me with large whips, one of them also carrying a coil of rope.

"Cross your hands," commanded Tibeats, with the addition of such a shuddering expression of blasphemy as is not decorous to repeat.

"You need not bind me, Master Tibeats, I am ready to go with you anywhere," said I.

One of his companions then stepped forward, swearing if I made the least resistance he would break my head—he would tear me limb from limb—he would cut my black throat—and giving wide scope to other similar expressions. Perceiving any importunity altogether vain, I crossed my hands, submitting humbly to whatever disposition they might please to make of me. Thereupon Tibeats tied my wrists, drawing the rope around them with his utmost strength. Then he bound my ankles in the same manner. In the meantime the other two had slipped a cord within my elbows, running it across my back, and tying it firmly. It was utterly impossible to move hand or foot. With a remaining piece of rope Tibeats made an awkward noose, and placed it about my neck.

"Now, then," inquired one of Tibeats' companions, "where shall we hang the nigger?"

One proposed such a limb, extending from the body of a peach tree, near the spot where we were standing. His comrade objected to it, alleging it would break, and proposed another. Finally they fixed upon the latter. . . .

At length, as they were dragging me towards the tree, Chapin, who had momentarily disappeared from the piazza, came out of the house and walked towards us. He had a pistol in each hand, and as near as I can now recall to mind, spoke in a firm, determined manner, as follows:

"Gentlemen, I have a few words to say. You had better listen to them. Whoever moves that slave another foot from where he stands is a dead man. In the first place, he does not deserve this treatment. It is a shame to murder him in this manner. I never knew a more faithful boy than Platt. You, Tibeats, are in the fault yourself. You are pretty much of a scoundrel, and I know it, and you richly deserve the flogging you have received. In the next place, I have been overseer on this plantation seven years, and, in the absence of William Ford, am master here. My duty is to protect his interests, and that duty I shall perform. You are not responsible—you are a worthless fellow. Ford holds a mortgage on Platt of four hundred dollars. If you hang him he loses his debt. Until that is canceled you have no right to take his life. You have no right to take it any way. There is a law for the slave as well as for the white man. You are no better than a murderer.

"As for you," addressing Cook and Ramsay, a couple of overseers from neighboring plantations, "as for you—begone! If you have any regard for your own safety, I say, begone."

Cook and Ramsay, without a further word, mounted their

horses and rode away. Tibeats, in a few minutes, evidently in fear, and overawed by the decided tone of Chapin, sneaked off like a coward, as he was, and mounting his horse, followed his companions.

I remained standing where I was, still bound, with the rope around my neck. As soon as they were gone, Chapin called Rachel, ordering her to run to the field, and tell Lawson to hurry to the house without delay, and bring the brown mule with him, an animal much prized for its unusual fleetness. Presently the boy appeared.

"Lawson," said Chapin, "you must go to the Pine Woods. Tell your master Ford to come here at once—that he must not delay a single moment. Tell him they are trying to murder Platt. Now hurry, boy. Be at the Pine Woods by noon if you kill the mule."

Chapin stepped into the house and wrote a pass. When he returned, Lawson was at the door, mounted on his mule. Receiving the pass, he plied the whip right smartly to the beast, dashed out of the yard, and turning up the bayou on a hard gallop, in less time than it has taken me to describe the scene, was out of sight.

51.

HENRY DAVID THOREAU:

"Show me a free state, and a court truly of justice, and I will fight for them, if need be"

Ralph Waldo Emerson felt a sense of pain that his much-admired friend Henry David Thoreau (1817–1862) had accomplished so little in life. All of Thoreau's fame was posthumous; in his lifetime he was at most no more than a friend of some notables. Yet the nature of his talents precluded fame. He judged events without concern for the commitments of the persons involved. A literary artist, he studied levels of meaning which were incomprehensible to general readers. An individualist, he was shy of such cooperative ventures as Brook Farm and most of the abolitionist crusade. The Fugitive Slave Law alarmed him, and the rendition of Anthony Burns in 1854 moved him to speak at Framingham on July 4 in words which Garrison and the would-be slave rescuers made deeds.

The judges and lawyers,—simply as such, I mean,—and all men of expediency, try this [Burns] case by a very low and incompetent standard. They consider, not whether the Fugitive Slave Law is right, but whether it is what they call *constitutional*. Is virtue constitutional, or vice? Is equity constitutional, or iniquity? In important moral and vital questions, like this, it is just as impertinent to ask whether a law is constitutional or not, as to ask whether it is profitable or not. They persist in being the servants of the worst of men, and not the servants of humanity.

SOURCE: Henry David Thoreau, *Miscellanies* (Boston: Houghton, Mifflin Company, 1893), pp. 188 ff.

The question is, not whether you or your grandfather, seventy years ago, did not enter into an agreement to serve the Devil, and that service is not accordingly now due; but whether you will not now, for once and at last, serve God,—in spite of your own past recreancy, or that of your ancestor,—by obeying that eternal and only just CONSTITUTION, which He, and not any Jefferson or Adams, has written in your being.

The amount of it is, if the majority vote the Devil to be God, the minority will live and behave accordingly,—and obey the successful candidate, trusting that, some time or other, by some Speaker's casting-vote, perhaps, they may reinstate God. This is the highest principle I can get out or invent for my neighbors. These men act as if they believed that they could safely slide down a hill a little way,—or a good way,—and would surely come to a place, by and by, where they could begin to slide up again. This is expediency, or choosing that course which offers the slightest obstacles to the feet, that is, a downhill one. But there is no such thing as accomplishing a righteous reform by the use of "expediency." There is no such thing as sliding up hill. In morals the only sliders are backsliders. . . .

What is wanted is men, not of policy, but of probity,—who recognize a higher law than the Constitution, or the decision of the majority. The fate of the country does not depend on how you vote at the polls,—the worst man is as strong as the best at that game; it does not depend on what kind of paper you drop into the ballotbox once a year, but on what kind of man you drop from your chamber into the street every morning.

What should concern Massachusetts is not the Nebraska Bill, nor the Fugitive Slave Bill, but her own slaveholding and servility. Let the State dissolve her union with the slaveholder. She may wriggle and hesitate, and ask leave to read the Constitution once more; but she can find no respectable law or precedent which sanctions the continuance of such a union for an instant.

Let each inhabitant of the State dissolve his union with her, as long as she delays to do her duty.

The events of the past month teach me to distrust Fame. I see that she does not finely discriminate, but coarsely hurrahs. She considers not the simple heroism of an action, but only as it is connected with its apparent consequences. She praises till she is hoarse the easy exploit of the Boston tea party, but will be comparatively silent about the braver and more disinterestedly heroic attack on the Boston Court-House, simply because it was unsuccessful!

Covered with disgrace, the State has sat down coolly to try for their lives and liberties the men who attempted to do its duty for it. And this is called *justice!* They who have shown that they can behave particularly well may perchance be put under bonds for *their good behavior.* They whom truth requires at present to plead guilty are, of all the inhabitants of the State, preëminently innocent. While the Governor, and the Mayor, and countless officers of the Commonwealth are at large, the champions of liberty are imprisoned.

Only they are guiltless who commit the crime of contempt of such a court. It behooves every man to see that his influence is on the side of justice, and let the courts make their own characters. My sympathies in this case are wholly with the accused, and wholly against their accusers and judges. Justice is sweet and musical; but injustice is harsh and discordant. The judge still sits grinding at his organ, but it yields no music, and we hear only the sound of the handle. He believes that all the music resides in the handle, and the crowd toss him their coppers the same as before.

Do you suppose that that Massachusetts which is now doing these things,—which hesitates to crown these men, some of whose lawyers, and even judges, perchance, may be driven to take refuge in some poor quibble, that they may not wholly outrage their instinctive sense of justice,—do you suppose that she is anything but base and servile? that she is the champion of liberty?

Show me a free state, and a court truly of justice, and I will fight for them, if need be; but show me Massachusetts, and I refuse her my allegiance, and express contempt for her courts.

The effect of a good government is to make life more valu-able,—of a bad one, to make it less valuable. We can afford that railroad and all merely material stock should lose some of its value, for that only compels us to live more simply and economi-cally; but suppose that the value of life itself should be dimin-ished! How can we make a less demand on man and nature, how live more economically in respect to virtue and all noble qualities, than we do? I have lived for the last month—and I think that every man in Massachusetts capable of the sentiment of patrio-tism must have had a similar experience—with the sense of having suffered a vast and indefinite loss. I did not know at first what ailed me. At last it occurred to me that what I had lost was a country. I had never respected the government near to which I lived, but I had foolishly thought that I might manage to live here, minding my private affairs, and forget it. For my part, my old and worthiest pursuits have lost I cannot say how much of their attraction, and I feel that my investment in life here is worth many per cent. less since Massachusetts last deliberately sent back an innocent man, Anthony Burns, to slavery. I dwelt before, perhaps, in the illusion that my life passed somewhere only *between* heaven and hell, but now I cannot persuade myself that I do not dwell *wholly within* hell. The site of that political organization called Massachusetts is to me morally covered with volcanic scoriæ and cinders, such as Milton describes in the infernal regions. . . .

52.

HARRIET BEECHER STOWE:
The Great Dismal Swamp

Harriet Beecher Stowe (1811–1896) was far from an insurrectionist. She was, however, caught up in the temper generated in the North by the Fugitive Slave Law and, in large measure, by her own Uncle Tom's Cabin. *Thus she could parley with violence in ways she had not previously allowed. Her novel,* Dred, *honored Denmark Vesey and Nat Turner and created insurrectionary figures.* Dred, *a mystic who dreamed of uprisings against slaveholders, was imagined to be the son of Vesey. Curiously, although there was a slave Dred involved in the Turner action (her novel reproduced Turner's "confession" in an appendix), Mrs. Stowe found her title in the pending Dred Scott suit which was soon to rock the nation. The case of infanticide was based on an incident of that year of 1856 when a slave family crossed the frozen Ohio River in an escape effort. Captured in Cincinnati, Margaret Garner attempted to kill her children and succeeded in killing one before being overwhelmed by slave catchers. Her subsequent attempt to drown herself and another child on the return to Kentucky was frustrated, and traces of her were lost following her sale farther south.*

On his return home, Clayton took from the post-office a letter, which we will give to our readers.

MR. CLAYTON: I am now an outcast. I cannot show my face in the world, I cannot go abroad by daylight; for no crime, as I can

SOURCE: Harriet Beecher Stowe, *Dred* (Boston: Phillips, Sampson and Company, 1856), pp. 201 ff.

see, except resisting oppression. Mr. Clayton, if it were proper for your fathers to fight and shed blood for the oppression that came upon them, why isn't it right for us? They had not half the provocation that we have. Their wives and families were never touched. They were not bought, and sold, and traded, like cattle in the market, as we are. In fact, when I was reading that history, I could hardly understand what provocation they did have. They had everything easy and comfortable about them. They were able to support their families, even in luxury. And yet they were willing to plunge into war, and shed blood. I have studied the Declaration of Independence. The things mentioned there were bad and uncomfortable, to be sure; but, after all, look at the laws which are put over *us!* Now, if they had forbidden them to teach their children to read,—if they had divided them all out among masters, and declared them incapable of holding property as the mule before the plough,—there would have been some sense in that revolution.

Well, how was it with our people in South Carolina? Denmark Vesey was a *man!* His history is just what George Washington's would have been, if you had failed. What set him on in his course? The Bible and your Declaration of Independence. What does your Declaration say? "We hold these truths to be self-evident, that *all men are created equal;* that they are endowed by their Creator with certain *inalienable* rights: that among these are life, liberty, and the pursuit of happiness. That *to secure these rights* governments are instituted among men. That *whenever any form of government becomes destructive of any of these ends, it is the right of the people to alter or to abolish it.*" Now, what do you make of that? This is read to us, every Fourth of July. It was read to Denmark Vesey and Peter Poyas, and all those other brave, good men, who dared to follow your example and your precepts. Well, they failed, and your people hung them. And they said they couldn't conceive what motive could have induced them to make the effort. They had food enough, and clothes enough, and were kept very comfortable. Well, had not your people clothes enough, and food enough? and wouldn't you still have had enough, even if you had remained a province of England to this day,—much better living, much better clothes, and much better laws, than we have to-day? I heard your father's interpretation of the law; I heard Mr. Jekyl's; and yet, when men rise up against such laws, you wonder what in the world could have induced them! That's perfectly astonishing!

But, of all the injuries and insults that are heaped upon us, there is nothing to me so perfectly maddening as the assumption of your religious men, who maintain and defend this enormous injustice by the Bible. We have all the right to rise against them that they had to rise against England. They tell us the Bible says, "Servants, obey your masters." Well, the Bible says, also, "The powers that be are ordained of God, and who so resisteth the power, resisteth the ordinance of God." If it was right for them to resist the ordinance of God, it is right for us. If the Bible does justify slavery, why don't they teach the slave to read it? And what's the reason that two of the greatest insurrections came from men who read scarcely anything else but the Bible? No, the fact is, they don't believe this themselves. If they did, they would try the experiment fairly of giving the Bible to their slaves. I can assure you the Bible looks as different to a slave from what it does to a master, as everything else in the world does.

Now, Mr. Clayton, you understand that when I say *you*, along here, I do not mean you personally, but the generality of the community of which you are one. I want you to think these things over, and, whatever my future course may be, remember my excuse for it is the same as that on which your government is built.

I am very grateful to you for all your kindness. Perhaps the time may come when I shall be able to show my gratitude. Meanwhile, I must ask one favor of you, which I think you will grant for the sake of that angel who is gone. I have a sister, who, as well as myself, is the child of Tom Gordon's father. She was beautiful and good, and her owner, who had a large estate in

Mississippi, took her to Ohio, emancipated and married her. She has two children by him, a son and a daughter. He died, and left his estate to her and her children. Tom Gordon is the heir-at-law. He has sued for the property, and obtained it. The act of emancipation has been declared null and void, and my sister and her children are in the hands of that man, with all that absolute power; and they have no appeal from him for any evil whatever. She has escaped his hands, so she wrote me once; but I have heard a report that he has taken her again. The pious Mr. Jekyl will know all about it. Now, may I ask you to go to him, and make inquiries, and let me know? A letter sent to Mr. James Twitchel, at the post-office near Canema, where our letters used to be taken, will get to me. By doing this favor, you will secure my eternal gratitude   HARRY GORDON.

Clayton read this letter with some surprise, and a good deal of attention. It was written on very coarse paper, such as is commonly sold at the low shops. Where Harry was, and how concealed, was to him only a matter of conjecture. But the call to render him any assistance was a sacred one, and he determined on a horseback excursion to E., the town where Mr. Jekyl resided.

He found that gentleman very busy in looking over and arranging papers in relation to that large property which had just come into Tom Gordon's hands. He began by stating that the former owner of the servants at Canema had requested him, on her death-bed, to take an interest in her servants. He had therefore called to ascertain if anything had been heard from Harry.

"Not yet," said Mr. Jekyl, pulling up his shirt-collar. "Our plantations in this vicinity are very unfortunate in their proximity to the swamp. It's a great expense of time and money. Why, sir, it's inconceivable, the amount of property that's lost in that swamp! I have heard it estimated at something like three millions of dollars! We follow them up with laws, you see. They are outlawed regularly, after a certain time, and then the hunters go in and chase them down; sometimes kill two or three a day, or something like that. But, on the whole, they don't effect much."

"Well," said Clayton, who felt no disposition to enter into any discussion with Mr. Jekyl, "so you think he is there?"

"Yes, I have no doubt of it. The fact is, there's a fellow that's been seen lurking about this swamp, off and on, for years and years. Sometimes he isn't to be seen for months; and then again he is seen or heard of, but never so that anybody can get hold of him. I have no doubt the niggers on the plantation know him; but, then, you can never get anything out of them. O, they are deep! They are a dreadfully corrupt set!"

"Mr. Gordon has, I think, a sister of Harry's, who came in with this new estate," said Mr. Clayton.

"Yes, yes," said Mr. Jekyl. "She has given us a good deal of trouble, too. She got away, and went off to Cincinnati, and I had to go up and hunt her out. It was really a great deal of trouble and expense. If I hadn't been assisted by the politeness and kindness of the marshal and brother officers, it would have been very bad. There is a good deal of religious society, too, in Cincinnati; and so, while I was waiting, I attended anniversary meetings."

"Then you did succeed," said Clayton. "I came to see whether Mr. Gordon would listen to a proposition for selling her."

"O, he has sold her!" said Mr. Jekyl. "She is at Alexandria, now, in Beaton & Burns' establishment."

"And her children, too?"

"Yes, the lot. I claim some little merit for that, myself. Tom is a fellow of rather strong passions, and he was terribly angry for the trouble she had made. I don't know what he would have done to her, if I hadn't talked to him. But I showed him some debts that couldn't be put off any longer without too much of a sacrifice; and, on the whole, I persuaded him to let her be sold. I have tried to exert a good influence over him, in a quiet way," said Mr. Jekyl. "Now, if you want to get the woman, like enough she may not be sold, as yet."

Clayton, having thus ascertained the points which he wished to know, proceeded immediately to Alexandria. When he was there, he found a considerable excitement.

"A slave-woman," it was said, "who was to have been sent off in a coffle the next day, had murdered her two children."

The moment that Clayton heard the news, he felt an instinctive certainty that this woman was Cora Gordon. He went to the magistrate's court, where the investigation was being held, and found it surrounded by a crowd so dense that it was with difficulty he forced his way in. At the bar he saw seated a woman dressed in black, whose face, haggard and wan, showed yet traces of former beauty. The splendid dark eyes had a peculiar and fierce expression. The thin lines of the face were settled into an immovable fixedness of calm determination. There was even an air of grave, solemn triumph on her countenance. She appeared to regard the formalities of the court with the utmost indifference. At last she spoke, in a clear, thrilling, distinct voice:

"If gentlemen will allow me to speak, I'll save them the trouble of that examination of witnesses. It's going a long way round to find out a very little thing."

There was an immediate movement of curiosity in the whole throng, and the officer said,

"You are permitted to speak."

She rose deliberately, untied her bonnet-strings, looked round the whole court, with a peculiar but calm expression of mingled triumph and power.

"You want to know," she said, "who killed those children! Well, I will tell you"; and again her eyes travelled round the house, with that same strong, defiant expression; "I killed them!"

There was a pause, and a general movement through the house.

"Yes," she said again, "I killed them! And, O, how glad I am that I have done it! Do you want to know what I killed them for? Because I loved them!—loved them so well that I was willing to give up my soul to save theirs! I have heard some persons say that I was in a frenzy, excited, and didn't know what I was doing. They are mistaken. I was not in a frenzy; I was not excited; and I did know what I was doing! and I bless God that it is done! I was born the slave of my own father. Your old proud Virginia blood is in my veins, as it is in half of those you whip and sell. I was the lawful wife of a man of honor, who did what he could to evade your cruel laws, and set me free. My children were born to liberty; they were brought up to liberty, till my father's son entered a suit for us, and made us *slaves*. Judge and jury helped him—all your laws and your officers helped him—to take away the rights of the widow and the fatherless! The judge said that my son, being a slave, could no more hold property than the mule before his plough; and we were delivered into Tom Gordon's hands. I shall not say what he is. It is not fit to be said. God will show at the judgment-day. But I escaped, with my children, to Cincinnati. He followed me there, and the laws of your country gave me back to him. To-morrow I was to have gone in a coffle and leave these children—my son a slave for life—my daughter—" She looked round the court-room with an expression which said more than words could have spoken. "So I heard them say their prayers and sing their hymns, and then, while they were asleep and didn't know it, I sent them to lie down in green pastures with the Lord. They say this is a dreadful sin. It may be so. I am willing to lose my soul to have *theirs saved*. I have no more to hope or fear. It's all nothing, now, where I go or what becomes of me. But, at any rate, they are safe. And, now, if any of you mothers, in my place, wouldn't have done the same, you either don't know what slavery is, or you don't love your children as I have loved mine. This is all." . . .

53.

JANE GREY SWISSHELM:
Carrying the War to the Foe

*Jane Grey Cannon Swisshelm (1815–1884) was another of the
great antislavery voices of her time which were neither feminist
nor confined to abolitionist sects. She was a writer and editor
whose sharp satire and independence made her formidable
among the increasing number of commentators and journalists
were reflecting changing northern opinion. Born and raised in the
Pittsburgh, Pennsylvania, area, she early learned hatred of
slavery. An unhappy marriage made her partial to married
women's rights. In 1847 her* Pittsburgh Saturday Visitor—*she
grimly cited Dr. Samuel Johnson in support of her spelling—
quarreled freely with those tolerant of slavery. She later fought as
uncompromisingly with Minnesota moderates through her newspapers and still later was embroiled in Reconstruction politics.
The following verse was aimed at the famous Kentucky editor,
George D. Prentice, who accused her of being a man in "all but
the pantaloons."*

Perhaps you have been busy
Horsewhipping Sal or Lizzie
Stealing some poor man's baby,
Selling its mother, maybe.
You say—and you are witty—
That I—and, 'tis a pity—
Of manhood lack but dress;

SOURCE: Jane Grey Swisshelm, *Half a Century* (Chicago: Jansen, McClurg
& Co., 1880), p. 49.

But you lack manliness,
A body clean and new,
A soul within it, too.
Nature must change her plan
Ere you can be a man.

Part V: Revolutions and Aftermath

We'll cross the prairies as of old
  The Pilgrims crossed the sea,
And make the West, as they the East,
  The homestead of the Free!

> The Hutchinsons

A uniform we *soon* shall see
  For true men; 'twill be seen,
Republicans! that garb must be
  Of sober Lincoln green!

> Lincoln campaign song

North and South now seethed with treason and solutions. Peaceful separation of the sections of the country seemed to many a tolerable answer to the dilemma of irreconcilable differences. Seward once more, in a speech at Rochester, New York, October 25, 1858, found an unfortunate phrase which raged throughout the country to the detriment of his political ambitions in his reference to an "irrepressible conflict." Like the more cautious Abraham Lincoln in Illinois, Seward meant only that the basic differences in sectional programs would have to be resolved to the satisfaction of one side or the other, and that he intended that Free Soil would not be subverted. But Lincoln's less sensational "House Divided" speech, with its staid expectations of a *national* decision on the problem of slavery and emphasis on slavery restriction in the territories offered less of a trumpet call than Seward's rhetoric. The country, fascinated by apocalyptical prospects, was preparing for the worst.

The worst presented itself in the poorly organized, weakly manned and badly planned attempt of "Captain" John Brown at Harpers Ferry in western Virginia. A nation truly determined on peace could have shrugged it off without trouble. It could have emphasized Brown's vulnerable record of mental and social stability and merely incarcerated him as an object of pity and insignificance. It could have been merciless in its intellectual awareness of the undistinguished nature of his few followers. Above all, it could have agreed in severe disapproval of the notable Northerners and abolitionists, including Gerrit Smith, one of the wealthiest men in New York State, and Dr. Samuel G. Howe—

men who had encouraged Brown with money in the formulation of his obscure stratagems.

Instead, the North swathed itself in crepe in memory of Brown and his men and called forth all its eloquence to lend dignity to their deed. Southern spokesmen and politicos, on the other hand, concluded to make Brown a legitimate representative of northern opinion. They enforced the extreme measure of capital punishment not only upon him but upon all dissenters wherever they could be reached. Abolitionists in more free border states heretofore granted some small leeway of expression, were persecuted and made outcast.

Outstanding was the fierce proscription in the South accorded Hinton R. Helper's *The Impending Crisis* (1857), a book intended to aid and reinvigorate the South, rather than demean it. Helper, a North Carolina poor white, despised Negroes but hated slavery, which he blamed for all his section's troubles. It oppressed poor whites he urged with eloquence and statistics. It wore out the land. It sapped ambition and enterprise. Lastly, it perpetuated a system which offended humanity and religion. The book, intended as a battle-cry of freedom for a new South, became instead a Republican party campaign document. Helper became himself a stranger to his homeland.

The country slid toward war, electing a President whom Southerners insisted on viewing as a sectional choice, though Lincoln was a minority victor and much of his party's campaign centered not so much on slavery as on industrial and free enterprise issues. Secessionists ignored Lincoln's pleas for national unity and his invocation, in his First Inaugural Address, of "mystic chords of memory, stretching from every battle-field and patriot grave to every living heart and hearthstone all over this broad land." The new Confederates also discounted Lincoln's offer to carry out the Fugitive Slave Law.

Whether, in fact, Lincoln deliberately maneuvered the issue of war at Fort Sumter, off Charleston, South Carolina, forcing the

South into a stance of rebellion,[1] must ever be a matter of interpretation. But he led a North which, despite "doughfaces" and
traitors, equated the Union with the nobler reaches of Federal
experience. The North denied the validity of southern particu-
larism. It made disreputable, in ways it had learned from abolitionists and reformers, the symbols of slaveholding, slave selling
and the sexual violations it associated with slavery.

The pacifist cause disappeared in the defense of the Union
with only a relatively few dissenters from military duty enduring
the rigors of military persecution on both sides of the lines. The
woman's cause was temporarily put aside in favor of support of
the armed forces, though a massive use of women in every department behind the lines constituted a revolution in itself.
Dorothea L. Dix became a superintendent of nurses, and Clara
Barton, out of a non-reform background, began a career which
would lead finally to the founding of the American Red Cross.

The temperance cause fought against overwhelming odds to
maintain its mission. Soldiers lived too close to life and death to
give serious regard to shibboleths which had loomed large in
earlier reform years, and encountered spirits more often than not.
(For example, whiskey was one of the few medicines available to
surgeons operating in the field.) Soldiers expressed different
degrees of religiosity, concern for Negroes and faithfulness to
their mission. But as they mustered to meet tests of strength
below Washington and in the West, they sang "John Brown's
Body Lies A-Moldering in the Grave."

The greatest revolution, however, was that which transformed
the North into an industrial terrain of mills, works and factories.
The result rendered obsolete the blacksmith, the apprentice and
the artisan. The hasty production of guns, military equipment
and mass quantities of food also resulted in a new type of businessman far in thought from the methods and goals which had
once produced the Tappan brothers.

1. Richard Hofstadter, *The American Political Tradition* (New York:
A. A. Knopf, 1948), pp. 120–122.

Reform slogans symbolizing piety, equalitarianism and social unity of all classes were taken wholesale out of the hands of reformers and became part of the verbiage of press and politicians. Lincoln could not afford to indulge in casual idealism. He felt his way among influential publicists and office-seekers, searching for competence but settling for apparent usefulness. Of necessity he often appointed "political generals" with no military experience yet holding the life and death of their troops in hand. He labored to balance friends and enemies in Congress. His entire concentration was upon holding Kentucky, Tennessee and Missouri where he feared secession and thus total defeat.

His tactics drew scorn from northern leaders of opinion who handled extremist slogans lightly and irresponsibly. They ignored the fact which haunted Lincoln: that the South did not have to *win* the war to attain its ends. It needed only to create a stalemate which would give it status and recognition from governments abroad. The North, on the other hand, had to rout the Confederates, and that task required unity, congressional funds and agreement on military objectives.

Northern enthusiasts drifted from one specious slogan to another. Greeley, speaking for many Northerners who were at first anxious to avoid carnage, had begun by demanding that the South be turned out of the Federal Union without war. His theory, and that of *Tribune* readers, had been that the South would feel lost without the Union and beg to be received back. Yet the Confederacy *might* have proceeded to prosper as a separate nation and riveted slavery or its equivalent into its way of life as was done in many parts of the world.

Greeley's peace slogan having failed, he proceeded to his equally notorious slogan of "On to Richmond!" It was a cry which, at Bull's Run, in Virginia, threw an untried rabble of Union soldiers against determined and resourceful Confederate troops and all but cost the Federal government control of its capital in Washington.

Meanwhile, dominant northern opinion, while rejecting the

abolitionist plan for Negro troops in Federal uniforms, made popular the slogan of immediate emancipation, though it would have immediately disaffected the Border States and torn the northern states apart into warring factions. Public opinion made heroes of commanders in the field, some of them ambitious demagogues, others sincere, who sought to use or emancipate Negroes in their military departments. Lincoln endured anger and opprobrium for overturning their orders. As Commander-in-Chief of the armed forces, he was put in awkward positions by opportunists of every stamp who imagined that liberation by fiat would unleash slave revolts throughout the South and so quickly end the war.

Ill-advised or genuine, the antislavery demands mounted and brought forth heroes of war and abolition. Among Negroes, they produced such persons as Robert Smalls, a South Carolina slave who delivered a Confederate transport ship, *The Planter,* to Union sailors; James Lewis, a Louisiana free Negro who raised Negro companies for service with Union military units; and Sojourner Truth, who performed variously in aid of the Union effort. Among whites were Thomas Wentworth Higginson, who put off ministerial duties to serve in the army and whose organization of a Negro regiment broke ground for further employment of Negroes eager, under Frederick Douglass's guidance, to prove their worth in battle.

Slavery crumbled not only under the impact of Emancipation Proclamation but of free employment created by enormous government contracts. But as slavery expired, so reform on the old model dwindled. War was too real to sustain abstract stances of reform. It offered too little occasion for transcendental apostrophes. The metaphysics of individualism, which were the essence of Thoreau's art, were too subtle for general interest or comprehension in an era requiring group effort and attention to material and administrative wants. Lincoln's reference, in his Second Inaugural Address, to "the progress of our arms, upon which all else chiefly depends," left no room for fanciful calculations. The new watchword, for Lincoln and for the nation, was survival, rather than reform.

Survival did indeed create an eloquence of its own but different in kind from that which had inspired the memorable phrases of Wendell Phillips, Whittier and even Thomas Corwin. The vengeful slogans of the Radical Republicans, the battle plans of Generals Ulysses S. Grant and William T. Sherman, the practical work of the United States Sanitary Commission in taking care of the troops in field and hospital diluted memory of the speeches and personalities previously exciting to watchers of events in Kansas and readers of *Uncle Tom's Cabin*.

And yet, from another point of view, reform did not so much disappear as it changed its form. Soldiers, whether pious or blasphemous, whether thoughtful or concerned only for the moment, whether respectful of Negroes or imbued with feelings of ethnic superiority, were engaged in defending the Constitution and opposing slavery. For that cause they died in the hundreds of thousands. More than a million of them would carry scars and other eloquent reminders of war for the remainder of their lives. In a substantial sense they, as well as the abolitionists, ended slavery in the United States.

The war ended, and the Thirteenth Amendment to the Constitution was passed December 18, 1865. It officially provided that "[n]either slavery nor involuntary servitude, except as a punishment for crime whereof the party shall have been duly convicted, shall exist within the United States, or any place subject to their jurisdiction." Accordingly, William Lloyd Garrison closed the *Liberator* and pronounced his crusade ended. The common soldier with equal justice could have joined in the ceremonies.

Garrison laid down his pen to become a legend of prophecy and firmness in the right. Other abolitionists, like Jay and Birney, died before the Union victory and were afterwards forgotten. Some, like Owen Lovejoy and Robert Dale Owen, won influence in Congress and the Administration as a result of the war. Still

other old-time reformers faded into a variety of pursuits. La Roy
Sunderland had been an evangelical minister who had contributed significantly to abolitionist agitation in the churches. He
became a mind reader claiming supernatural inspiration. He
emerged from this pursuit a cheerful and benign atheist. So did
John A. Collins, once a Garrisonian who had engineered the
brilliant victory of his group at the 1840 New York annual meeting of the American Anti-Slavery Society. Collins left reform to
seek gold in California. Another branch of the former antislavery-
reform alliance became spiritualists, notably Robert Dale Owen,
whose *Footprints on the Boundary of Another World* (1859)
gave the erstwhile freethinker an impressive success with readers
of his generation.

But if abolition seemed a completed cause, its component of
justice to the Negroes continued vigorous and demanding. The
former slaves were at first sustained as wards of the Republican
party and by philanthropists. The Freedmen's Bureau was too
prominently part of the tissue of Republican control in the South
to receive full credit for its complement of gracious ladies and
sincere gentlemen who gave sometimes unrequited toil to help
accustom former slaves to their freedom. Such judges as Albion
W. Tourgée, who helped break the Ku Klux Klan in North
Carolina, helped give some dignity to the carpetbagger. Such a
friend of Negroes as the young Boston attorney Edward L.
Pierce—later memorialist of Charles Sumner—did his best to
give strength and stability to freed Negroes of the Sea Islands off
the coast of South Carolina. The Fourteenth and Fifteenth
Amendments to the Constitution, securing Negro civil rights and
Negro male votes, were accepted in all good faith by numerous
Northerners grateful for the rescue of the Union.

Nevertheless, it was clear that the main current of northern
interest took the form of supporting Radical Republicanism,
which took credit for that rescue, and of dedicating itself to such
activities (heretofore repressed by war) as railroad building,
converting war industries to peace-time manufactures, western

settlement, speculation in stocks and entertainment on a scale which the new affluence permitted. New Republican leaders like James G. Blaine learned to "wave the bloody shirt" without discrimination at Democrats, though many had died to stop the rebellion. Idealistic ranters like Theodore Tilton of the ever-increasingly influential *Independent* mouthed abolitionism, rather than modernized it creatively. They denounced Horace Greeley for having helped raise bail for the captured Confederate chieftain, Jefferson Davis and continued to rage effectively at Greeley on the issue as late as 1872 when he conducted his catastrophic presidential campaign as a Liberal Republican.

Yet, though the Radicals could impeach and all but convict President Andrew Johnson and break up the Ku Klux Klan, they could not prevent the slow and steady social and political process which returned the South to white supremacists by 1876.

Only the Negro communities themselves remained steadfast to the abolitionist crusade and its implications, and worked to reestablish their old internal solidarity. Self-help enabled them to administer such friendship and philanthropy from white Northerners and Southerners as never flagged in the worst days of the reinvigorated white establishment. Douglass remained their peerless leader, but new leaders emerged in northern and southern cities who set up educational plants, administered such patronage as the Republican party had to give and worked to foster intellectual and commercial opportunities for Negroes. A milestone in their efforts was the election to the post of temporary chairman of the Republican convention of 1884 of John Roy Lynch, a former slave who had been the first Negro elected to Congress from Mississippi. Lynch, and others like him, could not in that era afford the rhetoric of their white Radical associates. They built for a future which placed clear-minded and judicious leaders of Negroes in communities everywhere in the Union and, nationally, forged the programs of Booker T. Washington, born a Virginia slave, and W. E. B. Du Bois, born free in Massachusetts.

Temperance lost some of the distinguished aura which the

great reformers had earlier given it. Typical of the new temperance were such platform heroes as John B. Gough, who offered "thrilling anecdotes," humorous stories and pathetic scenes with which to divert his simplistic audiences. Yet new organizers also picked up the cause, ultimately to elect Frances E. Willard as president of the Women's Christian Temperance Union: an educator, a suffragist and one of the great women of her time.

Education burgeoned, though with none of the reformist zeal which had characterized Horace Mann's crusade, and new institutional reformers appeared who, like Frederick Howard Wines, learned how to give life and urgency to more complex statistics than earlier reformers had needed.

Of all the old causes, none rebounded with more vigor than the woman's rights cause with all the old crusaders eager to gain from what they interpreted the war to have been—an emancipation movement. They quarreled over their stake in the Fifteenth Amendment, which enfranchised Negro men but not women whether white or black. Mrs. Elizabeth C. Stanton argued that this left half the human race "enslaved." Lucy Stone, in rebuttal, insisted that so forward-looking an Amendment could not be repudiated.

In 1869 the two factions separated. Mrs. Stanton, Susan B. Anthony and their followers formed the more "radical" National Woman Suffrage Association. Mrs. Stone, Julia Ward Howe and others set up the equally vigorous American Woman Suffrage Association. The movement raised new talents of every sort. These included the distinguished Belva A. Lockwood, who won laws favoring women, and herself ran a respectable campaign for President of the United States in 1884 and 1888, and also the clownish Victoria Woodhull, who advanced no one but herself.

The giant of prewar reformers who sustained his power and reputation in the postwar years was Wendell Phillips. Unlike Garrison, he refused to perceive that the Thirteenth Amendment furnished reason to leave public life. There had once been slavery. Now it was necessary to secure freedom by passing civil rights and voting laws. He fought for the amendments covering these but did not forget the woman's cause. With his easy, oratorical power, he found references, anecdotes and arguments to shake and challenge his audiences. "Women's sphere" he ridiculed, the alleged protection given them by society he scorned. He turned arguments around:

> I do not want to ignore the power of women; it is too great. I want it lessened. I am not going to give the sex any more influence; I am going to diminish it. Her influence is hidden and all but omnipotent. Uneducated and irresponsible, it is terrible. I want it dragged to the light of day; I want it measured and labeled; I want it counted and criticized. . . .

But his most stirring cause was labor. He saw a new "wage slavery" succeeding the old. Many of his former comrades turned from him, but Phillips, a veteran of riots and proscription, was undeterred. He talked to new associates of trades unions, who were honored and inspired by his presence. Phillips was the gift of the old reform movement to the new.

It was a large and complex arena which took in such varied personages as Rebecca Harding Davis, who wrote of oppression in the iron mills, and Helen Hunt Jackson, whose *A Century of Dishonor* (1881) told a sad tale of government policy toward Indians. It took in Josephine Lowell Shaw, whose hero-husband, Colonel Robert Gould Shaw, had died in the assault on Fort Wagner, and who had dedicated herself to social reform. It involved such labor organizers as Daniel De Leon, Samuel Gompers and Albert R. Parsons, whose thoughts moved between reform and revolution. It involved such imaginative and theoretic minds as those of Edward Bellamy (who at first seemed a successor of Hawthorne) and Henry George.

They seemed in many cases different in kind or perspective from William Jay, Thoreau, Elijah Lovejoy, Robert Owen, David Walker and John Humphrey Noyes, to say nothing of such forgotten crusaders as Elihu Burritt and George Ripley. Yet all of them would be recalled in causes involving peace, freedom of the press, Negro wants, and other continuing themes. Birney did not attain the presidency he imagined he was suited to fill. However, his 1844 campaign could remind future partisans that the Liberty party men had threatened both major parties and forced them to change their ways. Thus, one did not have to win power to affect society. This was the final heritage of the reformers. No one, they could assert, need be insignificant. So long as he had a true vocation, and the will to follow it, he could hope to advance his cause and perhaps even see it succeed.

INDEX